Ethics and Environmental Policy

Ethics and Environmental Policy

Theory Meets Practice

EDITED BY

Frederick Ferré and Peter Hartel

The University of Georgia Press

Athens and London

© 1994 by the University of Georgia Press
Athens, Georgia 30602
All rights reserved

Designed by Kathi L. Dailey
Set in Sabon by Tseng Information Systems, Inc.
Printed and bound by Thomson-Shore, Inc.

The paper in this book meets the guidelines for
permanence and durability of the Committee on
Production Guidelines for Book Longevity of the
Council on Library Resources.

Printed in the United States of America

98 97 96 95 94 C 5 4 3 2 1

98 97 96 95 94 P 5 4 3 2 1

Library of Congress Cataloging in Publication Data

Ethics and environmental policy : theory meets
    practice / edited by Frederick Ferré and Peter Hartel.
        p.   cm.
    Includes bibliographical references and index.
    ISBN 0-8203-1617-2 (alk. paper);
    ISBN 0-8203-1657-1 (pbk: alk. paper)
        1. Environmental ethics.   2. Environmental policy.
    I. Ferré, Frederick.   II. Hartel, Peter.
    GE42.E84   1994
    179'.1—dc20   93-21058

British Library Cataloging in Publication Data available

Title page illustration of sea oats by Allen Rowell.

To Ellen R. Jordan,
lawyer, environmentalist,
and former member of the
Faculty of Environmental Ethics

Contents

Practical Pressures on Environmental Ethics

What Should Environmental Philosophers Do?

Preface

Many people now talk about the need for a new ethics. The traditional ethics of the industrial world, the so-called global North, have been human centered (some would say *man* centered in the gender-specific sense of the term) and dominantly individualistic. With such defective ethical equipment we have squandered and insulted the nonhuman environment. We have violated the human community as well, through exploitative practices and the inequitable distribution of resulting wealth and harm.

But new ethics do not simply leap fully armed from Zeus's brow. They arise gradually, from somewhere or something deep and powerful enough to wrench us from our accustomed attitudes and practices. This is where our book begins. First, Victoria Davion gives an overview of the essays that follow and attacks the accustomed notion that there must be a deep split between theory and practice. Such traditional bifurcations are ill-conceived, Davion holds, and she insists that even philosophical theorizing itself is a kind of practice. She challenges thinkers to do their thinking well: in touch with praxis and as a kind of praxis.

The next four essays respond by offering four potent stimuli for needed changes in ethical theory. All four are different, but they seem not to lie in mutually exclusive directions. Perhaps all can work together to provide the needed new ethical viewpoint. Ecological science (Golley), feminist metaphysics (Gray), Chinese philosophy (Mao), and holistic postmodern technology (Callicott) may each have a vital role in nurturing the new ethics. Each author seeks a framework adequate for coping practically with the environmental and social challenges of the twenty-first century and beyond.

The challenges themselves, of course, are not the traditional ones. The second part of this book underscores that fact with four essays designed to expand awareness of practical problems crying for solution. The painful emergence of real international cooperation, its problems and possibilities (Musu); the inequitable but economically intractable issue of gaseous emissions in the shared global atmosphere (Simonis); the political and ethical challenges of wise city planning for the future (Poli); the growing evidence of the fundamental inappropriateness of treating land as legal private property (Varner)—all have the cumulative effect of convincing any remaining doubters that "business as usual" is not just bankrupt, it is impossible.

Finally, we offer prescriptions. All five essays in the third section were written by professional philosophers who want their profession to address more directly the pain and urgency of the new realities facing the world. One way to accomplish this is to explode all halfway "fixes" and focus relentless attention on the need for basic cultural reorientation (Kohák); another is to take sides openly on public environmental controversies, to enter frankly into the activist trenches (Shrader-Fréchette); still another is to instill self-critical cultural modesty, as scarce among philosophers as it is among the general public of the developed world (Gunn); a fourth way is to think with new philosophical depth about what is at stake in the struggle for saving nature—and ourselves (Rolston); finally, two philosophers emphasize opposite but complementary needs: environmental philosophers need to become more practical (Norton), and environmental practitioners need to become more philosophical (Hargrove).

This combination of insights from the world's leading philosophers and environmental experts would not have happened if, roughly a decade ago, a group of faculty members at the University of Georgia had not banded together into the Faculty of Environmental Ethics. A unique group of scientists and humanists drawn from more than a score of departments, programs, schools, and colleges of the university, the faculty offers a graduate Certificate of Environmental Ethics to students enrolled in any graduate program of the university. The Environmental Ethics Certificate Program (EECP) has made a difference to the university's faculty as well as to its students. We, the editors of this volume, would probably never have met if it had not been for the EECP. One of us (Ferré) is a member of the Department of Philosophy, located far away—in mental as well as geographical distance—from the Department of Crop and Soil Sciences where the other (Hartel) teaches in soil microbiology. But thanks to the regular activities of the EECP—our evening seminar programs, reading interest groups, guest lectures, and environmental outings—we not only leaped the large gap between "north campus" and "south campus" but (under the sponsorship of the EECP) came to design and teach together, for four consecutive years, a course in agricultural ethics.

The Faculty of Environmental Ethics served many such good bridge-making purposes during its first decade, but by spring 1990 there was a widely felt need for something more. Many of us simply could not bring environmental ethics into our daily lives. Part of the problem was that many of us were scientists who had difficulty considering qualitative aspects (e.g., aesthetics) of environmental decisions in our quantitatively grounded disciplines. We needed to stop and learn these aspects. Yet another part of the problem was environmental ethics theory: the theories seemed impractical or cloaked in impenetrable jargon. So, in the spring quarter of 1990, the EECP faculty decided to organize an international conference on environmental ethics to bring philosophers and scientists together with the purpose of turning environmental ethics theory toward practice.

Like a house, a good conference must start with a strong foundation. What were the central issues in environmental ethics theory and who could translate this theory into practice? We began a round-robin discussion within our EECP membership on these questions and the people who might best answer them. Unfortunately, the process seemed to work only in reverse—the names were easy but the questions were hard. The simplest solution seemed to be to pick a person within each specialized area of environmental ethics and have that speaker talk about his or her field. This unsatisfactory situation persisted until September 1990. Finally, in a long evening session, four central questions were hammered out:

What are the practical implications of new environmental ethics theories (e.g., deep ecology and ecofeminism) on environmental problems?

To what extent should legislation for ecological sustainability restrict property rights?

How can nations share responsibility for global environmental problems?

How can military and political threats to the environment be diminished?

These questions formulated in just this way did not survive unaltered into this book, but it was on the basis of these questions that all the speakers were finally selected for the conference.

The Second International Conference on Ethics and Environmental Policy was held April 5–7, 1992. The conference was attended by 109 registered persons representing twenty states of the United States and eight foreign countries.

This book, composed of the revised conference papers from the twelve major speakers and three of the four moderators (the fourth has his say here in the Preface and in the Epilogue), is ready to address a wider audience and meet a more general need. Reviewing the essays, rendering formats uniform, and keeping after all the details involved in international correspondence with far-flung, multilingual authors was the task of the incomparable Mona Freer. She has functioned brilliantly as "gatekeeper" in the passage between the conference and the book. Both editors are deeply in her debt.

Acknowledgments

Two things are important for a conference to be a success. First, no conference happens without funding. The EECP began with its own pockets: with the approval of our parent organization (the University of Georgia Graduate School), the entire EECP speaker budget for 1992 was committed to the conference. Additionally, Vice President for Academic Affairs William F. Prokasy awarded us funds through the University of Georgia's State-of-the-Art Conference Initiative. This gave us one-third of the necessary funds. The next step was more difficult. Environmental ethics is a relatively new discipline, and few organizations or foundations support conferences on this subject. In August 1990 the Fondazione Lanza (Padua, Italy) had sponsored the First International Conference on Ethics and Environmental Policy, in Borca di Cadore, Italy. When we asked them for support, they were delighted to assist with funding. To show further support they sent President Giancarlo Minozzi and Scientific Director Corrado Poli to the University of Georgia to assist with the planning. They wanted continuity with their first important effort, so they asked us to change our conference name to the Second International Conference on Ethics and Environmental Policy. We did this, and the conference name was chosen. With two-thirds of the funds in hand and additional backing from the Council of Educators in Landscape Architecture and the International Society for Environmental Ethics, a final grant application was submitted and approved by the Ethics and Values Studies Program of the National Science Foundation. It is these organizations that we now thank for their timely assistance.

Second, no conference happens without behind-the-scenes workers. These people make a conference pleasant and allow conferees to spend their time talking about the issues, not about uncomfortable surroundings or poor food. We thank the Georgia Center for Continuing Education, especially Joseph Allen, for helping to coordinate these aspects. We thank Holmes Rolston III and Eugene Hargrove for publicizing the conference in the *International Society of Environmental Ethics Newsletter* and in *Environmental Ethics,* respectively. We thank William Reeves of the Department of Agricultural Communications at the University of Georgia for producing a first-rate printed program. Thanks to Abner and Irene Schepartz of the Chocolate Shoppe, Athens, for catering the public reception—especially for the chocolate-covered strawberries! Finally we thank Jean Billingsley, Gail Jones, and Henrietta Tucker, all of the Department of Crop and Soil Sciences (and who wondered what crop and soil sciences ever had to do with environmental ethics), for taking care of registration, photocopying, and all the conference correspondence.

Ethics and Environmental Policy

VICTORIA DAVION

Introduction

Where Are We Headed?

In the essays that follow, readers will notice several themes emerging. All involve the importance of context for the field of environmental ethics. One principal theme emphasizes the context of theory in practice. In "An Apologia for Activism: Global Responsibility, Ethical Advocacy, and Environmental Problems," Kristin Shrader-Fréchette makes compelling arguments in favor of academic theorists taking political stands on environmental issues at least some of the time rather than attempting to remain neutral all of the time. She argues that in an atmosphere where private interest groups try to determine the direction of research in academic institutions, the context of academia can become highly politicized. Theorists can serve as a politically corrective force only if we recognize that we are not neutral when we are in search of the pure truth. We are often on a battlefield with special interest groups who want particular conclusions.

Shrader-Fréchette points out that objectivity does not mean neutrality when there are more reasons in favor of one position than another. One does not come closer to the truth by remaining neutral, but rather by taking a position on the issue. Thus, theorists should be prepared to take positions and engage in political advocacy.

One of the most important points made in this book, explicitly by Shrader-Fréchette and implicitly by a number of others (e.g., Elizabeth Dodson Gray in "Come Inside the Circle of Creation: The Ethic of At-

1

tunement"), is that there is no such thing as pure theory. To theorize is to practice. When we are trained as theorists we learn the rules of various practices within particular contexts, although these rules can be changed when we critique the practices themselves.

These practices are in need of change in several respects. The first, noted above, is the idea of objectivity as neutrality. This dangerous myth keeps us from saying what we think when what we think may be extremely important.

In addition, both Gray's essay and Corrado Poli's "The Political Consequences of an Environmental Question" point out that we theorize from within particular worldviews. We must, after all, start somewhere, with some assumptions. Sometimes, however, these assumptions play a part in creating the problems we are trying to solve. When this occurs we must step back and evaluate the assumptions themselves—an extremely difficult task given that it is often hard to isolate such assumptions.

Gray analyzes patriarchy, showing the dangerous unfounded assumptions that many theories incorporate because they have emerged from patriarchal worldviews. She shows the importance of looking at the way people treat each other as a clue to figuring out why people treat the environment in particular ways. The way people treat other people and the way people treat the environment are both parts of comprehensive worldviews; they are not isolated issues. Once again, this point underscores the need to examine the contexts in which various theories emerge and to analyze them accordingly.

Readers familiar with ecofeminism will recognize these themes.[1] For example, Karen J. Warren, in "The Power and the Promise of Ecological Feminism," argues that the domination of nature by human beings and the domination of women by men are justified by the same worldview, one based on the logic of domination.[2] The logic of domination sets up moral hierarchies and claims that whenever something ranks higher than something else on a moral hierarchy, it has the right to dominate that which is below it. Thus Warren argues that in worldviews that view human beings as above nature, the logic of domination confers on humans the moral right to dominate nature. When these same worldviews include the idea that women are closer to nature than men, the logic of domination confers on men the right to dominate women. Warren argues that the fight for women's liberation and the fight for respect for nature in general are conceptually linked. Both argue against the validity of the logic of domination.

Another theme concerning context addressed in this book is the question of relativism versus universalism. Both Alastair S. Gunn, in "Can Environmental Ethics Save the World?" and Frank B. Golley, in "Grounding Environmental Ethics in Ecological Science," emphasize the importance of maintaining respect for cultural differences as we theorize. A central problem in the field of environmental ethics is how to do this while simultaneously ensuring environmental protection.

Ignazio Musu, in "Efficiency and Equity in International Environmental Cooperation"; Udo E. Simonis, in "Toward a 'Houston Protocol': How to Allocate CO_2 Emission Reductions Between North and South"; and Yu-shi Mao, in "Evolution of Environmental Ethics: A Chinese Perspective," all make clear that many important environmental problems must be dealt with on an international level.

This raises interesting and disturbing questions about what to do in situations in which a certain group's practices are extremely detrimental to environmental well-being, but the group in question either denies that the practices are detrimental or does not seem to care. Golley's essay exemplifies one alternative, which is to try to find a universal basis for an environmental ethic. He suggests that perhaps ecologists can come up with a foundation for environmental ethics based on "authentic" experiences of nature, which could generate an ethic that is both attuned to the environment and respectful of cultural differences. I find the idea of "authentic" experiences of nature to be problematic because it so clearly implies that some experiences are inauthentic. Although Golley's aim is to construct something respectful, how can we construct an ethic that respects differences if we dismiss certain people's ("inauthentic") experiences from the start? This brings us to the problems of how to decide which experiences are authentic and which differences are ethically acceptable.

Gunn's essay represents an alternative approach. He advocates a pluralistic approach to ethics using the idea of "relativism of distance." This is not universalism, he says, but he also does not imply a mere value-as-preferences analysis of value. Gunn borrows the idea of relativism of distance from Bernard Williams and attempts to use it to argue against the idea that cultures have the right to impose ethical standards on one another.

Williams himself uses this term to discuss ideas concerning historical rather than spatial distance, claiming that in today's world we are fairly close to one another, and all confrontations must be seen as real rather than notional:

A real confrontation between two divergent outlooks occurs at a given time if there is a group of people for whom each of the outlooks is a real option. A notional confrontation, by contrast, occurs when some people know about two divergent outlooks, but at least one of those outlooks does not present a real option. . . . An outlook is a real option for a group either if it already is their outlook or if they could go over to it; and they could go over to it if they could live inside it in their actual historical circumstances and retain their hold on reality, not engage in extensive self-deception.[3]

If a confrontation is merely notional, it is not possible to make ethical judgments about the practices of the other group. Even if we accept this distinction, it may create more problems than it can solve. There may be disagreement about whether a certain option is real for a particular group, even within the group itself. Williams believes that in today's world, all confrontations must be seen as real. If this is so, the relativism of distance will not provide a defense against an attempt to change the values of other cultures, because in real confrontations groups can make moral judgments concerning one another's practices.

If we disagree with Williams and attempt to argue that even in today's modern world some confrontations are notional, we will need a much clearer idea of just what makes a confrontation notional rather than real. Again, there is likely to be disagreement; hence, there are problems with this approach to the ethical dilemmas posed by cultural differences as well.

Another theme of this book is that we face problems in attempting to design fair regulations in both national and international contexts. Gunn points this out by quoting a welfare organizer who tells some ecology radicals that welfare mothers still want what the ecology radicals are rejecting. This is an important point. All too often, environmentalists advocate policies and actions that put an unfair burden on the poor. Closing factories means eliminating jobs. Regulating the use of scarce resources by keeping prices high puts a huge burden on the poor while those with plenty can continue using the resources as before.

In "Red War, Green Peace" Erazim Kohák addresses just this problem, asking how we can expect others to conserve if we will not. Along similar lines, Gary E. Varner raises important legal issues concerning regulation within United States society in "Environmental Law and the Eclipse of Land as Private Property."

A central issue concerning distribution, the problem of intergenerational justice, is discussed by Ignazio Musu in "Efficiency and Equity in International Environmental Cooperation." Here we have all the problems of pluralism versus monism, but also the problem of the rights of future individuals versus the rights of existing ones, an issue that involves context in an intriguing way. What is the scope of our obligations to future individuals? Must our ethical theories consider them?

Both Kohák's essay and "The Role of Technology in the Evolving Concept of Nature," by J. Baird Callicott, point out that our consumer mentality is the source of many of our problems. The idea that technology can produce environmentally safe cars so that we do not have to think about whether to use cars at all expresses the fundamental problem. This is a finite planet, and we must change our consumer mentality. Callicott suggests that perhaps some developing technologies can help us change our fundamental values themselves rather than simply come up with new ways to serve the consumer mentality. At any rate, what emerges most clearly is that no Band-Aid solution will work. The domination of people by other people and the domination of the environment by certain people are both products of worldviews in need of change.

There is much work to be done conceptually, and this is part of the practical work, not mere theorizing. To return to the point with which I began, this is why it is important to critique various practices of theorizing as well as the results of that theorizing. If we accept the notion of theory as a kind of practice, we will have to ask questions of application a bit differently, but we will not lose the ability to ask them. We can still ask how useful various theories are in solving particular environmental problems. If international cooperation is necessary to peacefully solve certain problems, then theories that fail to respect cultural differences are not likely to be helpful in resolving these problems. In addition, theories that fail to respect the poor in distributing the costs of environmental protection are unlikely to lead to cooperation either at national or international levels.

In "Winning and Losing in Environmental Ethics," Holmes Rolston III suggests that a win-win situation is possible if humans do the right thing with respect to the natural environment. I hope he is right about this; however, we must take perceived losses seriously. It is a tricky matter to start telling others what their "real" interests are, as opposed to the interests they think they have. Rolston also maintains that we need not harm any more of the natural environment in the service of expanding human culture. Again this raises questions concerning the present distribution of the natural resources already in use. We cannot expect people to conserve natural resources if they are or see themselves as impoverished and no one is helping them to solve these problems without further depleting natural resources. Protecting the environment will cause many perceived losses; whether or not these constitute "real" losses in the sense discussed by Rolston, they will have to be distributed equitably if we expect cooperation with others on either a national or an international level.

Finally, in "Where Do We Go from Here?" Bryan Norton and Eugene Hargrove suggest future directions for theory and practice and for theory *as* practice. The book returns to the question of the practical context for environmental ethics, suggesting new ways of looking at what theorists do—or ought to do—so that their work can be applied more meaningfully and effectively.

NOTES

1 The term *ecofeminism* was first used by Françoise d'Eaubonne in "Feminism or Death," in *New French Feminisms: An Anthology,* ed. Elaine Marks and Isabelle de Courtivron (Amherst: University of Massachusetts Press, 1980). For a useful overview of ecofeminist philosophy, see Karen J. Warren, "Feminism and the Environment: An Overview of the Issues," APA Newsletter, *Feminism and Philosophy* (Fall 1991).
2 Karen J. Warren, "The Power and the Promise of Ecological Feminism," *Environmental Ethics* 12 (1990): 125–46.
3 Bernard Williams, *Ethics and the Limits of Philosophy* (Cambridge: Harvard University Press, 1985), 161.

Resources
for a
Practical
Environmental
Ethics

FRANK B. GOLLEY

Grounding
Environmental Ethics
in Ecological Science

My continuing objective is to build a foundation for an ethical relationship between human beings and the environment using selected concepts of ecological science. This effort began with an examination of how deep ecology, the ecological philosophy, uses the term *ecology*. As an ecological scientist I was concerned about how philosophers applied the name for my science to an environmental philosophy. My interest continued with a comparative study which determined that the ultimate norms of deep ecology—self-realization and biocentric equality—are consistent with the observations of ecological science.[1] This essay moves away from deep ecology to consider the relations between the scientific study of the environment and the value systems that underlie the application of ecological science to environmental management.

Environmental analyses are often organized hierarchically.[2] The largest scale in the spatial hierarchy is the global environment, my primary concern. Study of the global environment considers the properties of the atmosphere, oceans, and land that influence the capacity of living organisms—including humans—to live and prosper. At successively finer spatial scales one can consider the environments of continents and oceans, geographic regions, and local areas. Humans affect the environment at all levels, and an enormous literature based on long-term, intense ecological study at all levels describes these interactions. Because humans are organized most closely on local spatial scales, environmental management and concern are greatest at the smallest scale, becoming less important as one moves to the global scale.

Thus we have an interesting contradiction. Local problems frequently exhibit special, limited properties, but they elicit an intense response. Global problems, on the other hand, have much broader implications, but we know relatively little about them, and it is difficult to determine who is responsible for them. For a local example, let us imagine that a chemical waste dump is discovered. The dump lies in a former wetland, a waste area on the margin of economically useful land. The chemicals leak into the environment, contaminate the groundwater, and threaten human health. Local governments seek expert assistance to determine the extent of the damage and the specific types of poisons in the environment. State and federal agencies may be drawn into the study and may provide funds to isolate or even clean up the mess. Local governments may try to determine those responsible for the problem and force them to pay the costs of the cleanup or punish them with fines and jail sentences.

Many countries have mechanisms to deal with local problems of this type. If local and national authorities are honest and competent, the problems can be solved, the citizens protected, and the environment restored. But the costs of solving environmental problems may become astronomical, and it quickly becomes apparent that it is most cost-effective to prevent helter-skelter dumping of chemical wastes in marginal environments in the first place. Nevertheless, at this scale we have the experience and institutions to act effectively.

When the problems become regional or continental in scale they become much more intractable. Not only are different nations with different laws and administrations involved, but the environmental processes are highly variable seasonally and from year to year and may be stochastic or even chaotic in their behavior. A good example is the accident at the Chernobyl nuclear reactor. The explosion had intense local impacts, but its regional impacts were also significant. The economies of Scottish sheep farmers, Lapp reindeer herders, and Polish and German dairymen were all adversely affected. But the problem was spread even farther—to Africa—through the migration of birds from the Pripet marshes near Chernobyl.[3]

The impacts of the radiation contamination and its effect on the health of European human populations cannot be determined precisely. On a regional scale, it is difficult to chart the environmental flows and storages, and therefore to predict the impacts. And even more seriously, the government authorities responsible for public health—from those in the former USSR to the International Atomic Energy Agency—misunderstood, misled, and acted irresponsibly during and after the accident. Indeed, electric power authorities worldwide still ignore Chernobyl or declare it to be an aberrant case that cannot happen again. The public is justified in asking if it is adequately protected from environmental accidents of regional scale, especially those originating in other countries in industries managed by nonelected, self-regulated authorities. National governments try to deal with such problems through treaties and joint activities, and in many cases cooperation is an effective way to approach regional problems.

Let us move to the global scale, the major concern of this essay. Human activities are influencing global processes in the air, water, and land. Intensified efforts to feed the exploding human population are increasing rates of soil erosion worldwide and causing the transportation of the land surface to rivers and oceans. I live in such a region, the southern piedmont of the United States, and I demonstrate the impact of irresponsible farming practices on human and environmental well-being to my classes. Alteration of the chemical composition of the atmosphere as a result of human practices is another well-known example of a global environmental problem.

In these examples the environmental problem is generated by millions of small, local actions distributed globally. Here is an example of the link between the small and the large—an ecological principle. Yet how does one move from a global impact back through national and state governments to local people—in all their diversity—and change their behavior? The present United Nations is not capable of acting globally in the necessary way. Nations are seldom motivated to act cooperatively to solve global problems. Indeed, if one wishes, one can buy an expert who will testify that there is no environmental problem at all. But the issue is more complicated than lack of cooperation. Around the global conference table sit people from all the existing cultures, ideologies, religions, political theories and practices, and historical experiences. Not only do we not speak each others' languages, we do not even share common concepts of humanness and environment. The discussion about the global environment tends to be in the language of the materialistic, industrialized West. Even the environmental ethics that informs us in these developed countries is culturally contingent on Western history and experience. But the Western approach to the environment is foreign to most human inhabitants of the planet. This is part of the reason for the screams of outrage and the violence generated by frustrated, disenfranchised, marginalized people in so many parts of the earth. The global conference table is a most disorderly affair. But before we despair, we must try again to search together for a foundational experience that might provide a sufficiently common point from which to move from theory to practice as a global community. I am optimistic that we can find such a common ground.

Objectives

The problem of relativity seems so serious to me that I want to approach it in two steps. First, I want to focus on the authentic experience of the environment. That is, I propose to take seriously the Norwegian philosopher Arne Naess's approach to the problem and return to an environment where it is possible to experience the natural world directly and authentically.[4] I suggest that we begin with the observations of the field ecologist or the experiences of the naturalist, forester, or woods walker. In their authentic form, these experiences, while individually relative and personal, involve close interactions with the natural environment. Second, I want to turn to the method of ecological science, which, while culturally relative, attempts to be objective, and remove personal bias and contingency from the study of the environment. Ecological scientists seek interpretations that can be tested by further observation and experiment, and they rely on their peers to test, correct, support, or discard their observations. There is in ecological science, then, a crude form of self-correction that provides a foundation of common experience from which we can reason toward ethical rules for environmental behavior.

I shall now explore a fundamental concept in ecological science as a ground for a global environmental ethic. The task is a large one, beyond the limits of a single essay, but these words may point the way and suggest potential conclusions.

The Ecosystem Concept

Ecology is an active and complex science. Actually it is a discipline with many subdisciplines, each connected to different applications and having sometimes contradictory conceptual foundations. The British Ecological Society (BES), formed in 1913, was the first professional organization of scientific ecologists. Recently the BES celebrated its Seventy-fifth Jubilee with a symposium on the concepts of ecological science held at University College, London. As a preliminary activity (useful in organizing the symposium) the BES queried its members about the most important ecological concepts. Malcolm Cherrett collected these opinions and ranked them in his publication about the symposium.[5] Of 645 respondents, 447 ranked "the ecosystem" as the most important concept. Thus, we have a way into the analysis of ecological concepts that has the imprimatur of ecological scientists.

Ecosystem, a contraction of the words *ecological* and *system,* was coined by the British scientist Sir Arthur Tansley in 1935. Tansley stated:

> But the more fundamental conception is, it seems to me, the whole system (in the sense of physics), including not only the organism-complex, but also the whole complex of physical factors forming what we call the environment of the biome—the habitat factors in the widest sense.
>
> It is the systems so formed which, from the point of view of the ecologist, are the basic units of nature on the face of the earth.
>
> These ecosystems, as we may call them, are of the most various kinds and sizes. They form one category of the multitudinous physical systems of the universe, which range from the universe as a whole down to the atom.[6]

By calling units of nature "ecosystems" Tansley linked ecology with the conceptual developments of physics and preadapted ecology to the post–World War II developments in information theory, system science, and computer science. In 1953 Eugene Odum adopted the ecosystem concept as the core idea in his influential textbook, *Fundamentals of Ecology,*[7] and from that time to the present the concept has been a key element in ecological discourse.

Tansley's contribution was to give units of nature a useful name that linked them to the units studied in other sciences. Ecologists had been studying ecosystems for a long time, even before the science itself was named by Ernst Haeckel in 1866.[8] These natural units had been called by all sorts of peculiar names—holons, biogeocenoses, ecotopes, and so on—but none of these names achieved the widespread acceptance of ecosystem. Ecologists studying ecosystems had to face the problem of bounding their objects of investigation. Nature is seldom discrete, and depending on one's point of view, one system may seem to blend into another over space and time. This problem of boundaries is less serious for lakes and ponds, where the presence or absence of water is a good criterion for the system's border. Ecosystem studies of lakes took a major step beyond abstract ideas about the interrelatedness of nature to active scientific study of the relations themselves. Ecological studies of lake ecosystems began in northern temperate regions, where glaciation had left thousands of small lakes across the landscape. Research centers for lake studies developed in Europe in Germany and Sweden, and in America in Wisconsin, Michigan, and New York. Students of terrestrial ecology were less able to find easily bounded systems. These researchers tended to seek relatively simple, low-stature systems where the ecologist could look out and determine with the eye the boundaries of the system. Such landscapes occur in grasslands, deserts, and tundras, and these were the locations of the first ecosystem studies on land. The greatest advances in terrestrial studies were made in Russia, Great Britain, and the western United States; however, terrestrial ecosystem studies did not fully mature until the late 1960s when the American ecologists F. Herbert Bormann and Gene E. Likens demonstrated that each small watershed can be treated as a bounded ecological system.[9]

Sir Arthur Tansley's motivation in coining the term *ecosystem* was complex, but one of the prime influences was his irritation over a set of publications by a South African professor of botany named John Phillips. Tansley, a senior spokesman for English plant ecology, had spent his life struggling to see that ecological studies were made a part of the botanical curriculum and that ecology was respected as a serious science. In addition to being a superior teacher of ecology, Tansley wrote several textbooks and edited several influential journals of plant ecology and botany. He was deeply concerned that ecology be scientific in the sense that physics is scientific, and that it not be involved in speculations about the organization of nature or the relations between humans and nature. Tansley's concern must be seen against the background of British positivism and Continental romantic idealism, including Germany's national socialism, that characterized the period between the two world wars.

John Phillips was influenced by two people: Jan Christian Smuts, general, statesman, and premier of South Africa, who had advanced the philosophical concept of holism in 1926; and Frederic E. Clements, the American ecologist who proposed that the units of nature were organismic (he called them superorganisms) and went through a life cycle similar to that of an individual.[10] Phillips argued that ecological succession, the life cycle of vegetation, provides evidence that the biotic community behaves as a complex organism. Tansley was not wholly unsympathetic with the ideas of Clements, who was a personal friend, and he was aware that nature could be viewed as complexes of interacting systems. But Tansley wanted to avoid any taint of mysticism and romanticism and keep ecology focused toward the analytical study of nature, linking it with biology, chemistry, and physics. For this reason he opposed the holistic thinking of Phillips and Smuts. He developed a concept that bridged the gap between ecologists' tendency to reason from their studies of ecological relationships toward wholes and the need for ecology to identify with biology by deeper analytical study of ecological processes. This dualistic tendency is present in all disciplines but is particularly acute in ecology.

Tansley's solution still holds, although the ecosystem concept has been expanded since he formulated it in 1935. This expansion has created a confusion of usage. First, the term *ecosystem* may refer to a lake or a watershed, as described above, and it is in this sense that most philosophers use the term.[11] Ecosystem studies of this sort are concerned mainly with the flows of energy, materials, and information through networks of feeding relationships. A second definition, emphasized by the ecologist Francis Evans,[12] applies the term *ecological system* to any system in which the biota interacts with an environment. In this second sense, an individual can interact with its environment and be an ecosystem—as can a population, a community, or even the entire biota of the planet. I am using *ecosystem* in this second sense, and I am applying the concept to individual human beings.[13]

Application to an Environmental Ethic

This brief history of the ecosystem concept indicates the nature of the problem that must be solved. The ecosystem concept can be applied to any ecological system at any level of the ecological hierarchy, from the individual to the planetary. No matter the type of ecosystem, we begin by describing the interactions of the biological components and the environment. The environment of a biotic element may include other biological elements or the products of biological activity. Environment is not always physical, chemical, or material; it may be informational, too. It may involve the rules for the interaction of materials as well as the materials themselves.[14]

Every ecosystem also has an environment—the ecosystem of higher order in which it is located. Thus the individual is part of a population, the population occurs in a community, the community is part of a landscape, the landscape is part of a biome, and the biome is part of the biosphere. Each analysis involves three levels: the system of interest, the subsystems relevant to the question or issue, and the suprasystem that forms the environment of the system of interest.[15] Of course, an ecosystem might also be influenced indirectly by systems distant from it in the hierarchy, but this influence usually comes down through the series of systems and subsystems that make up the sequence.

My concern here is with the ecosystem of the human individual. This system includes all the elements of life that influence and shape human action and thought. It includes the built environment, family members, friends, foods, institutions, laws, and philosophical ideas. This individual ecosystem comprises all the individual's interactions with his or her environment.

We influence our environment and it influences us; the process is multidimensional and reciprocal, and it involves multiple direct and indirect feedbacks. Our well-being, health, productivity, and survival depend on a balance of positive interactions with our environment, otherwise our situation deteriorates and we die. It is in our self-interest to maintain positive relations with our environment. It is not enough to be passive, assuming that nature will take its course. Rather, we are obliged to actively maintain the environmental relationships, protecting ourselves in some cases, competing in others, mutually supporting other individuals in yet other instances, and so on. Relationships may be positive, neutral, or negative in the short or the long term. Living involves a dynamic environmental relationship.

Indeed, reflection on the information ecologists have obtained about environmental relationships raises questions about the real nature of the individual object in an ecosystem. For example, humans are distinct in the sense that we have a skin that separates us from the air and from other people, and we have a mind that recognizes an ego or self. In a chemical sense, however, we are exchanging chemical molecules continuously, and our skin is a sieve through which water vapor, gases, and energy pass readily. Mentally, we are acutely sensitive to the environment; our mental state is transformed by subtle signals from the environment. In a concrete physical sense, as well as in a subjective sense, each individual is one with the elements of his or her personal ecosystem. The real person may well be the entire ecosystem, not merely the biological organism that is the body. If one can understand and apply the knowledge of this ecosystemic character of being, then care of and respect for and love of one's environment is obviously self-interest.[16]

Ecosystemic self-interest is not selfish in the usual sense of the word because it involves as much concern for the other systems that make up the individual's environment as for the self. Clearly self-centeredness is counterproductive because eventually it results in negative interactions with others. Its survival value is only short term. Rather, the ecosystem concept is a foundation for will toward greater positive interactions, greater good—in a sense an extension of the Golden Rule. Self-interest supports the admonition to love one's neighbor, but it goes further to include as neighbors the physical, chemical, biotic, material, and subjective elements of the environment. Further, it leads to the recognition of forests, lakes, mountains, and deserts as other systems that deserve respect and moral consideration.

For this reason I propose that the ecosystem concept is a foundation for a global, as well as a local, environmental ethic. The ecosystem concept comes from scientific experience. It can be defined quantitatively if that is required. Many environmental interactions can be described concretely. If we hold the patterns described by science as real in a material sense, then we cannot ignore the implications of the ecosystem concept, even though I have extended the metaphor into the subjective and philosophical realms of discourse. The ecosystem as defined by ecological scientists provides a basis from which to reason toward a broader, more inclusive concept that undergirds an attitude that is deeply ethical. To paraphrase Aldo Leopold: When in doubt, preserve the integrity of the ecosystem![17] In educating people toward the ecosystem perspective, it is important that we show that selfhood is one end of a continuum of perception. Selfhood is important in a genetic sense because the genes and creativity reside in the self. At the other end of the continuum is generosity, altruism, immersion in the other, love in its deepest sense, meditation leading to identification with the all. During our lives we move between the ends of this continuum. In a life-threatening situation our tendency is to move toward the self; in life-enlarging situations our tendency is to lose the self. In this complex of potential actions, recognition of the ecosystem leads us to choose life-enhancing actions where we may. Thus, the ecosystem concept provides a rationale for ethical behavior.

The practicality of this suggestion has at least two components. First, an ecosystem-based environmental ethic is practical because it is rooted in actual experience with nature. In this sense it shares a foundation with deep ecology but does not depend on a concept of biocentric equality. Reasoning from the ecosystem concept makes us realize that all elements in our environment are not equal, nor are they all safe and positive. The individual must judge the significance of each element in the environment. Survival depends on making the right choices in the long and short terms. Right choices are enhanced by ecosystemic awareness, knowledge, humility, alertness, carefulness, caution, conservatism, and respect for traditionally successful patterns.

Second, the ecosystem concept is extensible. It can be applied to a family, a community, a city, a county, or to the human population as a whole. In the latter case, the human ecosystem is planet Earth—our home and the only place where life is known to exist in the universe. Thus the concept underpins the bioregional movement that seeks to fit culture to land socially, politically, and environmentally. While the ecosystem ethical approach is founded in ecological science, it seems to have close ties with the philosophical concepts of a variety of cultures. The connection seems to be through those cultures' concern regarding the relationship of the individual with society and nature, and the maintenance of a balance between positive and negative elements of the environment so that harmony (as health, well-being, and survival) is obtained. Thus we recognize links between modern science and traditional wisdom. I do not have the knowledge to describe these links in greater detail, but their presence is heartening.

Nevertheless, let us not discount the difficulty of the task. The ecosystem concept speaks directly against the countervailing separateness of humans and nature characteristic of Western industrialized societies; it speaks directly against further human population growth; it speaks directly against sciences and philosophies rooted in abstractions; it speaks against control of human beings and environments by power- and money-driven religions and ideologies. It is a linchpin in a truly subversive science. It is responsive to a trend that has dominated the human experience over more and more of the earth for about five hundred years, a trend that is directly responsible for the global environmental crisis. In the words of the American poet Robinson Jeffers:

> A little too abstract, a little too wise,
> It is time for us to kiss the earth again,
> It is time to let the leaves rain from the skies,
> Let the rich life run to the roots again.[18]

Because an ecosystem concept–based environmental ethic is deeply practical and linked to the wisdom of other cultures, it has potential for use in dealing with the global environmental crisis. The task remaining is to work out the meaning of an ecosystem-based environmental ethic in specific situations and to rebuild modern environmental wisdom.

NOTES

1 Frank B. Golley, "Deep Ecology from the Perspective of Ecological Science," *Environmental Ethics* 9 (1987): 45–55.

2 T. F. H. Allen and Thomas B. Starr, *Hierarchy: Perspectives for Ecological Complexity* (Chicago: University of Chicago Press, 1982); and R. V. O'Neill, D. L. DeAngelis, J. B. Waide, and T. F. H. Allen, *A Hierarchical Concept of Ecosystems* (Princeton: Princeton University Press, 1986).

3 I. Lehr Brisbin and Cham E. Dallas, "Estimation of the Uptake and Distribution of Radiocesium by Migrating Water Fowl Following the Chernobyl Incident," *Proceedings of the Society Environmental Toxicology and Chemistry* [SETAC] (1984): 41.

4 Arne Naess, "The Shallow and the Deep, Long-Range Ecology Movement: A Summary," *Inquiry* 16 (1973): 95–100; Naess and David Rothenberg, *Ecology, Community and Life Style: Outline of an Ecosophy* (Cambridge: Cambridge University Press, 1989); and Robert Aitken, "Gandhi, Dogen and Deep Ecology," *Zero* 4 (1980): 52–57.

5 J. M. Cherrett, "Key Concepts: The Results of a Survey of Our Members' Opinions," in *Ecological Concepts: The Contribution of Ecology to an Understanding of the Natural World*, ed. J. M. Cherrett (Oxford: Blackwell Scientific Publications, 1989), 1–16.

6 Arthur G. Tansley, "The Use and Abuse of Vegetational Concepts and Terms," *Ecology* 16 (1935): 284–307.

7 Eugene P. Odum, *Fundamentals of Ecology* (Philadelphia: W. B. Saunders, 1953).

8 Ernst Haeckel, "Generelle Morphologie der Organismen," in *Allgemeine Grundzuge der organischen Formen-Wissenschaft, mechanisch begründet durch die von Charles Darwin reformirte Descendenz-Theorie*, 2 vols. (Berlin: Reimer, 1866).

9 F. Herbert Bormann and Gene E. Likens, *Pattern and Process in a Forested Ecosystem* (New York: Springer Verlag, 1979).

10 See Jan C. Smuts, *Holism and Evolution* (New York: Macmillan, 1926); and Frederic E. Clements, "Plant Succession: An Analysis of the Development of Vegetation" (Washington, D.C.: Carnegie Institution of Washington, 1916).

11 J. Baird Callicott, "The Metaphysical Implications of Ecology," *Environmental Ethics* 8 (1986): 301–16; Harley Cahen, "Against the Moral Considerability of Ecosystems," *Environmental Ethics* 10 (1988): 195–216; and Holmes Rolston III, *Environmental Ethics: Duties to and Values in the Natural World* (Philadelphia: Temple University Press, 1988).

12 Francis C. Evans, "Ecosystem as the Basic Unit in Ecology," *Science* 123 (1956): 1127–28.

13 A reviewer asked that I make clear that my use of *ecosystem* is different from

that of other authors. For example, Joel Hagen interprets the history of the ecosystem concept as a contest between ecosystem and population community ecology, with ecosystem ecology eventually being reduced in emphasis. Karen J. Warren and Jim Cheney, in a comparison of ecosystem ecology and ecofeminism, point out that beyond this ecosystem-population contrast there is a third way to view ecological science. They emphasize a hierarchical approach to ecological systems, which they call "observation set theory." Their use of the ecosystem concept to expand understanding of ecofeminism parallels my use of the concept in this essay. See Joel B. Hagen, *An Entangled Bank: The Origins of Ecosystem Ecology* (New Brunswick: Rutgers University Press, 1992); and Karen J. Warren and Jim Cheney, "Ecological Feminism and Ecosystem Ecology," *Hypatia* 6 (1991): 179–97.

14 Biological science is materialistic, but its materialism has two forms. Mechanistic materialists think that all living phenomena are ultimately explained by the laws of physics and chemistry. Holistic materialists argue that in addition to understanding the implication of the rules of physics and chemistry as they apply to living organisms, it is also necessary to know the rules through which the physical and chemical parts interact to form wholes. That is, it is not enough to understand the chemistry and physics of cells if one wishes to construct a liver from liver cells, a human body from its tissues, or the biota of a lake from its populations; information about how the parts are organized is also required.

15 Arthur Koestler, *Janus: A Summing Up* (New York: Random House, 1978).

16 Callicott comments, "Ecology gives a new meaning as well as new substance to the phrase 'enlightened self-interest' " in "Metaphysical Implications," 316.

17 Aldo Leopold, *A Sand County Almanac and Sketches Here and There* (London: Oxford University Press, 1949). "A thing is right when it tends to preserve the integrity, stability, and beauty of the biotic community. It is wrong when it tends otherwise." Leopold used the more readily understood concept of biotic community. In the ecosystem concept the biotic community interacts with its environment to form an ecosystem.

18 Robinson Jeffers, "Return," in *Selected Poems* (New York: Vantage Books, Random House, 1963), 60.

ELIZABETH DODSON GRAY

Come Inside the Circle of Creation

The Ethic of Attunement

Our view of reality is basic to our ethic. Behind every ethical system there is what Walter Lippmann once described as "the pictures in our minds of the world beyond our reach."[1] Our Judeo-Christian tradition has given us one such picture in its mandate of "dominion" in Genesis 1:26, fleshed out in Psalm 8: "What is man that Thou art mindful of him? Thou has made him a little lower than the angels and put everything else underneath his feet" (Ps. 8:4–6). What is envisioned here is a cosmic hierarchical pyramid of value—called in the Middle Ages the Great Chain of Being—a pyramid with "Man" on top; a pyramid based on the illusion that one can rank the diversity of real life, putting that which is presumed to have more value "up" and in dominion over that which is perceived to be of less value and thus "below" (Figure 1).

This cosmic pyramid humans carry in our heads is basic also to another, more recent "picture in our minds of the world beyond our reach," the evolutionary picture. It is interesting that, a century after Darwin, the evolutionary picture is fundamentally this same pyramid of value. But now God is no longer at the top. And the human species is "ascending"— as Jacob Bronowski says in The Ascent of Man[2]—from the primordial oceans through the "lower" (simpler) species to the "higher" (more complex) species.

21

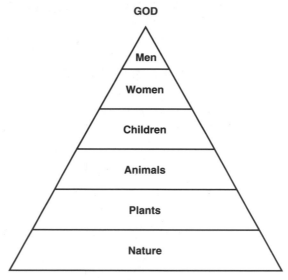

GOD

Men

Women

Children

Animals

Plants

Nature

Figure 1. The Pyramid of Value

In this evolutionary picture we have confused our human uniqueness with superiority—even though any biologist will tell you that *each* species is unique. We never ask ourselves if we, as a species, have the best eyes or ears or sense of smell or fleetness of foot, because the answer would be no. We never ask ourselves if what humans do is as remarkable as the photosynthesis plants do. Instead, we have convinced ourselves that big brains are the mark of a superior species. But recent research has revealed that cetaceans (whales, dolphins, and porpoises) have an equally large and convoluted brain cortex. Further, cetaceans, using the sonar of echolocation, can detect sickness, health, happiness, sadness, and sexual arousal in fellow cetaceans. If only we could echolocate, we would be certain we were the superior species!

Both the Judeo-Christian religious picture of cosmic hierarchy and the scientific evolutionary picture of species hierarchy manifest the self-serving nature of the game of ranking diversity. Always it is Man, the ranker, who just happens to end up at the top of his own ranking!

Where Does This Ranking Come From?

There is a cartoon in my book *Patriarchy as a Conceptual Trap* that gives us a clue to the answer to that question. Two men are standing on a suburban lawn and the snow is gently falling from a domed sky. One man is saying to the other: "How do we know we're not inside someone's paperweight?" [3]

The truth is we *are* inside someone's paperweight. We are within a bubble of assumptions, a social construction of reality built totally from the point of view of the male and male life experience.

We need to pause here to dip briefly into "the sociology of knowledge." In the period from 1909 into the early 1920s scientists peering into the very heart of matter were deeply puzzled. When they looked with the "eye" of one technology, light was a wave, but when they used the "eye" of another technology, the same light could be seen just as certainly to be made up of particles. But how, they asked themselves, could the same light be two (contradictory) things at once?

There was nothing in their Western intellectual heritage to prepare them for this seeming contradiction. One of them reports they had to become like Zen Buddhists to deal with this phenomenon.

What these scientists finally concluded was that *what* they saw depended on *how* they looked; or, to put it another way, the act of looking *affected* what was being looked at. What they had discovered was that the standing point of the observer deeply conditions what that observer can know. Thus, *knowledge is standpoint dependent.* How one thinks depends on what intellectual and cultural tradition one takes as a standing point. Let us look at some examples.

We all learned in school that Columbus discovered America. Does that mean America was lost until Columbus found it? That has indeed been our Western view. It was not until the World Council of Churches' General Assembly in Vancouver in the 1970s that a native American told the gathering that, from their point of view, "Columbus and his men were a few white men lost at sea." And they were! They were looking for India, and they had stumbled on a continent they had not known existed. When they got there, they did not know where they were. And they did not appreciate what it was they had found.

"Lostness" and "foundness" are standpoint dependent, profoundly so. Jan Struther, writing about travel in her book of essays, *Mrs. Miniver,* [4] makes a perceptive observation that the first few days after returning home are difficult because you as the traveler know you took the center of the world with you, but the people at home quaintly feel the center of the world stayed behind with them. Precisely!

The sociology of knowledge, therefore, tells us that anyone's reasoning will be deeply affected not only by assumptions like these but also by the realities of race and class and national, ethnic, and cultural origin. But it has only recently begun to dawn on us that reasoning as a standpoint-dependent activity is *also* deeply affected by sex and gender. The sociology of knowledge teaches us that all of us live within a social construction of reality, which I have named "Adam's World."[5]

Adam (the male) can say, as is said in Genesis 1: "I've named everything, thought everything, from *my* point of view." And *we*, men and women socialized into Adam's World since birth, feel: "*This* is the way the world is." We have never experienced another way.

It is no accident that the pervasive "ranking" of reality imaged in the pyramid of values came into being within what I call Adam's World and what feminists call patriarchy. I define *patriarchy* simply as a slanted society in which males are valued highly and females are valued less, in which men's prestige is up and women's is down.

Margaret Mead says that when she journeyed from tribe to tribe during her anthropological studies she discovered that it did not matter what was done in a particular tribe—it only mattered who did it. If the weaving in a particular tribe was done by men, it was an occupation of high prestige. If twenty miles away weaving was done by women, it was of low prestige. The important thing was which sex did it.[6] Think of cooking in our culture. If it is done by women at home, it is no big deal. If we go to a fancy restaurant, we find gourmet cooking done by a highly paid and honored chef—who almost invariably is male.

We all live within that slanted Adam's World, and it should not surprise us that this worldview, created by men, ranks and rewards highly what men do.

Patriarchy has been and is a problem for humans on this planet because it has been the seedbed of our near-fatal cultural need to rank diversity. Patriarchy's need to value men above women has set the *obsession* with comparison flowing within the patriarchy, and it has given us as our intellectual heritage a *mindset* of comparison. Men look at women and ask, "Which of us is better?" Whites look at people of color, straights look at gays, developed countries look at develop*ing* countries, humans look at plants, earth, and water and ask, "Which of us is better?"

Thus the problem patriarchy poses for the human species is not simply that it "ranks" and oppresses women—although that is bad enough. Patriarchy, with its obsessive need to rank diversity (beginning with male and female), has erroneously conceptualized and mythologized "Man's" place in the universe. Thus, by the illusion of dominion this ranking has legitimated, patriarchy has endangered the entire planet.

The Ethic from the Old Worldview

Now, if you were an ethic born of this worldview, what would you look like? From this hierarchical view of reality was born the ethic that humans can do anything we want on the planet, and that which is below us—animals, plants, nature—will accommodate to our wishes. This *anthropocentric illusion* about the human species and our place on planet Earth has unfortunately been the basis of Western science and technology. We never ask whether a particular invention or scientific advance fits in, because we have conceptualized ourselves as above, never as within. Mark Twain coined a great saying: "It ain't what you don't know that gits you into trouble. It's what you *think* you know that *ain't so!*"

This also has given us an atomized ethic of self-interest. When one takes isolated, autonomous entities and ranks them into pyramids of value—some up and into control, some down and supposed to obey and otherwise accommodate—then, within that worldview, self-interest can be imagined as stopping at each person's skin. I can maximize *my* self-interest—go further up the pyramid of status, power, and privilege—and never be touched or hurt by whatever happens to other entities.

Within such an atomized self-interest, what happens to blacks in the inner cities is of no concern to whites in the suburbs. Men are unconcerned about the pervasive male violence to women and children. Overstuffed Americans ignore the reality of hunger in their own country and in Third World countries. Those with homes step over the homeless on their way to work or to the theater. We send pollutants up the stack into the air as if we breathe in air made on some other planet.

The New Worldview

Into such a world have come new revelations about reality brought to us by the sciences of ecology and subatomic physics. In a multitude of ways, each of these disciplines has put out the startling news—*Reality is different from what you have imagined!*

Item: You can never do just one thing. Life is like sticking your finger into water; you always produce ripples.

Item: There is no *away* to throw things to. Even garbage ends up somewhere. So do social outcasts and people in prison.

Item: We humans are *within*—not atop—life. Life is a system of interconnections where everything ultimately affects everything else.

Item: We are actually like a fetus, maintained in life by the biospheral cycles that, functioning like a placenta, bring us our nourishment and also carry away our wastes.

Item: We are like Whos in Dr. Seuss's classic *Horton Hears a Who!*[7] We dwell within the five-mile-high "fuzz of life" on the tennis ball of the living earth.

We are living today (and have always lived) *within* an interconnected system. But we do not yet perceive or understand the component systems very well. We have a hard time *thinking systemically,* partly because many of these systems are so vast, but also because all our training teaches us to break problems into manageable parts rather than to see them and deal with them whole. Our entire formal education consists of experiencing knowledge divided into departments and specialties. We are taught to hold a tight and narrow focus and to value the intense tunnel vision of educational specialties, disciplines, and departments.

But the major problems of our day—whether they involve the health of individuals, the well-being of the economy and our society, or the environmental viability of the entire planet—suggest a new and different worldview. We are being compelled by the complexity of these problems to reimagine the character of our world and to look at reality as a whole rather than in parts. From within any of our specialties, we are being forced increasingly to construe our biological and social existence as a vast system, or system of systems, an extensive and complex network of relationships.

The Ethic from the New Worldview: Is It Stewardship?

Now, if you were an ethic born from this new worldview of the interconnected system, what would you look like? Some have advanced an ethic of stewardship. This is the new attempt within Christianity to deal positively with our environmental crisis. Those who espouse stewardship seem to be saying: "Yesterday we interpreted dominion as domination. We see now that was a mistake. But we do *not* repent of the illusion of dominion. We are still secure in our conviction that we have been given by God a primary place of authority and control as humans. But *now* we will wield that authority with *care*. We will be good stewards of the world entrusted to us. Tomorrow our hearts will be pure, and we'll do it *right!*"[8]

Stewardship is still steeped in hierarchy and paternalism. It takes for granted that we *know* what is right. Stewardship assumes that we both perceive and understand the intricate web of life that is complexly organized into ecosystems—of which humans are constituent parts.

Nor has stewardship yielded up one iota of patriarchy's illusion of dominion and superiority and smug self-assurance about its own goodness and good intentions. Stewardship is an ethic for those who will be good "husbands" of what is entrusted to them. The old patriarchal tradition, in which males used to own their wives, own their children, continues today as we "own" cars and animals and trees and farms, and nations "own" continents and even the two hundred miles of adjacent ocean and all that is in it.

Stewardship leaves these illusions of hierarchy, ownership, and dominion safe in our heads and hearts. Taking care of nature from above is not the ethic we need, because we simply do not know enough to do what is promised in the phrase *taking care*.

An Ethic of Attunement

What ethic do I think is adequate to express our true situation of interconnectedness and relationship? Instead of stewardship I would speak of *attunement*. In place of dominion, in place of illusions of control, I am suggesting attunement. Write it on your hearts. It means that we are to open ourselves, we are to listen and look, we are to pay attention.

Why? Because we are *within* life, not above it, and we see life incompletely and often dimly, and we cannot afford *not* to attune ourselves. Not paying attention to our life-support systems in the earth's biosphere will no longer work for us.

Is it *possible* to attune ourselves to trees and rivers? After all, they do not talk. Christopher Stone, in *Should Trees Have Standing?* says:

Natural objects *can* communicate their wants (needs) to us, and in ways that are not terribly ambiguous. I am sure I can judge with more certainty and meaningfulness whether and when my lawn wants (needs) water, than the Attorney General can judge whether and when the United States wants (needs) to take an appeal from an adverse judgment by a lower court. . . . For similar reasons, the guardian-attorney for a smog-endangered stand of pines could venture with more confidence that his client wants the smog stopped, than the directors of a corporation can assert that the corporation wants dividends declared.[9]

What Stone is proposing for natural objects is similar to what parents do when they attune themselves to the nonverbal body language of infants. All life is not bound up in words. Body language speaks volumes in parenting, in sexuality, in friendship. The earth also has nonverbal body language, as Stone points out. When the air smells bad, when the trees on the crests of hills and mountains die, when the waters are foul to the eye and nose, it does not take a genius to know that we are doing something wrong—and that we must *stop* doing it.

Paying Attention When We Hear Crying

Shortly after my daughter was born I discovered that she cried intensely every time I tried to put her in water to bathe her. So I stopped bathing her that way and kept her clean with baby oil and cotton. In that era of correct child rearing I did not talk about this with anyone, I just did it.

My daughter's body language was absolutely clear to me, and, attuned, I accommodated. Her hair did not fall out, her skin did not rot, and she grew up to be an athletic young adult who takes at least two showers a day. But when she was an infant, bathwater was not for her, and I attuned myself to her crying.

"What we most need to do," says the poet Thich Nhat Hanh, "is to hear within ourselves the sounds of the Earth crying."[10] Can we hear the plant in the tropical rain forest, the plant that may have the cure for cancer or for AIDS? Can we hear that plant calling out just before the bulldozers reach it? The extinction of species is silent. We did not hear a cry then. Can we listen now? Can we hear and attune ourselves at all?

Fitting In

How do we do this attuning—in practical terms? Well, the overall task is largely to redesign our technologies, indeed, our whole industrial system, so that it fits within the biological fabric that is life rather than blasts gaping holes in it. Let me first explain what I mean and then give several examples of this being done.

Humans are impressed by our worldwide industrial and economic system and by the measures of national GNP by which we gauge it. But the greatest productivity on earth is not industrial or even human; it is the producing and reproducing done by the biosphere (Figure 2).

All life starts with the energy from the sun, the source of all production in the biosphere. Green plants join oxygen atoms and hydrogen atoms to make carbohydrates, what you and I know as food and use in our cars as hydrocarbons, or gasoline. This energy of the sun captured in photosynthesis provides the foundation of all nonplant life and all human civilizations and technologies. So the green plants are *producers*.

The wastes of the producers are food for the *consumers*. In the food chain, green plants become food for mammals, birds, fish, and reptiles. Small animals are eaten by larger animals, and these in turn are eaten by still larger animals. Humans sometimes speak of ourselves as top carnivores because we eat all classes of other organisms. But we are *not* at the top, because we need these other organisms to exist; they do not need us. We are at the *bottom* of the food chain—the most vulnerable organisms of all.

The wastes of all the consumers, including eventually their bodies, flesh, and bones, become food for the *decomposers*—fungi, bacteria, and insects. In scavenging their own life energy, the decomposers continue the process of breaking down complex molecules and returning them as simpler molecules and atoms to the resource pool, where they can again cycle through the producer green plants in photosynthesis, flowing to the consumers and then to the decomposers. It is a cycle that repeats itself, mostly without human intervention or management and certainly without any reliance on government subsidies. From the perspective of the industrialized economies this is truly an underappreciated miracle.

By contrast, the industrial model of production (Figure 3) is linear rather than cyclical. For its inputs it depends on geologically concentrated deposits of raw materials and energy, and it depletes these. Its intentional and unintentional outputs (i.e., its products and its wastes) are complex chemical compounds such as chlorofluorocarbons (CFCs) and polychlorinated biphenyls (PCBs), and heat—vast quantities of heat.

I am asserting that our task in the next generation is to redesign that industrial model of production, changing it from an unsustainable straight-

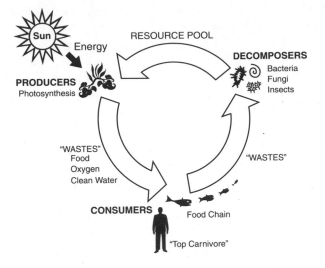

Figure 2. The Biosphere Model of Production

line method to a system that is sustainable and circular, one that cycles and recycles, mimicking the cyclical processes of the biosphere. We need to convert from an arrow that disrupts and overloads natural systems and biospheral cycles to a circle fitted within the cycles that characterize the biospheral model of production.

Why? Because we *exist within* these biospheral cycles, and when we finally come to understand that, and only then, we will design ourselves within it. *This* is the challenge of the future: redesigning our industrial system to fit *within*. And this is a work that stems only from the environmental ethic of attunement.

Technology That Fits Like a Hand in a Glove

The ecologist Bettie Willard has said of our technology that it must be like a hand in a glove. It must be designed and used with such sensitivity and attunement that it fits within the biospheral systems just as a hand fits into a glove without destroying that glove.

Be clear that the ethic of attunement is not against technology. It is not

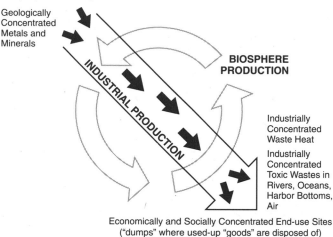

Figure 3. The Industrial Model of Production

Luddite. We need technology to help us redesign our industrial system. But it must be technology used with sensitivity, technology that is carefully and consistently monitored to track its impacts on air and water and natural systems and habitats. What is needed is technology motivated not only by profit but by a profound appreciation of our true place within the living earth system and marked by a commitment to stop using any technology if it proves harmful.

How do we do that? Willard suggests using "ecological reconnaissance." By this she means sending out ecologically trained advance patrols to scout what lies ahead of us. Usually a project is conceived because of some human or regional or national need (and the possibility of profit). Then the project is designed by engineers or architects or economists or other planners (usually untrained with regard to considering the ecology of the particular natural systems involved). All those involved use their usual professional skills, but these do *not* include ecological scouting.

Only after the project, at great expense, has been fully designed is it time for the legally mandated environmental impact statement. Never having enlisted ecologists to "listen" to the environment, it should come as no surprise to discover that we must then choose between, say, a massive dam project and the tiny endangered snail darter; or between a logging industry and the forest that is the last remaining habitat of an endangered owl species.

But these choices we have generated for ourselves are stupid ones. They are the alternatives we created when, by inadvertence and by a lack of ecological expertise at the start, we created a faulty original design that could have been vastly improved by adequate anticipatory ecological reconnaissance.

Attuning a Pipeline to the Dynamic Mystery of Permafrost

Perhaps you remember the Alaskan pipeline stretching from Prudhoe Bay on the Arctic Ocean across Alaska to the southern coastal port of Valdez. Oil was discovered at Prudhoe Bay in 1966, and early in the 1970s the trans-Alaska pipeline was being planned by engineers to lie directly atop the permafrost. Under the usual Arctic conditions, permafrost, the swamplike land found in parts of Alaska, is permanently frozen.

I was told (again by Bettie Willard) that early in this enormous pipeline construction project, Max Brewer approached the engineers in charge and suggested that there were some things they needed to know about permafrost. Brewer's specialty was permafrost engineering, and at that time he was director of the Naval Arctic Research Laboratory several hundred miles to the west in Barrow, Alaska.

Brewer was brushed off by the engineers, who assured him they had built many such pipelines in some of the most hostile environments on the planet. What Brewer knew was that permafrost *looks* hard and solid when it is frozen. But even when it is solid the permafrost is still a dynamic medium. It looks rock-hard, but it does not behave like rock. And when permafrost is warmed, it melts to a marshlike state.

The high viscosity of the crude oil from the North Slope meant that it had to be pumped out hot, at 180°F. The designs called for the pipeline to transmit this hot oil through a four-foot-wide pipe of half-inch-thick steel. The pipeline was to be 781 miles long, laid on top of the ground.

Can you see this coming? The Alyeska Pipeline Construction Company started construction in the summer of 1974. One portion of the pipeline was laid on permafrost across the bottom of a river. The engineers' first interest in the unusual properties of permafrost came the following spring when they found that the portion of the pipeline attached to the bottom of the riverbed had been twisted and curled like copper wiring by one winter's shifts in the permafrost.

Suddenly everyone could imagine what Max Brewer already knew. They could now envision what would have happened to the permafrost (and the pipeline) if it had been subjected to heat lost from uninsulated steel pipes transporting high-temperature oil. Suddenly everyone could foresee the pipeline sinking into a swamp of its own making. Approximately 60 percent of the pipeline had to cross permafrost.

The right-of-way for the trans-Alaska pipeline was nearly all on federal land, and it was the responsibility of the U.S. Department of the Interior to protect the land during this use. Retired General Andrew Rollins, formerly of the U.S. Army Corps of Engineers, was appointed to act for Interior on behalf of the environment.

Rollins assembled a sizable multidisciplinary team to do an extensive assessment of the environment through which the pipeline was being constructed. Willard, an Alpine ecologist, was at that time one of three members of the Council on Environmental Quality in the Executive Office of the President. She has told me how finally the pipeline was built on a pad of gravel to sit wrapped in thermal insulation atop holders that elevated it six to eight feet in the air. As it was finally constructed, she regards the pipeline as one of the most environmentally sensitive major construction projects to date.

There is a parable here. Remember the permafrost. Imagine the heated oil and the original design. This sinking pipeline is a microcosm of what happens when we do not attune ourselves to a complex and dynamically changing natural world.

The Port of Miami Story

Move in your mind now to the subtropical waters of southern Florida in the mid-1970s. The population of Miami has grown from 200,000 in the early 1960s to nearly 3 million, and Biscayne Bay is in deep trouble from filling, sewage, and thermal pollution from nuclear power plants, as well as from dredging by the Port of Miami.[11]

"The South Florida coastline is a fragile and sensitive subtropical environment," says my colleague and friend Anitra Thorhaug, a specialist in subtropical marine ecosystems. "There are three critical habitats: the mangrove trees, from the Everglade estuaries to the shoreline; the coral reefs; and the sea grass, from the shoreline to the continental shelf. These areas are home to thousands of species: the roseate spoonbill, the manatee, the great blue heron, eagles, pink shrimp, stone crab and rock lobster."[12]

In 1976 the Port of Miami needed to double its size. In two earlier expansions the port authorities had designed construction without considering the environment, and environmental groups had gone to court to stop the projects, resulting in highly publicized fights and costly delays. The Port of Miami now wanted to enlarge and deepen the shipping channels.

This time port officials decided to try to do things right. They recognized the need for ecological reconnaissance, and they approached Thorhaug, who was just establishing herself as an expert in a new specialty, subtropical marine coastal ecosystems.

She surveyed the sea life on the bottom of Biscayne Bay. During 1976–78 she negotiated and renegotiated the plans for the dredging with the project engineers, reducing the total amount of dredging that would be done. Finally, after the third or fourth revision, the expansion needs of the port and the survival needs of marine life and ecosystems in Biscayne Bay had been brought into an acceptable economic and ecological balance.

Thorhaug did her job well—so well that when she and the Port of Miami met with representatives of the Biscayne Bay environmental groups, they all "signed on" in about twenty minutes. In two years of work, Thorhaug saved the Port of Miami about $10 million and a great deal of time. The point is not that $10 million was saved, but that with design teams that involve appropriate ecological experts, it is possible to design major industrial projects *within* fragile ecosystems *without* destroying or disrupting them.

The Experiment in Ecology at Henderson Mine

The "experiment in ecology" at AMAX/Henderson Mine high in the Colorado Rocky Mountains is an account of an early corporate decision to try ecological reconnaissance.

In 1966, AMAX, Incorporated, determined that the Henderson deposit could be a profitable molybdenum mine. The mine and the mill to process the ore were to be located in fragile ecosystems just at the timberline. "These altitudes [10,300–11,300 feet above sea level] result in severe winters and very short growing seasons. The average annual temperature is slightly below freezing. The growing season, as depicted by consecutive frost-free days, can be expected to last only six to eight weeks. Seed of grass species native to these elevations is not commercially available."[13] So the ecology of the site was challenging.

To get a pound and a half of molybdenum it is necessary to mine, crush, and process five hundred pounds of ore. Thus the process of mining and milling is very energy-intensive, and, high in the Rockies, it takes place far from energy sources. And afterward there is the problem of what, in this environmentally sensitive setting, to do with the enormous volume of waste in the form of mine tailings. Furthermore, the molybdenum is separated from the rock by a water-based process. This takes place in a water-scarce setting and must not pollute local watercourses.

Colorado was at that time (and still is) a state very conscious of the environmental and aesthetic aspects of the lives of its citizens. Jobs and prosperity are important, but things also have to be good for nature and must look good to the human eye from highways, airplanes, mountaintops, and valleys.

How, then, was a mining company best to perform an essentially industrial process in a remote setting that was both ecologically and aesthetically fragile?

Along with the decision to develop the Henderson mine and mill, a related decision was made at the highest levels within AMAX to seek out prominent local environmental activists and specialists in what AMAX at the time described as "an experiment in ecology." To AMAX management, this meant trying to meet the highest environmental standards while at the same time meeting the corporate objective of developing a technologically and economically effective new mine. Bettie Willard was one of the prominent Colorado environmentalists they sought out, and she and her files are my source of this information.

The molybdenum deposit lay two thousand feet underground. It was beneath a smaller deposit that was already being mined, and the small valley would soon begin filling with mine tailings left after the molybdenum had been extracted from the older, smaller mine.

So where could AMAX locate the processing mill for the new mine? There would be acres of mine tailings. It would be an energy- and water-intensive process, and the ore would need to be transported some distance to it.

A committee composed of ten upper-level AMAX decision makers and environmentalists developed and evaluated potential sites for the mill, listing sites from A to Z and then AA on to JJ as they considered them. "AMAX officials knew that there were engineering limitations that could not be violated. And the environmentalists were firm in their convictions that there were ecological principles that should not be violated in the construction of a mine." [14]

Site JJ, they all agreed, worked for the company, for the ecology, for transportation, and for aesthetics. There was also sufficient space there for the vast volume of sandy wastes left after processing at the mill, and there would not be any disturbance of water through pollution. The solution they arrived at together, commented a writer for the *Journal of Metals* shortly thereafter, is "unusual in that the mill, which for obvious reasons of transportation economics should have been located at the mine mouth, was actually installed *15 miles away* at the end of a railroad line that *includes a 9.6 mile tunnel under the [Continental] Divide.*" [15]

Learning to See and Work with the Grain

The first step was the ecological inventory, to determine with animal ecology and plant studies what species and what quantities were present at the site before work began. The site of the Henderson mine and mill comprises some 22,750 acres. The mine is in Clear Creek County east of the Continental Divide; the mill was to be west of the divide in Grand County.

AMAX fostered an attitude of doing everything possible to minimize disturbance of the site. This extended to the more than two hundred separate contracts let in connection with the development of the mine, including that to the Public Service Company of Colorado (PSCo), which was supplying power to the site. In conferences with the environmentalists PSCo officials came up with the criteria for the design, location, and construction of the transmission lines. Today such criteria are commonplace, but they were highly innovative then.

The power company also learned what areas to avoid passing through. Most of the timber on and around Henderson is quite young because it has been periodically wiped out by fire, ranching, or timbering. During the environmental inventory, plant ecologist John Marr found a climax (mature) stand containing several hundred-year-old Douglas firs. In the fragile ecosystems of the high Rockies this is a rare and important habitat. PSCo rerouted power lines around it, choosing instead a route through faster-growing lodgepole pine.

PSCo also shifted from hauling cut trees out on trucks to dragging such trees out with horses, their hoofprints being less destructive in that fragile terrain than truck tracks. To put transmission poles in place with the least environmental disruption, PSCo used helicopters in what was then a very innovative procedure but has since become common for utility companies working in remote locations.

Above the timberline, where tundra growth is measured not in years but in decades and centuries, AMAX wrote the power company contracts specifying that displaced tundra would be set aside on burlap and replaced after each pole was set in place.

Bill Distler, AMAX vice president of western operations, saw mining as "a temporary use of the land. . . . We may be there for 50 or 60 years, carrying on mining activities." In the view of AMAX the environmental objective was to cause as little disturbance as possible while AMAX was there, and when the firm was finished mining, to restore the site as nearly as possible to the way it was before.[16]

AMAX had grasped the meaning of "using technology like a hand in a glove."

A New View of Self-interest

The Alaskan pipeline, the Port of Miami, AMAX and PSCo at the Henderson mine—these case studies each illustrate that attunement carries with it a radically new view of self-interest. If life really is an interconnected system—if we really live on a finite and intricately interrelated planet—then the only ethic that works is a whole-system or all-win ethic.

Every decision we make, to be a good decision, must be good for the whole system. If a decision is good for the corporation but not for its environment, then it is a bad decision and we will come to regret it. If a decision is good for humans but not for trees or tundra or permafrost or marine life, it is a bad decision.

If a decision is good for men but not for women, then it is a bad decision and we will regret it. The truth is, we cannot affirm life unless we affirm women, because women are the life-bearers of the human species. This is why the so-called Pro-Life movement is not really pro-life—because it is not pro-women.

But also, if a decision is good for adults but not for children—good for whites but not for people of color; good for rich but not for poor; good for the First World but not the Third World; good for humans but not good for plants, animals, the ozone layer, and air and water; good for the present but not the future—it is a BAD decision and we will come to regret it.

The alternative whole-system ethic can say, with Native American spirituality, "With all beings and all things we shall be as relatives." It is foolishness to say, "Your end of the lifeboat is sinking." Do we really comprehend the full absurdity of a wealthy corporation on a dying planet? I once saw a sign in a vegetarian restaurant that read, Only when the last tree is cut down, when the last river is poisoned, and the last fish is caught, will we realize we can't eat money.

A New View of Diversity

Attunement also carries with it a new view of all kinds of diversity. The old ethic ranked diversity so that some human and biological diversity was rendered invisible, devalued, abused, and subjected to violence and extinction. When we exorcise from our hearts and minds the culturally taught obsession to rank diversity, we can then internalize the truth that ecology has learned—namely, that diversity is what keeps a dynamic system stable.

Richard Austin writes: "The more diverse a particular ecosystem is, the more stable and healthy it is likely to be; the greater the variety of species within the system, the more resistant the system is to blight or attack, and the more resources it has to recover from attack. . . . Life is best supported by diversity."[17] So, ranking diversity is not only illusion, it is also life threatening.

The ethic of attunement *within* an interconnected system calls us to become comfortable with diversity, to praise and celebrate it, and to honor the diversity that holds all life in place. Diversity is life affirming, so to affirm diversity, whether human or nonhuman, is to affirm life.

The All-Win Ethic

If we look at game theory, we can see what we are changing. With patriarchy we have played our lives like a zero-sum game: if I win, it's plus one—and if I win, then you have to lose, which is minus one. Plus one and minus one add up to a zero-sum game. Our patriarchal culture has played life as though it could *only* be a zero-sum game. I can gain only at your expense. It is like a teeter-totter or seesaw: if I am up, you must be down.

This is the moral essence of the Superbowl and competitive games in general in the male world. These win/lose games socialize continuing generations of males into believing this is the only game in town, and that this I-win/you-lose game is what one can (and must) play even within an interconnected system. This seesaw understanding of things also leads some men to fear feminism, thinking that if women come up, then men will have to go down.

But in truth, the way of all-win is like a cartoon by Shirvanian that I included in *Patriarchy as a Conceptual Trap*. [18] It shows a husband and wife dancing about just inside their front door, saying, "We did it! We did it! You had a good day and I had a good day—both in the same day!"

Exactly! Within an interconnected system everything, and everyone, wins—or nothing wins. We, the human species, are like the huge elephant in the forest: we can act out that all-win ethic only by an exquisite dance of attunement, trying hard to pay attention to what is so that we may walk very lightly upon the earth.

Seeing What We Have Never Seen Before

A headline in the *Harvard Gazette* proclaimed "Chimpanzees Use Plants as 'Medicine,' Research Finds." Twenty years earlier, in 1971, Richard Wrangham first watched a chimpanzee carefully select leaves from *Aspilia,* a plant of the sunflower family, and swallow them without chewing. Wrangham, a Harvard anthropologist and specialist in primate behavior, knew chimps did not normally eat this plant, and when they did they acted like children taking castor oil. Wrangham had a hunch the chimp was doctoring himself.

According to the *Gazette* account, it was 1984 before Wrangham found someone who would take the time to analyze *Aspilia*. "Eloy Rodriguez of the University of California, Irvine, chemically analyzed the leaves and found that they contain an oil that kills bacteria, fungi, and parasitic worms. What is more, he told a meeting of the American Association for the Advancement of Science [February 1992], the same compound kills cancer cells that are particularly resistant to drugs."

Wrangham described two additional plants he had discovered with the help of chimps. One is a potent antibiotic, the other induces labor or abortion. At the same session various researchers reported on medicinal plants used by bears, monkeys, and elephants in the United States, South America, and Africa.

"We don't yet know how widespread the practice of animals doctoring themselves is," Wrangham said. "But the idea that they could reveal to us a storehouse of new drugs is an incredible and wonderful one." [19]

The close of the article reports Wrangham contemplating the evolutionary meaning of it all: "Chimps, capuchins, elephants, and bears boast the biggest brains in their beastly categories. 'Does this mean,' he mused, 'that finding and using natural medicines is a product of greater intelligence? Or is it a broad phenomenon spread over the entire animal kingdom from butterflies to the closest relatives of humans—a phenomenon of which we have been ignorant until now?' "

I would ask: Were we ignorant because we never bothered to look? Did we fail to pay attention because we did not think animals could teach us something we didn't know? Such looking would be an outgrowth of attuning ourselves, an outgrowth of knowing ourselves to be within and therefore in need of paying attention, learning.

Where you stand, physically and mentally, affects what you see and where you look. The ethic of attunement calls us to come inside the circle of creation and find our unique place, but we must give up our arrogance.[20] Having eyes, do we not see? Having ears, do we not hear?

Can we attune ourselves to life before it is too late? Only time will tell.

NOTES

1 Walter Lippmann, *Public Opinion* (New York: Macmillan, 1922).

2 Jacob Bronowski, *The Ascent of Man* (Boston: Little, Brown, 1973).

3 Bill Maul cartoon (1981), in *Patriarchy as a Conceptual Trap,* by Elizabeth Dodson Gray (Wellesley, Mass.: Roundtable Press, 1982), 38.

4 Jan Struther, *Mrs. Miniver* (New York: Grosset & Dunlap, 1940), 269.

5 "Adam's World" is a concept first developed in *Patriarchy as a Conceptual Trap*. It was then used as the title for a twenty-minute movie (1988) by the National Film Board of Canada about Elizabeth Dodson Gray and her work.

6 Margaret Mead, *Male and Female: A Study of the Sexes in a Changing World* (New York: Morrow Paperback, William Morrow, 1949, 1975), 159–60.

7 Dr. Seuss, *Horton Hears a Who!* (New York: Random House, 1954).

8 See, for example, Douglas John Hall, *Imaging God: Dominion as Stewardship* (Grand Rapids, Mich.: W. B. Eerdmans; New York: Friendship Press, for the Commission on Stewardship, National Council of Churches of Christ, 1986).

9 Christopher Stone, *Should Trees Have Standing? Toward Legal Rights for Natural Objects* (Los Altos, Calif.: William Kaufmann, 1974), 24.

10 Thich Nhat Hanh, quoted by Joanna Macy in *Thinking Like a Mountain,* by John Seed et al. (Philadelphia: New Society Publishers, 1988), 102–3.

11 Anitra Thorhaug, Eugene Man, and Harvey Ruvin, "Biscayne Bay: A Decade of Restoration Progress," in *Environmental Restoration: Science and Strategies for Restoring the Earth,* ed. John J. Berger (Washington, D.C., and Covelo, Calif.: Island Press, 1990), 192–95.

12 Thorhaug, in "Local Heroes: A Special Environmental Series Sponsored by Amway" [advertisement], *U.S. News and World Report,* December 17, 1990, 90.

13 Larry F. Brown, "Reclamation at Climax, Urad and Henderson Mines," *Mining Congress Journal* (April 1976).

14 Jonijane Paxton, "An Experiment in Ecology: AMAX/Henderson Meeting the Environmental Challenges," *Editorial Alert* (1974): 8.

15 "The Henderson Mine/Mill/Concentrator: Fifty Million Pounds of Molybdenum per Year from a Successful Experiment in Ecology," *Journal of Metals* (October 1977).

16 Paxton, "Experiment in Ecology," 27.

17 Richard Cartwright Austin, *Beauty of the Lord: Awakening the Senses* (Atlanta: John Knox Press, 1988), 32.

18 Gray, *Patriarchy as a Conceptual Trap,* 71.

19 *Harvard Gazette,* February 7, 1992.

20 Elizabeth Dodson Gray, *The Energy Oratorio* (New York: Energy Study Project of the National Council of Churches of Christ, 1978), 18.

YU-SHI MAO

Evolution of Environmental Ethics

A Chinese Perspective

The longevity of Chinese civilization is due in part to sustainable environmental practices in agriculture. Starting three thousand years ago the Chinese people gradually learned the relation between farming methods and sustainability, which was documented in the ancient classic *Si Shu Wu Jing* and other books. Although the ancient Chinese philosophies, Confucianism and Taoism, emphasize the harmonious existence of human beings with other creatures, current population growth in China threatens this harmony.

The current concept of ethics in China has evolved from these older philosophies. The evolution of ethics not only helps keep society in good order but also promotes the development of human society; however, at the same time some changes in ethics can damage the environment. Therefore we need not merely a *new* ethics but an *appropriate* ethics. I discuss the possibility of such an ethical evolution below.

Ancient Chinese Environmental Ethics

Chinese written documents more than three thousand years old and archaeological evidence record a history of five thousand years of cultural development. The ancient Chinese ceased to be a nomadic tribe as early as 3000 B.C. and settled down to develop their agriculture.[1] While the Babylonians and Assyrians mismanaged their croplands and turned them into deserts, the Chinese cultivated and recultivated their own fields in certain areas for forty or fifty centuries. The longevity of Chinese civilization must be attributed in part to these sustainable agricultural practices.[2]

Mengfucius (372–289 B.C.), the most influential student of Confucius, said when he was approaching the king of Liang: "Plant your crops according to the changes of season, you will have more food than you want; limit the size of holes in your net, you will have more fish than you want; bide your time to fell the trees, you will have more fuelwood than you want." Even earlier, Guan-zhong (?–645 B.C.), the minister of Kingdom Qi, taught his people not to raise too many cattle on the grassland, lest it fail to recover from overexploitation; and not to plant crops too close together, otherwise the fertility of the soil would be insufficient. He also advised the people to utilize the forest and the fisheries, but only to a reasonable extent. Although the major points of *Si Shu Wu Jing* (Four Books and Five Classics; Mengfucius is one of the authors) are social ethics and philosophy, it mentions the right way to take from nature. Because *Si Shu Wu Jing* served as the central government's standard textbook for selecting officials, it was the most important book for every Chinese intellectual. Thus sound environmental practices have been taught in China for more than two thousand years. Some ancient Chinese physicians did not charge their patients but asked them to plant trees instead,[3] and this tradition still exists in rural areas. Even today the proverb You will never face shortage of fuelwood as long as the hills are green remains one of the best-known sayings in China.

Environmental aesthetics has its earliest record in *Zhou Yi* (anonymous), a book written even before the time of Confucius, which deals with the nature, society, and performance of the universe. Its theme treats the dynamic balance between human beings and nature.[4] Other ideas developed into the mysterious knowledge called geomancy, which relates the natural scene to an individual's fortune. Some Chinese locate houses or tombs or even the position of a desk in the office according to the principles of geomancy. Though there is little sound evidence to show that geomancy can ensure one's fortune, it has helped to create environmental aesthetics. To a certain extent, thanks to geomancy, the layout of the beautiful gardens in Suzhou, the magnificent Forbidden City in Beijing, and many other ancient buildings are in wonderful harmony with their surroundings. Almost all the distinguished poets in Chinese history left elegant poems depicting the beauty of nature, and these too have fostered environmental aesthetics. On the other hand, rules to despoil an area have also been summarized. The poet Li Shang-yin (813–858) criticized the nine ways to damage a scenic spot; in doing so he made another kind of contribution to environmental aesthetics.

These older cultures could not withstand the pressure exerted on the environment by the growing population. Before the eighteenth century the Chinese population fluctuated due to political unrest, foreign invasion, natural disaster, and disease.[5] When the Qing dynasty was established (1636) China's population was 100 million. A sudden increase occurred in the mid-eighteenth century, and within one hundred years the population jumped from 140 million to 430 million (partly because of adjustment for statistical error), while cultivated land increased from only 46 to 50 million hectares.[6] This population increase created the tremendous land shortage that was one of the leading causes of the Taiping revolution. Almost one-third of the population was killed during fourteen years of turmoil (1851–65). But the most intense population pressure occurred after the founding of the People's Republic in 1949. The population has more than doubled since then, and the current figure is 1.2 billion. China has 7 percent of the world's cultivated land to feed 22 percent of the world's population. Now there is no way to follow the ancient Chinese instruction; vast forests have disappeared, grasslands are overgrazed, rivers and lakes are polluted, underground water is depleted, deserts have expanded. In short, China's environment is in extreme danger.

Chinese Philosophy of the Relation Between Nature and Humans

The damage to the environment, some argue, can be attributed to anthropocentrism, which asserts that human beings are the rightful possessors of the universe and other creatures and plants are only servants to the owners. Humans can use the environment at will, without concern for the needs of others. These background beliefs about the relation between nature and humanity have clearly affected environmental conservation.

In the years of Confucius (551–479 B.C.) there were beliefs, but no religion in the strict sense existed. The ancient Chinese took Heaven as the Almighty, a counterpart of God in other nations' religions, but Heaven was never personalized. Animals, plants, rocks, and humans were different parts of nature and were governed by Heaven. Humans seemed to be at the same level as all other beings in the composition of nature. The emperor was the most powerful person in the society, but even the imperial power was thought to be conferred by Heaven,[7] and in fact, the emperor was called the Son of the Heaven. If even the emperor was small compared with Heaven, so much the smaller was the average person. Such an idea continued and dominated Chinese history until recent times. The relative positions of humans and nature are best illustrated by ancient Chinese paintings in which human beings often occupy a tiny space while the mountains, rivers, and trees take a much larger space. The sharp contrast in size is deliberately exaggerated to show the painter's philosophy.

In Western paintings the objects depicted are usually in exact proportion, the more accurate the better, and exaggerations are rarely used. Western painters learn perspective, geometry, and anatomy, but the ancient Chinese painters, even the greatest ones, knew little about these things. Their aim was not to reproduce the objective world but to transfer their understanding of the universe to the viewer through their paintings. The exaggerated proportions of nature relative to humans shows the philosophical idea: Humankind can never be positioned at the center of the universe. In addition, portrait painting and religious painting, major compositions in Western art, have rarely been important in Chinese art; on the contrary, mountains and rivers generally dominate Chinese pictures, followed by flowers, bamboos, fishes, and other small creatures. The contrast can be seen as another example illustrating different ethical cultures in West and East.

Six centuries after Confucius, in A.D. 67, Buddhism entered China from India, though it gradually declined and even disappeared between the thirteenth and nineteenth centuries in India itself. The essence of Buddhism is *equity,* an equity not only between individuals but also between humans and other creatures. Buddhists conceive of reincarnation after death. Tibetans believe that the Lama never dies; when his body becomes silent his soul goes into a newborn baby's body. For the average person, however, the next life may be as a pig, a dog, or even an insect. Therefore, Buddhism prohibits killing creatures and requires monks to be vegetarians. Today, older Chinese still believe that freeing captive animals is a merciful practice.[8]

In both doctrine and practice Buddhism emphasizes the harmonious coexistence of all the components of the environment. In China today, the best-protected environments are Buddhist temples and emperors' mausoleums and their surroundings. The former were protected by monks and the latter by soldiers. About one-third of the most famous scenic areas in China are Buddhist temples surrounded by ancient trees. If there had been no Buddhism, none of these beautiful places would have been preserved. Thus, one could say that Buddhists are the oldest environmentalists.

Taoism is a religion rooted in China itself. It was established in A.D. 142, after Buddhism had arrived. Founded by Zhang Dao-ling, Taoism venerates the ancient Chinese philosophers Lao Zi, who lived at the same time as Confucius, and Zhuang Zi, a follower two or three hundred years later. Taoism was the only religion strong enough to challenge Buddhism before Christianity was imported on a large scale in the eighteenth century. The fundamentals of Taoism are, first, strict restriction of material desire; and, second, rigorous obedience of natural law. With regard to daily life, one should live as simply as possible; with regard to social order, the best way of managing a nation is to do nothing. Such a conservative ideology was conducive to environmental protection, but it delayed economic development.[9]

The Development of Ethics Before the Market Economy

Besides deforestation due to population pressure, the environment has been damaged by industry that encourages the wanton use of natural resources and sets no restriction on pollutant discharge. In terms of ethical consideration, damage to the environment is due to the attraction of material enjoyment driven by self-interest. Although postindustrial population growth is an important factor, it is an effect, not a cause, of industrialization.

Ethics has evolved over thousands of years. The idea of good versus evil seems to be inherent in human nature, not the result of education. Although there are minor differences in ethics among different peoples, fundamental common points are shared, including benevolence, sympathy, honesty, and generosity. This is perhaps the result of evolution: groups with an antisocial notion of ethics would die off. For example, a people who believed that killing female babies was good would not survive. That is to say, different races of people may have very different notions of ethics, but only those which pursue pro-social morality can survive. Therefore, today the same basic ideas of good and evil are found among different nations, just as the biological human appearance is the same: both are the results of evolution.

In the primitive stage of Chinese history, social unrest was caused by the oppression of tyrants, fights with neighboring countries for land or wealth, and internal conflicts for power or population. It was natural that ancient wise men thought that the best way to win peace was to limit material desires and to consider others' benefits before one's own. These ideas are the essential points of Chinese ethics and, more or less, are shared by ancient Western ethics, too.

Such an ethics contains a logical contradiction, however: If the purpose of ethical rules is to advance everyone's well-being, why should these rules limit material enjoyment and ask everyone to sacrifice private benefits? Means and ends seem mutually exclusive. But within the context of a zero-sum game, in which no net benefit can be created, there is no other choice in setting ethical rules, even for the wisest sage of ancient times. In that context, to be rich is an evil thing. Since the pie is constant, any extra wealth has to come from stealing or exploitation of others.

During the Qin dynasty (221–206 B.C.), the first emperor of Qin ordered the rich people all over the country to move to the capital to facilitate close supervision; in the following dynasty, Han the emperor decreed a law prohibiting merchants from wearing silk clothes and riding on sedan chairs or horses. Since then a stringent policy toward merchants has been pursued in China. Although everyone likes to be rich, displays of great wealth are disdained. The only rich people tolerated were the emperor and associated officials, who held privileged rights that—before the idea of democracy emerged—were thought to be necessary for the stable structure of a society.

Indeed, it was an unfortunate misunderstanding that deemed that all riches come from stealing or exploitation. In fact, merchants can make themselves rich without stealing, provided that trade is voluntary, simply because trade that brings benefit to both sides brings agreement. Trade or exchange has a magic character that creates a net benefit and breaks through the zero-sum game rule. This was a discovery made by Adam Smith. Any policy that attacks merchants and cracks down on trade must result in harm to the common people. But traditional ethical thinking, based on zero-sum games, dies hard; until the 1980s, long-distance trading was thought to be profiteering in China. Speculation is illegal today.

The Industrial Revolution opened a new era of human history and a tremendous potential in productivity. Some think that the revolution was brought about by the invention of the steam engine and other machines, but technological change was not the real cause of the Industrial Revolution. China had a well-developed manufacturing industry as early as the eleventh century, when the output of iron is estimated to have stood at five to six times that of Europe's.[10] By the thirteenth century China had already developed a hydro-powered spinning machine.[11] This did not help China enter into industrialization, however, because the division of labor and the associated exchange between sectors of industry were repeatedly hindered by a policy hostile toward merchants. Even today merchants often become the target of riots, not only in China but also in other Asian countries such as Indonesia, Malaysia, and Vietnam. The new attitude, which recognizes one's right to pursue one's own interest in economic activities, has been encouraging the evolution of traditional ethics into modern market ethics. Such an evolution of ethics is based on the recognition that the destructive force of self-interest in ancient society has turned into a locomotive of economic development. The conservatism of ethical change in all countries with long cultural histories might be one of the principal retardants of market economies.

Market Ethics and Its Impact
on Environment

Ancient (or autarkic) ethics is different from market ethics. The former developed under the circumstances of household management; the latter under the circumstances of market exchange. The major difference between them lies in whether it is considered right or wrong to pursue one's own interest. Market ethics recognizes everyone's right to pursue one's own interest, provided the same right of others is observed. It is dangerous to think that all the moral constraints of seeking advantage can be abandoned during the process of transition from a nonmarket economy to a market economy, however. Traditional ethics is like a barrier that prevents conflicts among individuals. When such a barrier is demolished, people may behave without due restraint. At the beginning stage of a market economy one sees chaos mixed with good and evil, a desire to produce wealth and to share in others' wealth. Only after hundreds of years do people learn the correct way of transacting business; only then is a market economy on the right track. In the case of a sudden transition from a planned economy (which I prefer to call a household economy) to a market economy (as we see in Eastern European countries in the early 1990s), there is no time to foster market ethics. This results in confusion.

Market ethics is ideally characterized by responsibility, high-quality work, punctuality, credibility, and, above all, a respect for the equal rights of others. Ethics is different from a legal system, which, if violated, imposes punishment. Immoral behavior does not induce a direct penalty, although it may be confronted by public criticism. Although some immoral behavior may bring at least short-term advantages to the perpetrator at the expense of others, people avoid such activity, partly due to conscience and partly due to fear of public criticism (both can be categorized as ethics). Therefore, ethics can be seen as a form of public service: one is ready to follow ethics not for direct private advantage but because of a larger public good. Ethics requires everyone to sacrifice self-interest because doing so results in a better situation for the society in which all reside.

Market ethics has an implicit and profound connection with human rights that traditional ethics lacks. Here I define *human rights* as a host of rights contrary to privileged rights. Human rights can be enjoyed by everyone without conflict, whereas privileged rights can be enjoyed only by a specific group of people, otherwise conflict will occur. Earlier I mentioned that market ethics is characterized by the recognition of self-interest—particularly the recognition of others' self-interest. The general rules of exchange develop into market ethics. These rules require equal social status between trade partners to ensure voluntary and free negotiation and to avoid the domination of one side by the other. The conflict between those who have privileged rights and those who do not has hampered the establishment of market economies and market ethics.

Contrary to the common wisdom that judges self-interest to be the origin of social turmoil, self-interest combined with moral constraint ensures a better social order than one arranged by moral constraint alone. In fact, almost all the rules for constructing a modern society involving banking, insurance, contracting, law, and trade are based on the assumption that each person will take care of his or her own self-interest; otherwise all the rules would collapse. For example, when one withdraws money from one's bank, the bank requires a properly signed slip; but when one deposits money no signature is required. A police detective can track a criminal by following clues linked to selfish motives. If there were no self-interest, police would have far fewer clues. These examples illustrate the importance of the role self-interest plays in society.

The famous Chinese novel *Jing Hua Yuan* (literally, A Course in the Mirror and Flower) describes a country of gentlemen where people quarrel with each other because the buyer insists on paying more and the seller insists on receiving less.[12] It reveals a profound principle: The equilibrium of a society is established through self-interest. This is a more general statement than economists' assertion that the "economic man" is essential in order to have demand and supply curves (the intersection of which gives a balanced price). In a household economy, although there are trades, no real price can be formed because everybody is asked to work for the whole household, not for self-interest. The lack of a real price system is the reason why household economies have a low economic efficiency. Centrally planned economies (household economies) usually are successful in the beginning stage, but the economic efficiency gradually erodes because the fixed prices send a wrong signal to those allocating resources in planning.

Market principles ensure benefits to those on both sides of a transaction, thus directing the powerful force of self-interest on both sides to boost economic development. But this is true only when the transaction has no negative externalities; that is, when it does not impose losses on any third party outside the transaction. Environmental pollution, however, does impose losses on the public. On the production side, too, economic development requires vast amounts of natural resources, including forests, oil, land, minerals, and fresh water, all extracted without paying the full environmental price. Meanwhile, the remaining resources become scarcer and scarcer. Thus the problem of sustainable development—even a viable human future—is raised. It is becoming clearer and clearer that the present pattern of economic development cannot continue forever, and immediate measures must be taken.

Market ethics, still developing after two hundred years, suffers from inertia. People continue to make judgments using familiar old criteria; they find nothing wrong in daily business. From the giant manufacturers—powerful multinational corporations—to small retailers and governmental departments, profit maximization still motivates market practices. Although laws have been decreed to protect the environment, the cost of implementation is high because law, like ethics, has not evolved to keep pace with modern societies. In recent years, thanks to education and the media, people are beginning to realize that new rules must be established, yet a sound environmental ethics is far from well recognized.

Economic Policies to Protect the Environment and Their Limits

When complaints of environmental damage become loud enough to attract government's attention, the usual response is to promulgate regulations. Regulation may be effective in the beginning, but problems gradually reveal themselves. First, polluters can easily find loopholes in statutes, resulting in huge litigation expenses for the government—a wasteful, nonproductive activity. Second, government agencies often have difficulties in enforcement, particularly when the polluter is another governmental agency.[13] Third, protecting the environment requires the diversion of scarce funds. Finally, there is the problem of how to use funds efficiently. Regulation ignores the cost of pollution treatment, so it is far from an economical method.[14] Therefore, economic instruments that can provide an effective policy at minimum cost must come into consideration.

Theoretically, it may be true that economic policy is a better regulator than legislation. First, it is necessary to determine the environmental quality at the point where the marginal cost for reducing pollution equals the marginal willingness of the public to pay for enjoying (incrementally) a higher-quality environment while they are also allowed a choice of goods and services. This means that the optimum environmental quality should not be determined arbitrarily; it depends on the income level of households, the price structure, and the cost of pollution treatment. But in practice it is very difficult to obtain data on willingness to pay, because everyone likes a free ride; people hope the quality of the environment will be improved but the cost paid by others. In reality, policymakers can only guess the appropriate quality of environment through observation and indirect estimation. For example, some international organizations infuse funds into developing countries to improve the environment (as judged by the donor's own priorities) when the most urgent need there is not environmental quality but rather food and peace. In general, the consumption patterns between rich and poor differ greatly in terms of environment. Some extremist environmentalists consider the environment to be the only criterion and ignore the necessity of balanced development. Nobody knows how much waste has resulted from such a distortion.

Second, economic policy requires a unified marginal cost of pollution treatment. Discharge fees and tradable pollution rights are designed to achieve a unified marginal cost. But these economic instruments imply a number of practical and administrative efforts in terms of money and manpower. In the case of discharge fees, an aggregated charge might cause strong opposition because firms often have to pay for costs of calculation and related procedures. In contrast, simplified charges might be considered unjust. In the case of tradable pollution rights, the administrative cost is also high; legal uncertainties make this policy even more complicated.[15] Furthermore, all economic instruments depend on expensive, secured, continuous monitoring of pollution discharge. Thus economic instruments may become uneconomic.

Economic instruments are even more problematical when dealing with international environmental problems. For example, cutting a certain amount of carbon dioxide (CO_2) emissions at minimum cost requires marginal costs across countries to be equal. A carbon tax has been suggested as an instrument for this; however, several problems might arise in implementation.[16]

1 The optimal tax rate is determined by finding the intersection of the marginal cost curve (of reducing CO_2 emissions) with the marginal benefit curve. Differences in natural resources, energy, geography, and degree of economic development mean that the marginal cost curve and the marginal benefit curve will be different for each country. Therefore, the optimal reduction of CO_2 emissions or the optimal tax rate for each country will be different. The result is that every country would complain about contributing too much or benefiting too little.

2 The per capita GNP for rich countries is almost fifty times higher than that for poor countries. A carbon tax amounting to one-fiftieth of the GNP might not create enough incentives in rich countries but would sweep away all the means of subsistence for a poor country.

3 Some experts have suggested that the tax base should be the marginal increase or the annual carbon emission; others hold that a tax should be levied on the total or accumulated carbon emission. Taxing based on lump sum emission or per capita emission is another debated issue. Every country reaches its verdict based on self-interest; compromise is immensely difficult.

4 Should the collected tax be used domestically or redistributed among international communities? In the former case, the comparative advantage for each country might change, which could be criticized as unjust; in the latter case, what is the principle of redistribution and who will be in charge of implementation?

5 In what currency is the tax to be paid? Domestic or hard currency? Many countries pursue foreign currency control, and their official exchange rates differ by many times from the real rate or shadow rate. If hard currency is to be used, which currency will be chosen and how should the authorities deal with volatile exchange rates? The country whose currency is chosen will enjoy an extra benefit because the tax will create a demand for its currency.

6 Will a country's contribution of absorbing carbon be rewarded or used to compensate for its emission?
7 How can the quantities of emission and absorption of carbon be monitored and at what cost?
8 If a violation occurs, who is in charge of enforcement?

None of the aforementioned problems is easy to solve. Udo Simonis, after discussing various criteria regarding the distribution of CO_2 emission, concludes that "these negotiations center on a new distribution problem, the solution of which is utterly difficult; some points of orientation have emerged, but a final solution is not yet in sight." [17] Ignazio Musu analyzes the difficulties encountered in reaching an international agreement to address the problems of global warming, ozone layer protection, and conservation of biological diversity. His basic conclusion is that due to the temptation of a free ride, any international agreement—should it ever be signed—would be unstable. [18]

In fact, all the economic instruments have similar problems. Only within the national context can governments supervise implementation. If transferred payments remain within the nation, people do not care very much. Within the international context, however, if people take the national benefit seriously, there can scarcely be an acceptable solution for all nations. Some suggest that the United Nations should play the role of a world government. This would be fine if the United Nations were always right. If it makes a mistake, however, who can rectify it? To think further, how does one distinguish between right and wrong in judging a conflict of benefit?

Protecting the Environment: More Reliance on Ethics

We have seen the limitations of economic instruments, especially in dealing with international environmental problems, so what *is* the remedy? We admit that economics is a useful tool in policy design. A price system is necessary for efficient utilization of resources, and prices are formed by the forces of supply and demand, which are driven by self-interest. What we should recognize, however, is that human beings are ethical as well as selfish. The task of our generation is to develop a prevailing environmental ethics by which people will protect the environment, sacrificing their immediate benefit in the context of a price system.

I am not saying that current economic institutions are perfect; on the contrary, some kind of fundamental overhaul is required. In the developed world there is tremendous wastefulness in the prevailing consumption pattern, although the production process is precisely designed and highly efficient. In almost every household there are clothes rarely worn, books rarely browsed, small ornaments covered with thick dust—items that eventually go to yard sales. These items were purchased on impulse, because of a "sale," or just from some quirky desire for possession. It is impossible to estimate how much is wasted in this way; there are no statistics available. In economic theory, the value of a product is realized the instant it is exchanged on the market but not at the time it is consumed. A product finishes its journey in the economy once it is bought; after that it goes beyond the horizon of the economist. Thus the purpose of production is sale, not consumption. This absurd logic turns out to be a common rule in the market economy. One of the other results of the divorce of production from consumption is the huge waste of resources in advertising and packaging. If our aim were for the people in the Third World to become rich and to enjoy the current life-style of those in the developed world, the limitations of natural resources would not allow such a change. Even for the developed world itself, further change in this direction seems impossible in terms of available resources. Therefore it is vital that a close link be forged between production and consumption. Which policies could accomplish this goal? Nobody knows; however, conservation as an ethical virtue might provide the key.

Let us imagine what could happen if a conservation-based environmental ethics were generally accepted. Self-restraint resulting in conservation of natural resources could provide sustainable development; moreover, people would be willing to pay to improve the environment despite someone's free ride. But in fact, if everyone were to think in this way, that would be the end of free riders! In addition, people would pay as much as they value the environment, taking into account their earning capacities and the prices of other commodities. They would pay not only in money but also in physical effort, time, and wisdom—in the best combination, led by their consciences. The condition of optimal environmental quality would then be reached automatically, since if marginal benefit is larger than marginal cost, individuals will choose to improve the environment by payment of money or effort. If the marginal cost were larger they would choose to spend less on the environment. Therefore, everyone would use a combination of efforts in the most efficient way, implying an efficient use of resources combined with knowledge. Not incidentally, voluntary contributions to protect the environment involve no administrative expenses, monitoring costs, red-tape formalities, litigation, or negotiation. Therefore, conservation of the environment through ethics is economically efficient in terms of goals and the means to achieve them.

Many of us may doubt whether such an environmental ethics could be established. If there is no supervisor, how do people voluntarily contribute money and effort? If we look at how the chores are done in a household we can probably find an answer. There is no regulation, tax, or reward for chores, but the family members voluntarily do their household work. Though the burden of chores may not be justly divided, and sometimes quarrels arise, the institution still functions. In a community—a group larger than a family—it is not unusual for people to help each other by contributing money and effort. People send signals to each other that they will keep an ethic, a public service from which everyone benefits. People give up money and leisure, but in fact, everyone's condition is improved. Moreover, a contribution can create an internal pleasure in one's soul in the same way a good deed does.

In a family or small community, people know each other well and an ethical signal sent can be easily received, so a common ethics can be established readily. For large-scale environmental protection, however, many more people must be involved; therefore we must discover a way to let people know how others are protecting our common environment. Long-distance communication is not difficult with the support of modern technology, and it is feasible that an environmental ethics in the "global village" could be established and maintained.

Good news about environmental protection will encourage others to join the common cause; but bad news also needs to be publicized so that people who damage our common environment can be warned and restrained. Ethics is not a totally soft constraint; it exerts pressure on those who do not care about environmental protection. Penalties are not directly levied, because (as mentioned earlier) ethics differs from law. Nevertheless, clauses concerning penalties for violations should be explicitly included in business contracts, even though they may not always be effective, particularly for minor violations when the community's economic loss is less than the cost of litigation. Penalty clauses provide a clear line on what is right and what is wrong. They clarify the ethical line of defense. In disseminating environmental knowledge, environmental ethical advocacy is of prime importance. Kristin Shrader-Fréchette presents an excellent argument on this point.[19]

Nongovernmental organizations dedicated to environmental protection have mushroomed in recent years. Large sums have been collected and much effort has gone toward protecting the environment. Many consumers refuse to buy products such as leaded gasoline or detergents containing phosphate. Giant corporations, such as Du Pont, are cutting production of chlorofluorocarbons and other environmentally harmful products, not because these products earn less profit but at least in part due to the corporations' sense of responsibility to the environment. Some European countries have imposed taxes on energy in an effort to reduce energy consumption and carbon emission. All these events happened without external mandates but because of a moral sense, an internal self-constraint.

Pollution cut in this way incurs no transaction cost, litigation, or complaints concerning equity; economic efficiency still is possible. This is a sign that environmental ethics is evolving. I agree with Shrader-Fréchette that "the worst environmental pollution is perhaps mind pollution, and the rarest global resources are well-thought ethical principles."[20]

NOTES

1 Fan Wen-lan, *The General History of China* [in Chinese], vol. 1 (Beijing: People's Publishing House, 1965), 84.

2 Christopher Elliott, Foreword to *Natural History of China* (London: William Collins, 1990).

3 One example is Dong Feng (ca. A.D.), who asked patients to plant one to five trees, according to the seriousness of the patient's disease. After several years a forest of apricot trees was growing. See *Ci Hai* [Encyclopedia of Words; in Chinese], ed. Shu-Xin-chen, Chen Wang-dao, et al. (Shanghai: Shanghai Encyclopedia Publisher, 1985), 1257.

4 Li Yang, "Zhou Yi and Ecology," in *Zhou Yi and Chinese Medicine* [in Chinese] (Beijing: Beijing Science and Technology Publisher, 1990).

5 Liang Fang-zhong, *Historical Statistics of Chinese Households, Cultivated Land and Tax* [in Chinese] (Shanghai: Shanghai People's Publishing House, 1989), 4–6.

6 He Qing-lian, *Population, a Suspended Sword Toward China* [in Chinese] (Chongqing, Sichuan: Sichuan People's Publishing House, 1988), 44.

7 Chinese history records many stories about power. For example, when a general tried to usurp power, he might fabricate evidence that Heaven had chosen him as the emperor. One of the stories is about Han Tong-shan (1351), who

laid a stone stele underground inscribed with sentences implying that he would be the emperor, then pretended to discover it.

8 A picture in the newspaper *China Daily* [in English], December 25, 1991, titled "Animal Lover," shows a man of eighty-two who has spent the past fifty years performing small acts of charity in the animal kingdom. He regularly walks five miles to the market to buy animals to free them in the wild.

9 Mao Zhi-cheng, "To Learn a Little Bit of 'Anti-Culture,'" *China Environmental News* [in Chinese], January 14, 1992. Mao studied the philosophy of Zhuang Zi and expounds the belief that Taoism contains the highest wisdom of returning to nature.

10 E. L. Jones, *The European Miracle* (Cambridge: Cambridge University Press, 1981), 202; Paul Kennedy, *The Rise and Fall of the Great Powers* (New York: Random House, 1987), chap. 1, sec. 1.

11 Mark Elvin, *The Pattern of the Chinese Past* (Stanford: Stanford University Press, 1973), 195.

12 Li Ru-zhen, *Jing Hua Yuan* [in Chinese] (Beijing: People's Literature Publishing House, 1955), chap. 11.

13 One such case was studied in detail by Barbara A. Finamore; see "Regulating Hazardous and Mixed Waste at Department of Energy Nuclear Weapons Facilities: Reversing Decades of Environmental Neglect," *Harvard Environmental Law Review* 9 (1985): 83–141.

14 Richard B. Stewart, "Economics, Environment, and the Limits of Legal Control," *Harvard Environmental Law Review* 9 (1985): 1–22. The paper thoroughly explores the economic inefficiency of regulation control for environmental protection.

15 J. B. Opschoor et al., *Economic Instruments for Environmental Protection,* OECD Publications (London: Royal Institute of International Affairs, 1989), 19, 92.

16 Such as Michael Grubb, *The Greenhouse Effect: Negotiating Targets* (New Haven: Yale University Press, 1989), 27–45.

17 See his essay "Toward a 'Houston Protocol': How to Allocate CO_2 Emission Reductions Between North and South" (this volume).

18 Ignazio Musu, "Efficiency and Equity in International Environmental Cooperation" (this volume).

19 See "An Apologia for Activism: Global Responsibility, Ethical Advocacy, and Environmental Problems" (this volume).

20 Kristin Shrader-Fréchette, "Environmental Ethics and Global Imperatives," in *The Global Possible,* ed. Robert Repetto (New Haven: Yale University Press, 1985), 97.

J. BAIRD CALLICOTT

The Role of Technology
in the Evolving Concept
of Nature

In a notorious passage of *The Gay Science,* Friedrich Nietzsche graphically portrays a madman carrying a lantern in broad daylight and searching for God. While Nietzsche's mirthless character actually declares that "God is dead"—an exaggerated report, according to Erazim Kohák (this volume)—and says that we have murdered Him, what the philosopher meant, of course, was that the *concept* of God, the *idea* of God, was no longer alive and well (Nietzsche 1974: 181). Seventeenth-century astronomy and eighteenth-century physics had undermined belief in God's existence. "By the end of the eighteenth century," reports Thomas Kuhn (1957: 263), "an increasing number of men, scientists and nonscientists alike, saw no need to posit the existence of God." Nineteenth-century geology and evolutionary biology delivered the coup de grace (Ruse 1979). Certainly as Nietzsche was writing in the 1880s, the concept of God was definitely ill, if not dead and buried.

Read the medieval philosophers. Not one expresses the least doubt that God exists. Most even undertook to prove it (Oates 1948; Barrett 1940; Bett 1925; Anselm 1903; Aquinas 1955a; Ockham 1957). Differences of opinion were confined to God's attributes and relationship to His creation. The early modern philosophers also took the existence of God for granted, and some also tried to prove it, however much they reshaped Him to suit their purposes (Descartes 1911b). They transformed God into the designing engineer of a clockwork universe (Koyré 1965). But as the workings of the world machine were explored in ever-increasing detail, God receded further and further into the background and finally faded from the scientific and philosophical scene altogether (Passmore 1968). By the mid-twentieth century hardly any scientists or philosophers found a practical use for God in their systems of physics or metaphysics (Passmore 1968).

As the twentieth century now grinds to a close, many contemporary environmentalists fear that nature is dead. Of course the sun still rises and sets, the seasons continue to revolve, the winds blow, rain falls, and plants and animals flourish. But one can no longer find any place on earth untrammeled by the works of man.[1] Temperate forests, lakes, and streams the world over are ubiquitously affected by acid rain. In addition to such evident works of man as the trans-Alaska pipeline, the permafrost in the erstwhile Arctic wilderness is everywhere contaminated with measurable traces of toxic chemicals—everything from DDT to PCBs (Brown et al. 1984–92). There is a hole in the ozone layer over Antarctica created by fugitive chlorofluorocarbons (Brown et al. 1984–92). And nature can only become more anthropomorphized as the greenhouse effect kicks in followed by a higher sea level, changed weather patterns, hotter summers, milder winters, desiccated forests, enlarged deserts, irruptions of weedy fauna and flora, and impoverished ecosystems (Brown et al. 1984–92).

Nature as free, wild, and independent is gone. Everywhere man's works insidiously pervade, if they do not palpably dominate, the landscape. Nowhere is the earth and its community of life unaffected by man. There are precious few places where man is a visitor who does not remain. Even the South Pole has a permanently inhabited research station (U.S. Central Intelligence Agency 1990). The once impenetrable and mysterious Amazon basin is riddled with roads, power plants, gold mines, boomtowns, cattle ranches, settlers' swiddens, and coca plantations (Hecht and Cockburn 1989). In the United States, visitation of designated wilderness areas is so intense that permits are required to limit density, and the restrictions on what backpackers can and cannot do make a mockery of Bob Marshall's equation of wilderness with freedom and the absence of constraints (Nash 1982).

In language reminiscent of Nietzsche, Bill McKibben (1989) poignantly describes these and other enormities and eloquently voices the epidemic fear of an impending environmental apocalypse in his best-seller *The End of Nature*. Few contemporary writers are quite as audaciously dramatic as

Nietzsche, however. McKibben makes it clear that he is claiming that the *idea* of nature has ended, not nature per se. But what idea of nature? The idea, as McKibben also makes clear, of nature as Other, as a world existing apart from us and our artifice. Before we all go into mourning, however, let me suggest that nature as Other is a distinctly *modern* notion—though deeply rooted in the ancient soil of the Western intellectual tradition—and let me also suggest that the modern representation of nature as Other is false and that its historical tenure has been pernicious. Perhaps we should celebrate this momentous passage rather than mourn it.

The modern idea of nature as Other is one-half of a phony dualism, a dichotomy between man and nature. Indeed, the radical bifurcation of man and nature is a hallmark of modernism. But it flows from both well-springs of the Western intellectual heritage. In the first book of the Bible God makes man alone in His own image and gives him dominion over and charges him to subdue the earth and all its denizens. In ancient Greek philosophy, humans are set apart from nature because we alone among the animals are supposed to be rational (Aristotle 1941).

In the late medieval and early modern periods, thinkers as different from one another as Thomas Aquinas, the officially sanctioned perennial philosopher of the Catholic church, and René Descartes, the reputed father of modern philosophy, synthesized these two strands of thought—the Judeo-Christian and the Greco-Roman. According to Thomas Aquinas (1955b), God created nature as a life-support system for rational man. According to Descartes (1911b), reason is the *imago dei,* the respect in which man resembles God. Thus, by a purely rational method, man may discover the fully intelligible order—the master plan—according to which God fashioned nature (Descartes 1911b). Descartes's contemporary, Francis Bacon, set the modern agenda for the scientific conquest of nature by man. If we can discover the working principles—the divinely ordained laws—of nature, he presciently pointed out, we can bend it to our will (Bacon 1960).

My purpose here is not to vilify the Bible, the *De Anima,* the *Summa Contra Gentiles,* the *Meditations,* the *New Organon,* the *Principia,* and the rest of the Western intellectual canon. For better or worse, our civilization, with all its wonders as well as its perils, is the material legacy of this brilliant and powerful philosophical heritage. Moreover, until only a century or so ago, practically no one questioned the wisdom or the morality of conquering nature. John Stuart Mill's (1969) essay "Nature," originally published in 1874, provides a breathtaking example by a Victorian philosopher of lasting repute of an express injunction to thoroughly conquer nature. Thoreau's (1962) essay "Walking," published in 1862, is a rare exception to the general tenor of the times and expresses a keen and clear sense that the author represents a tiny minority. Only by the turn of the century could John Muir (1901:1) claim that "thousands of tired, nerve-shaken, over-civilized people are beginning to find out that going to the mountains is going home." Indeed, practically no one in the horse-and-buggy era imagined that the conquest of nature could become so complete that nature could seem mortally wounded, could seem indeed to have come to an untimely end. On this point McKibben (1989:62) comments, "Even the most farseeing naturalist of an earlier day couldn't comprehend that the atmosphere, the climate, could be dramatically altered. Thoreau, complaining about the logging that eventually destroyed virtually every stand of virgin timber between the Atlantic and the Mississippi, . . . [remarked], 'Thank God, the sky was safe.'" Until recently, man seemed to be the up-and-coming hero armed with Promethean science in the struggle with Titanic nature. Man was cast in the role of David to nature's Goliath.

But today, to many people, the spectacular technological achievements of the twentieth century appear grotesque (McKibben 1989). Victorious man seems to be a tyrant, and nature the hapless victim. Yet, for many ardent environmental Jeremiahs, although the roles of hero and villain are certainly reversed, the underlying dualism—the radical man/nature dichotomy—goes unchallenged (McKibben 1989). A wilderness advocate lamenting man's total reduction of nature to possession and a timber industry CEO gloating over it share the same underlying assumption that man is a case apart from the rest of nature. The difference is that one sides with nature while the other sides with man.

Descartes was the midwife who assisted the complete parturition of modern man from the natural matrix. He gathered all conscious experience into the *res cogitans*, the thinking thing—or, in ordinary language, the mind or soul (Descartes 1911b). Descartes did not dispute the orthodox Christian doctrine that only human beings have immortal, rational souls. Quite the contrary, he emphatically affirmed it (Descartes 1911a). He argued that all other natural entities, including animals and plants, are part of the *res extensa*, the extended or material realm. Every nonhuman natural entity "out there" in the "external world" is devoid of conscious experience and subjectivity. Only man is alive in the inner, felt, experiential sense of the term (Descartes 1911a).

Descartes (1911c) and his cohorts believed that the material realm consists, in the last analysis, of stripped-down atomic particles moving in

Euclidean space.[2] Each atom has only a few simple, mathematically expressible features or properties, famously identified by Descartes's older contemporary, Galileo (1957), and called "primary qualities" by Descartes's younger contemporary, John Locke (1961). Each has a mass, or solidity, a shape, a size, and a variable speed. The "secondary qualities"— color, sound, flavor, odor, and the like—were imagined to be the confused effects of the real or primary qualities on our organs of sense (Galileo 1957; Descartes 1911b; Locke 1961). All natural phenomena, the early moderns thought, can be reductively explained in terms of these elemental bodies with their primary qualities and their mechanical interactions (Descartes 1911c).

The mechanistic project that Galileo and Descartes had begun was completed by Isaac Newton at the end of the seventeenth century (Newton 1962). During the eighteenth century, the self-congratulatory Age of Enlightenment, nature was generally believed to be a perfectly intelligible clockwork, thanks to Newton's intellectual triumph (Kuhn 1957), and all nature's moving parts were thought to be automata or mechanisms in miniature (Kuhn 1957).

In this respect man is no different, except that a conscious, rational soul is supposed to inhabit the purely mechanistic human body (Descartes 1911c). Crowded into human consciousness are all the secondary qualities, the rich and diverse sensory readouts of the dull quantitative variables that actually exist in objects. Sound and color are the subjective register of frequencies of air and ether waves, respectively; hot and cold, the sensuous interpretation of molecular oscillation; odor and flavor, the subjective impression made by the chemical effluences of various materials (Galileo 1957). In this modern point of view, values are even more patently subjective. Not only beauty and ugliness but good and evil, right and wrong, are in the eye of the beholder—in man's mind, not in the objective world (Hume 1960). Thus nature became wholly object and only man was also a subject. As subjects, humans exist "in here," in our bodies, dispassionately looking out on impassive nature, which is thoroughly alien to the enveloped and isolated essential self.

In the twentieth century, hard-nosed scientists continued to hew pretty faithfully to the basic modern worldview. Scientific "resource management" is a perfect example. The very concept is tendentious. It treats nature as a raw material, valuable only as a pool of commodities for human use (Pinchot 1947). Why only for *human* use? Because only human beings are fully conscious subjects. Deer, ducks, fish, and trees are just so many mindless automata furnishing an inert physical landscape of mineral masses, soil, water, and air. Or so the received scientific wisdom would have it.

Touched by the Romantics' revolt against the Enlightenment, twentieth-century environmentalists in the tradition of Thoreau and Muir granted a modicum of consciousness to animals and celebrated the qualitative richness and diversity of the natural world (Fox 1981). Though few doubted that beauty is in the eye of the beholder, nevertheless they argued that the nonconsumptive aesthetic experience afforded by nature can equal or surpass that occasioned by works of art (Fox 1981). But the man/nature dichotomy and the sense that nature is radically other than fully self-conscious, rational man were too deeply ingrained to be rejected altogether.

Also very deeply ingrained was an essentially static sense of the "balance of nature," a concept that ecologists by mid-century had adapted from classical physics (Botkin 1990). Like a thermostat, ecosystems were represented as having a set point—a climax state—to which they return, through negative feedback mechanisms, if disturbed by drought, flood, fire, or similar perturbations (Botkin 1990). From the point of view of steady-state ecology, however, if ecosystems are subjected to too frequent or too intense disturbance, then they are liable to break down, driven by runaway positive feedback processes. Human activities, particularly industrial mining, agriculture, and logging, are, according to this way of thinking, prime examples of "unnatural"—because they are anthropogenic—impacts on ecosystems that are too great for them to absorb and which thus threaten to destroy them.

So, what is false about this modern picture of self-conscious rational man set over against an objective, essentially mechanistic nature? Let us reexamine the human side of the man/nature dichotomy first.

It should not surprise us that the philosophical implications of Darwin's great works, *The Origin of Species* and the *Descent of Man,* took more than a century to sink in, even among scientists and philosophers. As I just pointed out, the idea that man is spiritually or intellectually unique and thus discontinuous with nature has enjoyed a nearly three-thousand-year tenure in Western intellectual history. For this reason, and because it is so self-congratulatory and self-serving, the view has not been readily or gladly surrendered. Thus, while twentieth-century biologists greatly extended Darwin's theory of evolution by natural selection and ingeniously applied it to agronomy and resource management, its deeper implications about man's relationship with nature seem, until only recently, to have been conveniently ignored (Ruse 1986; Rachels 1990). But as Darwin (1874) himself elaborately argued, there is a seamless continuity between gradually evolved man and our fellow voyagers in the odyssey of evolution.

Bluntly put, we are animals ourselves, large omnivorous primates; very precocious to be sure, but just big monkeys nevertheless. We are, therefore, a part of nature, not set apart from it. We are one sort of living, feeling being among many others.

If the theory of evolution "naturalizes" man, then by the same token it also "humanizes" the other animals in the sense that they are, like us, conscious beings with more or less rich subjective lives. When we look out on the world, many subjects, each with its own distinct consciousness, are looking back at us.

Lots of authors (among them Rachels 1990) have gravely explored the expanded ethical responsibility that this Darwinian realization implies. But it also implies something liberating as well: Human works are no less natural than those of termites or elephants. Chicago is no less a phenomenon of nature than is the Great Barrier Reef, a vast undersea coral condominium, or limestone sediments formed by countless generations of calciferous marine organisms. If we are a part of nature, then the transformations we effect in the natural realm are not necessarily destructive, nor must they, simply by definition, diminish its naturalness.

If this seems a strange and implausible inference to draw, consider how we regard the transformations imposed on nature by aboriginal *Homo sapiens*. Consider, for example, the Kayapo Indians living in the Amazon basin (Hecht and Cockburn 1989). We do not think that their garden clearings violate the naturalness of the forest, but we think that the clearings of Euro-Brazilian peasants most certainly do. Note that this disparity of attitude suggests that we regard only "modern man" and our ancient European and Asian antecedents to be truly human. By implication, we regard "primitives"—the divers inhabitants of Africa, Southeast Asia, Australia, and North and South America—as just another kind of wildlife.[3] But all *Homo sapiens* are, biologically speaking, one species. All *Homo sapiens*, moreover, are equally cultural animals. And while our many cultures exhibit an astonishing diversity, they are, one and all, phenomena of nature.

Under the sway of the apparently ethnocentric as well as anthropocentric modern man/nature dichotomy, we have minimized the historical environmental impacts of aboriginal *Homo sapiens*, whom we tacitly think of as on the nature side of this Great Divide (Callicott 1991a). We generally acknowledge that the Old World has long been cultivated, civilized, and otherwise anthropomorphized, but we like to think that Columbus discovered a virgin New World only five hundred years ago, and that when the English colonists came to North America a century later, they stepped off the *Mayflower* into a vast, pristine "wilderness" of continental proportions (Callicott 1991b). But the North and South American continents had actually been discovered ten thousand or more years earlier by eastward-migrating pedestrian *Homo sapiens* (P. S. Martin 1973). Soon thereafter the Western Hemisphere was fully, if not densely, populated by Indians—from the Brooks Range in Alaska to Tierra del Fuego at the tip of South America and from Manhattan Island to San Francisco Bay (P. S. Martin 1973).

We properly lament the recent extirpation of native species such as the passenger pigeon by our Euro-American forebears, but we forget that the extinctions coinciding with the arrival of the original Siberian immigrants were of much greater magnitude (Wright and Frey 1965). What happened to the two species of elephant that roamed the Western Hemisphere before and for a little while after the Siberian big game hunters arrived? In the Americas, these spearmen also found horses, camels, yaks, and other beasts that were absent in 1492.

The flora of the New World was also transformed by the original pioneers, principally by their judicious use of fire (Day 1953; Pyne 1982). The Indians in temperate latitudes regularly and universally burned the countryside (C. Martin 1973; Lewis 1973). North America's Great Plains are believed to be anthropogenic, as are most of the world's grasslands (Heizer 1955). Anthropogenic fires in wetter regions altered the composition of forests just as in drier regions they created prairies and savannas. In the moist tropics, agroforestry, gardening, and sophisticated plant breeding occurred on a vast scale (Gomez-Pompa and Kaus 1988). The American paradise lost was not a pristine sanctuary where, as wilderness defender David Brower once supposedly said, "the hand of man had never set foot" (Cohen 1991); it was the tragically depopulated home of a culturally diverse and pluralistic race that thoroughly, though quite variously, transformed its habitat (Butzer 1992; Deneven 1992).

In short, if nature ended, it ended a long time ago. The only extensive virgin wilderness left in 1492 was Antarctica. *Homo sapiens* has been a global force altering the biota during the entire Holocene.

Now let us take the nature side of the modern man/nature dichotomy. The emerging postmodern concept of nature differs from the modern mechanistic model in at least two important ways.

First, from a contemporary ecological point of view, as Frank Golley (this volume) eloquently argues, nature is systemically integrated and its components are internally related. The obsolete mechanistic concept of nature invited a tinkering, engineering approach to settlement, development, and resource management. Thus we believed that if we wished, we could replace native species with exotics and need fear no adverse systemic effects. We could replace elk and buffalo with cattle and sheep, prairie grasses with wheat and corn, and so on, without affecting the native soils and waters—just as we can replace a two-barrel carburetor with a four-barrel or replace a radio with a tape deck in an automobile without affecting the tires, the radiator, and the chassis. But we have learned the hard way that nature functions more like an organism than a mechanism (Callicott 1986). Deliberately changing one component of an ecosystem often causes unanticipated and unwelcome side effects throughout the whole. The untoward systemic effects of introduced species are infamous (Mooney and Drake 1986). One need mention the names of only a few such transplants to make the point: carp, kudzu, Johnsongrass, starlings . . . and the list goes on and on.

A second, recently much bruited, feature of the postmodern concept of nature is change (Botkin 1990). Mid-twentieth-century ecologists were much impressed by the untoward effects of biological tinkering, but most did not reject the mechanical model (Odum 1971); they just gave it a different spin. Species in nature were represented as coupled in balanced opposition. Deer were supposed to be held in check by wolves and other predators. Thus they stayed in balance with their browse. Periodic fires apparently enabled the grasses to hold their ground against encroachment by forests. Nature was thus maintained in a delicate equilibrium by the competition and cooperation among its tightly linked component parts and processes. Nature undisturbed by man, it was accordingly believed, will remain stable, in a "steady state." So the ecologists of Barry Commoner's (1971) era warned us, in effect, to let well enough alone; if Spaceship Earth (note well the mechanistic metaphor) ain't broke, don't fix it.

But nature is inherently dynamic; it is constantly changing and ultimately evolving. Change at every frequency—diurnal, meteorological, climatic, geological, and astronomical—is inevitable and natural (Botkin 1990). Even designated wilderness areas would not stay the same if, per impossible, they could be protected from all human modifications. Quite recently, in geological measures of time, much of North America was under a glacier. As the ice retreated, forest communities very different from those that we find now sprang up (Botkin 1990; Brubaker 1988; Webb 1986, 1987). The Indians, as I mentioned before, used fire to manage the forests and plains for game. After the Indians were removed, fire was suppressed and exotic grasses, trees, plant and animal pathogens, insects, fish, birds, and mammals invaded even the most remote and uninhabited places (Usher 1988). In the absence of acid precipitation and global warming, "vignettes of primitive America" (as the Leopold Report of 1963 called the United States national parks—that is, nineteenth-century American scenery) could be maintained, but only by proactive ecological restoration and intensive wilderness management (Commission on Research and Resource Management Policy 1989). Merely protected or preserved, they would become something different yet.

I may seem to be headed toward a betrayal of environmental ethics. If humans are a part of nature, and if change is natural, then it would appear that we have no means of objectively evaluating the entirely natural changes that we hypercultural primates impose on the rest of nature. What is wrong—objectively wrong—with urban sprawl, habitat fragmentation, oil slicks, global warming, or, for that matter, abrupt, massive, anthropogenic species extinction, other than that these things offend the quaint tastes of a few natural antiquarians? Most people apparently prefer shopping malls and dog tracks to wetlands and old-growth forests. Why shouldn't their tastes, however vulgar, prevail in a free-market democratic society? Kristin Shrader-Fréchette (1989:76) explicitly brings us to this omega point: "Ecosystems regularly change and regularly eliminate species. How would one . . . argue that humans should not modify ecosystems or even wipe out species, for example, when nature does this itself through natural disasters, such as volcanic eruptions and climate changes like those that destroyed the dinosaurs? . . . One cannot obviously claim that it is wrong on ecological grounds for humans to do what nature does— wipe out species." Or can one? I think that one can. The key concept that saves environmental ethics from such skepticism and cynicism is the concept of "ecosystem health."

The emerging postmodern model of nature is more organismic than mechanistic. Organisms proper are integrated wholes with systemic integrity. And organisms change: from zygote to embryo to fetus to infant to child to adolescent to adult to senescent; or, even more dramatically, from ovum to larva to pupa to imago.

Now, organisms are either objectively well or ill. Physicians and veterinarians, further, can specify indexes of organic health; for example, 98.6°F and a blood pressure and pulse rate within certain ranges are all indexes of human health.

But health is also intrinsically good. Except in the most unusual circumstances, one never prefers to be sick rather than well.

The 1980s saw the creation of a new theory of ecosystems called hierarchy theory that is more rigorous than the older thermostatic models (O'Neill et al. 1986). Hierarchy theory enables ecologists to define nested ecosystems according to temporal and spatial scale. Hierarchy theory may also be sufficiently robust to enable ecologists to specify norms of ecosystem health.

Indeed, work is proceeding rapidly on this front. In February 1991, a symposium devoted to the concept of ecosystem health was convened at the annual meeting of the American Association for the Advancement of Science in Washington, D.C. It included ecologists, economists, and environmental philosophers. A book on the subject has been published by Island Press (Costanza et al. 1992). Health is at once descriptive and normative, an objective condition that is also indisputably good. If ecology can successfully specify indexes of health for ecosystems as unambiguously as medicine has for organisms, then ecology will also have specified objective standards for evaluating anthropogenic change in nature.

Thus we can, quite apart from the vagaries of personal preference, pronounce changes that we (or for that matter any other organisms) impose on nature to be objectively good or objectively bad. Good changes are those that do not impair ecosystem health. Bad changes are those that have the opposite effect, those that cause ecosystem morbidity. Chicago may be as natural as the Great Barrier Reef, but it certainly is not as ecologically salubrious. And the real difference between Kayapo and Euro-Brazilian slash-and-burn agriculture is not that one is natural and the other is not, but that one is symbiotic and sustainable while the other is not (Hecht and Cockburn 1989).

Further, the concept of ecosystem health makes it possible for us to envision ourselves affecting nature as much to improve as to harm it—judged not by subjective and instrumental but by objective and intrinsic standards of value. It should, in other words, be just as possible for us to actively enhance ecosystem health as to impair it. After all, we take human health enhancement programs for granted. We can similarly envision ecosystem health enhancement programs in which we—as active players, parts of nature—pursue our own interests, as the other parts also do, and at the same time, like many of the other parts, benefit rather than harm the health of the whole of which we are a part.

One hundred centuries after the depredations of the Siberian immigrants to the Western Hemisphere, the North, Central, and South American aborigines had evolved cultural adaptations to their environments that were symbiotic and sustainable rather than parasitic and destructive (Hughes 1983). Earlier I pointed out that, contrary to popular opinion, the New World was not a virgin wilderness when Columbus rediscovered it. But I would now point out that it was, nevertheless, in the poetic words of Aldo Leopold (1987:286), "a biota in perfect aboriginal health." After the catastrophic extinction of the Pleistocene megafauna, new, healthy ecological regimes were established during the Holocene that included the new keystone primate (P. S. Martin 1973). Thus it would seem that if illiterate and unscientific peoples can perceptively and self-consciously reinstitute ways of living in and with nature without impairing ecosystem health, then surely a technologically sophisticated culture can, too.

Ah, but isn't technological sophistication precisely the problem? The answer to that question is yes and no.

The modern technology of the nineteenth and twentieth centuries is certainly part of the problem, indeed the whole of the problem, not the solution. Go back to the litany of ecological ills recited at the beginning of this essay. Virtually every one is an untoward side effect of some modern mechanical or chemical technology: no chlorofluorocarbon refrigerants and propellants, no hole in the ozone; no coal and oil burning, no acid rain and greenhouse effect; no chain saws and bulldozers, no massive rain forest destruction.

But is modern technology the only technology conceivable? It may be true that, as Gertrude Stein said, a rose is a rose is a rose. But I don't think it would be equally true to say that technology is technology is technology. Now emerging on the horizon is something called "appropriate technology" (Schumacher 1973). An appropriate technology is one that is environmentally benign. To cite a couple of very limited and insignificant cases in point: chlorofluorocarbon propellants in spray cans are being replaced by non-ozone-threatening substitutes, and polychlorinated biphenyls in electrical machinery are being replaced by less toxic lubricants. These examples are limited because, among thousands of kinds of synthetic chemicals, two especially noxious classes are being phased out. And they are insignificant because they are cases in which a less environmentally harmful chemical is being substituted for a more environmentally harmful one without any real change in the basic technological modus operandi. In order to begin a genuine symbiotic reintegration of man with nature, we need a wholesale shift of technological esprit or motif. The much-discussed shift from a fossil fuel to a solar energy base would represent such a profound structural change (Barbour 1982).

A massive shift from hydrocarbon fuels to solar energy is indeed much discussed, but so far little progress seems to have been made. The obstacles to progress have been less technical than social and political. People are accustomed to personal cars, and heavy, peppy ones to boot. We do not want to change to something less convenient and familiar. Furthermore, solar development is poorly supported with public research dollars, tax incentives, and subsidies (Executive Office of the President of the United States 1991). We are dependent on the petroleum economy. Oil barons, automobile makers, assembly-line workers, chauffeurs—all those whose livelihood, one way or another, depends on cars, trucks, tractors, airplanes, and recreational vehicles—exert direct and indirect political influence. Their legislative representatives make policies, laws, and regulations designed precisely to thwart the development and implementation of alternative energy technologies, however more "appropriate" they may be. Getting from here to ectopia will require political will. But in a quasi democracy such as the United States, overcoming the special interest groups who influence the professional politicians, effecting real political change, takes such an enormous grass-roots effort that change seems hopeless (Phillips 1990).

The furthest thing from any expertise I may have is alternative technology design. The next furthest thing from my ken is an analysis of the economic, social, and political obstacles to alternative technology development and how to overcome them. What I think I can contribute, however, is some historical insight into how, after scientific paradigms shift, cultural worldviews change and realignments of the man-nature relationship take shape.

I am no more a certified futurist than I am an engineer or political scientist. I have no better idea than anyone else what the coming century will bring. Naturally, I have hopes as well as fears. Whatever the future holds, however, the one thing we can be absolutely sure of is that the future civilization will differ from the present one. Nature is not static. Culture is even more demonstrably dynamic. I recall witnessing environmental historian Donald Worster during a 1988 colloquium at Berkeley being wearied by students who insisted that American agriculture was doomed to eventual collapse because capitalistic forces relentlessly pressured farmers to adopt unsustainable practices. Finally, Worster waved his hand and said, "Look, capitalism came from somewhere and it's going to go somewhere." Similarly, modern twentieth-century technology, so ill-adapted to the ecological exigencies of nature, came from somewhere and is going to go somewhere.

Maybe if we understood where it came from we could get a feel for where it may go next. The answer to the first question is easy. Historians of technology are virtually unanimous in the opinion that modern technology is the translation into hardware of the laws, principles, and methods of modern classical science (Mumford 1934; Ducasse 1958). In fact, science and technology became so closely allied during the twentieth century that today most people do not distinguish between them. Newton portrayed the universe as a vast machine. Steeped in and inspired by Newtonian science, engineers went on to make machines that were images in miniature of the world machine. The longer ordinary people lived in an increasingly mechanized world—a world of steam engines, cotton gins, factories, and, later, tractors, automobiles, and airplanes—the more widespread and deeply ingrained, I suggest, the mechanical worldview became.

You may notice that throughout this essay I have blithely supposed that the people who have wielded the greatest power for the longest time (indeed, long after their deaths) are not kings, popes, dictators, conquerors, prime ministers, crime bosses, tycoons, inventors, and their ilk (persons of action and affairs), but natural philosophers—Galileo, Descartes, Newton, and all the others I have mentioned—intellectuals. I quite agree with Ludwig von Bertalanffy, who wrote: "The *Weltanschauung*, the view of life and the world, of the man in the street—the chap who repairs your car or sells you an insurance policy—is a product of Lucretius Carus, Newton, Locke, Darwin, Adam Smith, Ricardo, Freud and Watson—even though you may safely bet that the high school or even the university graduate has never heard of most of them or knows of Freud only through the *Dear Abby* column of his newspaper" (von Bertalanffy 1967:51–52).

Eugene C. Hargrove, my colleague at the University of North Texas, had to suppress an insurrection led by a militantly ignorant "Introduction to Philosophy" student who challenged the relevancy of Descartes to his undergraduate education—you know, "Why do we have to read this stuff?"—on the ground that neither he nor any of his friends had ever heard of "the guy" (Hargrove 1992). So how could Descartes have shaped that benighted kid's Weltanschauung? Adopting a metaphor from the Reaganomics of the 1980s, Hargrove (1992) suggests that the ideas of Galileo, Descartes, Newton, and the rest "trickled down," anonymously, to the person in the street. But how? Evidently not because ordinary people study modern philosophy and form their worldview by its light.

I think the influence is through the technological application of the modern mechanical concept of nature. Technologies are not only conveniences, they are also communicators. We live in a machine-saturated environment, so naturally the machine has become the pervasive metaphor for all reality in the collective modern mind.

Among the most deeply insightful treatises on the machine as metaphor is Charlie Chaplin's aptly named film *Modern Times* (1935), which opens with the face of a clock, symbol of the mechanical worldview, occupying the whole screen. In it, the familiar tragicomic character played by Chaplin is a factory employee whose working life becomes a mechanical nightmare. Chosen to be the subject of an experiment to increase efficiency by eliminating the worker's need to stop working long enough to eat lunch, a feeding device tips soup into his mouth and turns an ear of corn on a spindle against his teeth. Naturally, the mechanical feeder runs amok, with the intended comic effect. Turning two bolts with a wrench in each hand as the assembly belt speeds by ever faster, Chaplin falls further and further behind and eventually is swept perilously into the huge cogs and wheels of the factory. Expressing the ambivalent modern romance with the machine as well as his own lyrical genius, the artist turns his predicament into a kind of macabre dance with the gargantuan gears. But the lingering impression of this surreal transmogrification of a delicate and ever-so-human organism first into a reluctant robot and then into fodder for the behemoth apparatus of modern industry is tinged more with horror and pathos than with humor and hope.

Chaplin's satirical caricature of modernity has become a hellish reality for many nonhuman animals. Regarded as senseless automata to begin with, they have become milk-, egg-, and meat-producing machines on factory farms (Harrison 1964). I once presented a paper critical of the mechanical motif as it has been expressed in twentieth-century industrial agriculture to an international conference on technology held on the campus of Guelph University (Callicott 1990). In the process I managed to outrage the dean of a Canadian university's college of agriculture, who vehemently protested that he and his fellow "animal scientists" most certainly did not consider factory farm animals to be Cartesian automata or machines. Rather, he said, they are (and I quote) "production units."[4]

Though most of us who can afford to do so take care to insulate ourselves from the most egregious insults of the man-made mechanical and chemical

environment, so insidious is the machine metaphor that we often voluntarily submit ourselves to mechanical reduction. Since, as faithful Cartesians, we regard our bodies as nothing but elaborate machines, we dutifully
take them to high-paid mechanics for repair when they malfunction—for
kidney transplants and bypass surgery—just as we take our simpler man-
made machines to less-well-paid mechanics for clutch replacements and
brake jobs.

The history lesson seems to be this: The original scientific revolution was
followed by a technological application of the Newtonian paradigm, which
was followed in turn by a revolution in the popular worldview. The mystical, religious worldview of the Middle Ages was thus gradually replaced by
modernism as the then-new science was translated into hardware during
the Industrial Revolution. By now, practically every person in the street
has become, quite unwittingly, a Cartesian and Newtonian: a modern, in
short. They are buying the modern classical worldview like it's going out
of style.

Theoretically speaking, mechanism and dualism *are* going out of style
and have been for most of the twentieth century (Heisenberg 1962). Modern classical science is defunct. A second scientific revolution has already
occurred—effected by Albert Einstein, Max Planck, Niels Bohr, Werner
Heisenberg, and Ilya Prigogine in physics; and by Frederick Clements,
Charles Elton, Aldo Leopold, Raymond Lindeman, Eugene Odum, T. F. H.
Allen, and Robert O'Neill in ecology (Gribben 1984; Worster 1977). Relativity and quantum theory portray a universe that is systemically integrated
and internally related (Bohm 1980; Capra 1975). The objective world of
nature cannot be completely isolated from its subjects (Heisenberg 1962).
Even in the apparently innocent act of knowing nature we change it. Theoretical ecology posits a similar, conceptually resonant, holistic, interactive,
interdependent, and organically unified portrait of terrestrial nature (Callicott 1986). Gradually, this new scientific paradigm is being technologically
applied.

Television, for example, is a direct application of quantum theory; so is
the compact disk player (Fromhold 1981). We all sense what a profound
force television technology has already become in transforming the collective consciousness of Western civilization. To academics, it appears to be a
mostly evil force responsible for rendering a whole generation nearly illiterate. But it has also helped to create the global village. And TV may have
played a major role in the recent spectacular collapse of communism. Try
as they might, communist dictators could not keep the seductive (and, one

might add, largely illusory) image of the Western consumer society from beaming through the iron curtain.

I would like to distance these comments as much as possible from Marshall McLuhan's (1965) speculations in the 1960s about media and messages. His distinction between "hot" and "cool" communications technology was entirely impressionistic and totally vague. Today, similar— though more definite—speculations abound about how television has shortened the attention span of children to the length of a thirty-second commercial spot and, further, about how within such abbreviated program units the rapidly changing, fragmentary, and disconnected images deconstruct the modern sense of a synoptic spatially and temporally continuous reality (Lake 1981). Obviously, rigorous research into the effects of television on normal human consciousness (here please read "normal" as in "normal science") is needed before any specific conclusions can be drawn.

As in the case of the inevitability of cultural change, however, I think that one can confidently assert at least a few general principles regarding the link between technology and worldview. Surely history amply indicates that information technologies do profoundly affect normal human consciousness and that a major shift in a culture's primary medium of information transforms its erstwhile normal human consciousness into another mode. As Walter Ong (1982) and Eric Havelock (1963) persuasively argue, literacy revolutionized the human mind. Doubtless electronic communications technology will too, though I hesitate to say just how.

In a single decade, personal computer technology has become ubiquitous. Computers do not apply the new physics as directly as do television and laser technology, but they beautifully translate systems theory into hardware . . . and software. Think about your old Underwood typewriter. One keystroke, one mark on the paper. The typewriter, with its linked rods transferring the motion of the finger to the motion of the rods to the motion of the metal letter, is a mechanism par excellence. With a PC, one keystroke can dramatically and instantaneously change the whole configuration of a paragraph or a spreadsheet or a graphic. Here we have a technological analogue of an ecosystem in which the extirpation of a single keystone species can precipitate cascading reverberations throughout a biotic community (Soulé and Kohm 1989). People who use PCs have grown accustomed to systems experience. The present generation of kids, growing up with computers in their bedrooms, will think systemically—including, hopefully, ecosystemically.

These are just a few obvious examples of how new technologies insidiously change our concept of nature as they saturate our living space. While we still love our cars and other mechanical transportation technologies, in some aspects of life there seems to be emerging a contempt for the old mechanical appliances. For example, a vinyl long-playing record album is so inferior—not just in sound but in technical elegance—to a CD that people are literally throwing out their records and turntables. In the first decade of the twenty-first century, will solar voltaic lighting, space-heating, and transportation technologies make oil furnaces and gasoline automobiles equally uncool? Will people be taking to solar energy devices like they now take to TV, PCs, CDs, and microwave ovens?

I don't know. All I can offer is some scant, local anecdotal evidence for the possibility that they might. Among my rural friends in central Wisconsin a quiet revolt against conventional electrical energy is taking place. A group calling itself POWER has been organized to fight the up-scaling of existing transmission lines and the installation of new routes (C. Mitchell, pers. comm., 1992). The point of attack is the danger to human and animal (wild as well as domestic) health posed by errant electromagnetic fields. But the deeper concerns are social (the arrogance of centralized, monopolized utility companies) and environmental (the fact that energy is squandered and that modest efforts at conservation could offset the need for more electrical generation). Several households in the county are already nearly energy self-sufficient. As one person put it, "When there is an outage, we're not even aware of it until we hear about it next day from the neighbors" (T. Pease, pers. comm., 1992). The shift to solar energy was certainly not forced on these people by economics. Those who have changed over have not done so cheaply (R. Ramlow, pers. comm., 1992). For them, it is primarily a matter of conscience . . . and style. Nowadays, it's very hip to have solar panels on your roof.

Suppose there does develop an intuitive, wholesale appetite for the now-emerging postmodern solar-electronic genre of technologies. Obviously, that would be a plus for ecosystem health. A global transition to appropriate technology is the only way we can maintain a mass consumer culture and a functioning, healthy biosphere; the only way we can achieve a sustainable society. Just as important, however, is the bootstrapping effect of such technologies. I believe that they will communicate the postmodern holistic, systemic, dynamic concept of nature with us smart monkeys as creative, interactive components of it. That will lead to further technological breakthroughs in the same motif and esprit and, ultimately, to corresponding changes in politics, economics, agriculture, medicine, and other primary aspects of civilization.

Hints of things to come are both ominous and hopeful. In addition to the previously mentioned bad effects of television, its negative impact on politics in liberal democracies, especially in the United States (Kellner 1990), is increasingly clear. Evidently, television has reduced public discussion and debate of complex issues to thirty-second sound bites and iconography—like George Bush's infamous Willie Horton commercial during the 1988 presidential campaign. Television encourages just such packaging and advertising of candidates. And it forces professional politicians to sell out to special interest groups in order to have enough money to buy TV time (Kellner 1990). On the other hand, I tend to think that TV has done more good than harm for the environmental movement by bringing sympathetic images of wildlife and nature generally into our living rooms, in gorgeous color, accompanied by very didactic editorializing on the prudential, aesthetic, and moral necessity of preserving our magnificent natural heritage.

Even among neoclassical economists there is a new willingness to quantify and count the environmental and ecological costs of industrial agriculture and other forms of destructive development (Passell 1990). Steady-state and ecological economics are changing from concepts called for by environmental philosophers to fields articulated in some detail—theoretically, to be sure, but at least some movement in these directions is afoot, as evidenced by the recent establishment of the journal *Ecological Economics* and the appointment of Herman Daly to a post with the World Bank as senior economist (Daly and Cobb 1989).

The assumption that the human body is a microcosm—a miniature image of the macrocosm, or general world system—has characterized Western natural philosophy from its inception (Guthrie 1962–78). The four bodily humors of ancient medical theory mirrored the four elements of ancient cosmology (Clagett 1963). I remember how, as an undergraduate philosophy student, I was puzzled to find Descartes, in part 5 of the *Discourse on Method,* embarking on a long medical discussion, the whole purpose of which seemed nothing more than to show that the heart is just a mechanical pump (Descartes 1911a). I now see the passage as integral to Descartes's mechanistic project. Future undergraduates may be just as puzzled to find the current generation of environmental philosophers going to great lengths to argue what will doubtless then seem obvious—that the human body is an organism, not a mechanism, internally related to its environing ecosystem (Callicott 1986).

Indeed, it seems not to be entirely accidental that the holistic health and wellness movement began to gain momentum about the same time that *ecology* became a household word (Kirk and Hayshark 1972). Here, admittedly, we appear to have a classic case of one domain of theory (ecology) indirectly fertilizing another (medicine), not of the technological application of theory insidiously changing the cultural construction of reality. But I want to make the allied point that changes in medical thinking are a weather vane for shifts in the prevailing intellectual winds of the cognitive culture. The growing popular suspicion of surgery, chemical medicines, and radiology, and the increasing turn to such "conventional" treatments as a last resort—after the failure of diet reform, exercise, visualization, meditation, homeopathy, and the like—signal a shift from the modern mechanical to a postmodern organic worldview (Meeks 1991).

Getting sick is a human universal. Because being ill is an abhorrent state of existence, it is not surprising that all peoples try to understand the cause of disease. Naturally, their medical etiologies are consonant with their larger worldviews. Obtaining food is also a human universal. And agricultural beliefs, no less than medical ones, are indicative of a culture's Weltanschauung. Thus changes in the philosophy of agriculture, no less than changes in medical theory, are symptomatic of sea changes in a culture's Zeitgeist (Callicott 1990).

The winds of change blow in contemporary agriculture even more strongly than in contemporary medicine. Over the last two decades it has become common knowledge that industrial agriculture is unsustainable. Wendell Berry (1977), industrial agriculture's eloquent and devastating critic, and organic agriculture's equally eloquent and persuasive prophet, Wes Jackson (1980), have become folk heroes and celebrities. In 1989 the National Academy of Sciences' Board on Agriculture recommended a massive shift away from increased scale, mechanization, and use of chemical fertilizers, pesticides, and herbicides toward "alternative" organic farming techniques for agriculture in the United States (Committee on the Role of Alternative Methods in Modern Production Agriculture 1989).

                In conclusion, let me say that nature is not dead. Rather, the modern man/nature dualism and the mechanical concept of nature are dead. The ubiquity of man and his works has made the illusion of nature as Other all but impossible to maintain as the twentieth century gives way to the twenty-first. But the modern concepts of man and nature and the relationship between the two had already been invalidated by developments in science that occurred between the mid-nineteenth and the mid-twentieth centuries—by the theories of evolution and ecology in biology, and by relativity and quantum theory in physics. The new concept of nature is more organismic than mechanistic and includes man as, in Leopold's (1949:204) words, "a plain member and citizen of the biotic community." It is theoretically conceivable, therefore, that we may become good, law-abiding citizens of the natural world rather than brutal and ultimately self-defeating conquistadors. The new understanding of nature, human nature, and the man-nature relationship may trickle down into the popular mind through its representation in postmodern solar-electronic technology. The growing public interest in holistic medicine and sustainable organic agriculture is evidence that a shift in the prevailing cultural worldview is already well under way. The new solar-electronic technologies have already shown themselves to be seductive. People want them. These technologies may thus inspire further application of the systemic ideas they embody, and our present unsustainable mechanistic civilization may rapidly evolve into a new, more sustainable, systemic configuration, not only technically but socially, politically, and economically as well.

NOTES

1 Keenly aware that it is gender biased, I use the term *man* throughout, both deliberately and apologetically, to refer generically to the sexually dimorphous species *Homo sapiens* because I wish to evoke the historical connotations that the term *man* carries, including its decided sexist connotation. Further, the language here and in the next paragraph alludes, with deliberate irony, to the Wilderness Act of 1964, which reads, in part, "a wilderness, in contrast with those areas where man and his own works dominate the landscape, is hereby recognized as an area where the earth and its community of life are untrammeled by man, where man himself is a visitor who does not remain" (Nash 1982:5).

2 Principle 20, part 2, of *The Principles of Philosophy* (Descartes 1911c:264) says, "That from this may be demonstrated the nonexistence of atoms." What Descartes meant was that the material particles or corpuscles, of which he was an enthusiastic advocate, were not indivisible, or "atomic" in the literal sense of the Greek word *atom*. In principle 201, part 4, Descartes (1911c:297) affirms "that . . . sensible bodies are composed of insensible particles."

3 As in the earlier instance of gender bias, I shall only critically note and not pause to comment further on the ethnic slur implied by this exclusion.

4 Name withheld as a professional courtesy.

REFERENCES

Anselm. 1903. *Proslogium*. Trans. S. N. Dean. La Salle, Ill.: Open Court.

Aquinas, T. 1955a. *Summa Contra Gentiles*. Book 1. Trans. A. C. Pegis. Garden City, N.Y.: Doubleday.

———. 1955b. *Summa Contra Gentiles*. Book 3, part 2, chapter 112.

Aristotle. 1941. *De Anima*. Trans. J. A. Smith. In *The Basic Works of Aristotle*, ed. R. McKeon, 535–640. New York: Random House.

Bacon, F. 1960. *The New Organon*. New York: Library of Liberal Arts Press.

Barbour, I. 1982. *Energy and the American Values*. New York: Praeger.

Barrett, H. M. 1940. *Boethius: Some Aspects of His Times and Work*. Cambridge: Cambridge University Press.

Berry, W. 1977. *The Unsettling of America: Culture and Agriculture*. San Francisco: Sierra Club Books.

Bertalanffy, L. von. 1967. *Robots, Men, and Minds*. New York: Braziller.

Bett, H. 1925. *Johannes Scotus Eriugena: A Study in Medieval Philosophy*. Cambridge: Cambridge University Press.

Bohm, D. 1980. *Wholeness and the Implicate Order*. London: Routledge and Kegan Paul.

Botkin, D. 1990. *Discordant Harmonies: A New Ecology for the Twenty-first Century*. New York: Oxford University Press.

Brown, L. R., et al. 1984–92. *State of the World*. New York: W. W. Norton/World Watch Institute.

Brubaker, Linda B. 1988. "Vegetation History and Anticipating Future Vegetative Change." In *Ecosystem Management for Parks and Wilderness*, ed. J. K. Agee and D. R. Johnson, 42–58. Seattle: University of Washington Press.

Butzer, K. W. 1992. "The Americas Before and after 1492: An Introduction to Current Geographical Research." *Annals of the Association of American Geographers* 82:345–68.

Callicott, J. B. 1986. "The Metaphysical Implications of Ecology." *Environmental Ethics* 8:301–16.

———. 1990. "The Metaphysical Transition in Farming: From the Newtonian-Mechanical to the Eltonian-Ecological." *Journal of Agriculture Ethics* 3:36–49.

———. 1991a. "That Good Old-Time Wilderness Religion." *Environmental Professional* 13:378–79.

———. 1991b. "The Wilderness Idea Revisited: The Sustainable Development Alternative." *Environmental Professional* 13:235–47.

Capra, F. 1975. *The Tao of Physics: An Exploration of the Parallels Between Modern Physics and Eastern Mysticism*. Boulder: Shambala.

Chaplin, C., director, producer. 1935. *Modern Times*. Hollywood, Calif.: United Artists.

Clagett, M. 1963. *Greek Science in Antiquity*. New York: Collier Books.

Cohen, M. P. 1991. "John Muir, the Sierra Club, and Paradigms for Amateur Environmental Activism." Paper presented to the Fifth Annual Cassassa Conference on Ecological Prospects: Theory and Practice, 14 March, Los Angeles.

Commission on Research and Resource Management Policy. 1989. *National Parks: From Vignettes to a Global View.* Washington, D.C.: National Parks and Conservation Association.

Committee on the Role of Alternative Methods in Modern Production Agriculture. 1989. *Alternative Agriculture.* Washington, D.C.: National Academy Press.

Commoner, B. 1971. *The Closing Circle: Nature, Man, and Technology.* New York: Knopf.

Costanza, R., B. G. Norton, and B. Haskell, eds. 1992. *Ecosystem Health: New Goals for Environmental Management.* Washington, D.C.: Island Press.

Daly, H. E., and J. B. Cobb. 1989. *For the Common Good: Redirecting the Economy Toward Community, the Environment, and a Sustainable Future.* Boston: Beacon Press.

Darwin, C. 1874. *The Descent of Man and Selection in Relation to Sex.* 2d ed. London: John Murray.

Day, G. M. 1953. "The Indian as an Ecological Factor in the Northeastern Forest." *Ecology* 34:329–46.

Deneven, W. M. 1992. "The Pristine Myth: The Landscape of the Americas in 1492." *Annals of the Association of American Geographers* 82:369–85.

Descartes, R. 1911a. "Discourse on the Method of Rightly Conducting the Reason and Seeking for Truth in the Sciences." In *The Philosophical Works of Descartes.* Vol. 1. Trans. E. S. Haldane and G. R. T. Ross, 81–130. Cambridge: Cambridge University Press.

———. 1911b. "Meditations on First Philosophy in Which the Existence of God and the Distinction Between Mind and Body Are Demonstrated." In *The Philosophical Works of Descartes,* 1:131–99.

———. 1911c. "The Principles of Philosophy." In *The Philosophical Works of Descartes,* 1:200–302.

Ducasse, P. 1958. *Histoire du techniques.* Paris: Presses Universitaires de France.

Executive Office of the President of the United States. 1991. *Budget of the United States Government, Fiscal Year 1992.* Washington, D.C.: U.S. Government Printing Office.

Fox, S. 1981. *John Muir and His Legacy: The American Conservation Movement.* Boston: Little, Brown.

Fromhold, A. T. 1981. *Quantum Mechanics for Applied Physics and Engineering.* New York: Academic Press.

Galilei, G. 1957. "The Assayer." In *Discoveries and Opinions of Galileo.* Trans. S. Drake. Garden City, N.Y.: Doubleday.

Gomez-Pompa, A., and A. Kaus. 1988. "Conservation by Traditional Cultures in the Tropics." In *For the Conservation of the Earth,* ed. V. Martin, 183–89. Golden, Colo.: Fulcrum.

Gribben, J. 1984. *In Search of Schrödinger's Cat: Quantum Physics and Reality.* New York: Bantam Books.

Guthrie, W. K. C. 1962–78. *A History of Greek Philosophy.* 5 vols. Cambridge: Cambridge University Press.

Hargrove, E. C. 1992. "Weak Anthropocentric Intrinsic Value." *Monist* 75:183–207.

Harrison, R. 1964. *Animal Machines: The New Factory Farming Industry.* London: Stuart.

Havelock, E. A. 1963. *Preface to Plato.* Cambridge: Harvard University Press.

Hecht, S., and A. Cockburn. 1989. *The Fate of the Forest: Developers, Destroyers, and Defenders of the Amazon.* London: Verso.

Heisenberg, W. 1962. *Physics and Philosophy: The Revolution in Modern Science.* New York: Harper and Row.

Heizer, R. F. 1955. *Primitive Man as an Ecologic Factor.* Kroeber Anthropological Society Papers, no. 13, Berkeley, Calif.

Hughes, J. D. 1983. *American Indian Ecology.* El Paso: Texas Western Press.

Hume, D. 1960. *A Treatise of Human Nature.* Oxford: Clarendon Press.

Jackson, W. 1980. *New Roots for Agriculture.* Lincoln: University of Nebraska Press.

Kellner, D. 1990. *Television and the Crisis of Democracy.* Boulder: Westview Press.

Kirk, R. H., and C. Hayshark. 1972. *Personal Health in Ecologic Perspective.* St. Louis: Mosby.

Koyré, A. 1965. *Newtonian Studies.* Chicago: University of Chicago Press.

Kuhn, T. S. 1957. *The Copernican Revolution: Planetary Astronomy in the Development of Western Thought.* Cambridge: Harvard University Press.

Lake, S. 1981. *Television's Impact on Children and Adolescents: A Special Interest Resource Guide in Education.* Phoenix: Oryx Press.

Leopold, A. 1949. *A Sand County Almanac and Sketches Here and There.* New York: Oxford University Press.

———. 1987. [1947.] Foreword [to the MS of "Great Possessions"; later titled *A Sand County Almanac*]. In *Companion to a Sand County Almanac.* Ed. J. B. Callicott, 286. Madison: University of Wisconsin Press.

Leopold, A. S., S. A. Cain, C. M. Cottam, I. N. Gabrielson, and T. L. Kimball. 1963. *Wildlife Management in the National Parks.* Washington, D.C.: U.S. Department of the Interior.

Lewis, H. T. 1973. *Patterns of Indian Burning in California: Ecology and Ethnohistory.* Ballena Anthropological Papers, no. 1, Berkeley, Calif.

Locke, J. 1961. *An Essay Concerning Human Understanding.* Vol. 1. London: J. M. Dent.

McKibben, B. 1989. *The End of Nature.* New York: Random House.

McLuhan, M. 1965. *Understanding Media: The Extensions of Man.* New York: McGraw-Hill.

Martin, C. 1973. "Fire and Forest Structure in the Aboriginal Eastern Forest." *Indian Historian* 6:38–42, 54.

Martin, P. S. 1973. "The Discovery of America." *Science* 179:969–74.

Meeks, L. B. 1991. *Health: A Wellness Approach.* Columbus: Merrill.

Mill, J. S. 1969. "Nature." In *Three Essays on Natural Religion.* New York: Greenwood Press.

Mooney, H. A., and J. Drake, eds. 1986. *Ecology of Biological Invasions of North America and Hawaii.* New York: Springer Verlag.

Muir, J. 1901. *Our National Parks.* Boston: Houghton Mifflin.

Mumford, L. 1934. *Technics and Civilization.* New York: Harcourt, Brace.

Nash, R. 1982. *Wilderness and the American Mind.* 3d ed. New Haven: Yale University Press.

Newton, I. 1962. *Mathematical Principles of Natural Philosophy.* Trans. A. Motte, ed. F. Cajori. Berkeley: University of California Press.

Nietzsche, F. 1974. *The Gay Science: With a Prelude of Rhymes and an Appendix of Songs.* Trans. Walter Kaufmann. New York: Random House.

Oates, W. J. 1948. *The Basic Writings of Saint Augustine.* 2 vols. New York: Random House.

Ockham, W. 1957. *Philosophical Writings: A Selection.* Ed. P. Boehner. Edinburgh: Thomas Nelson.

Odum, E. P. 1971. *Fundamentals of Ecology.* 3d ed. Philadelphia: W. B. Saunders.

O'Neill, R. V., D. L. DeAngelis, J. B. Waide, and T. F. H. Allen. 1986. *A Hierarchical Concept of Ecosystems.* Princeton: Princeton University Press.

Ong, W. 1982. *Orality and Literacy: The Technologizing of the Word.* New York: Methuen.

Passell, P. 1990. "Rebel Economists Add Ecological Cost to Price of Progress." *New York Times.* 27 November, B5–B6.

Passmore, J. 1968. *A Hundred Years of Philosophy.* Harmondsworth: Penguin Books.

Phillips, K. 1990. *The Politics of the Rich and Poor: Wealth and the American Electorate in the Reagan Aftermath.* New York: Random House.

Pinchot, G. 1947. *Breaking New Ground.* New York: Harcourt, Brace.

Pyne, S. J. 1982. *Fire in America: A Cultural History of Wildland and Rural Fire.* Princeton: Princeton University Press.

Rachels, J. 1990. *Created from Animals: The Moral Implications of Darwinism.* New York: Oxford University Press.

Ruse, M. 1979. *The Darwinian Revolution: Science Red in Fang and Claw.* Chicago: University of Chicago Press.

———. 1986. *Taking Darwin Seriously: A Naturalistic Approach to Philosophy.* New York: Basil Blackwell.

Schumacher, E. F. 1973. *Small Is Beautiful: Economics As If People Mattered.* New York: Harper and Row.

Shrader-Fréchette, K. 1989. "Ecological Theories and Ethical Imperatives: Can Ecology Provide a Scientific Justification for the Ethics of Environmental Protection?" In *Scientists and Their Responsibility,* ed. W. R. Shea and B. Sitter, 73–104. Watson Canton, Mass.: Publishing International.

Soulé, M. E., and K. A. Kohm. 1989. *Research Priorities for Conservation Biology.* Washington, D.C.: Island Press.

Thoreau, H. D. 1962. "Walking." In *Excursions,* 161–214. New York: Corinth Books.

U.S. Central Intelligence Agency. 1990. Map of Antarctic Research Stations. Washington, D.C.: Central Intelligence Agency.

Usher, M. B. 1988. "Biological Invasions of Nature Reserves: A Search for Generalizations." *Biological Conservation* 74:119–35.

Webb, T. 1986. "Is Vegetation in Equilibrium with Climate?: How to Interpret Late-Quaternary Pollen Data." *Vegetatio* 67:75–91.

———. 1987. "The Appearance and Disappearance of Major Vegetational Assemblages in Eastern North America." *Vegetatio* 69:177–87.

Worster, D. 1977. *Nature's Economy: The Roots of Ecology.* San Francisco: Sierra Club Books.

Wright, H. E., and D. G. Frey, eds. 1965. *The Quaternary of the United States.* Princeton: Princeton University Press.

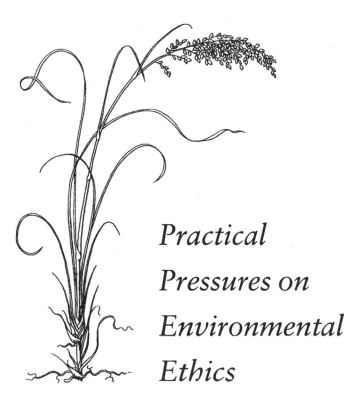

Practical
Pressures on
Environmental
Ethics

IGNAZIO MUSU

Efficiency and Equity in International Environmental Cooperation

International Environmental Problems and Sustainable Development

If the problems raised by the interdependence between economic development and environmental protection are to be faced in an appropriate way, they must be handled within an international framework. A planetary point of view makes it clear that merely worrying about the impact economic growth can have on the environment and on the quality of life is not enough today; we must also consider the impact ecological constraints may have on the prospects for future economic development (Brundtland 1987).

It is generally recognized that environmental resources, while they are regenerable according to biogeochemical cycles, are ultimately finite, and exploiting them above their regeneration rate may lead to their irreversible exhaustion. We may legitimately ask ourselves if a widening of economic growth to include the whole planet can take place without endangering the stock of environmental resources available to humankind, which would in turn impair the possibility of continuing the economic growth process.

The very existence of a north-south gap in the world economy complicates the ecological issue because it favors overexploitation of the common property resources of the world environment. Although the developing countries tend to specialize in the production and export of goods that use natural resources more intensively, environmental resources are basic factors in any kind of economic process. Some developing countries (for example, Brazil, Nigeria, Indonesia, and the Philippines) are particularly well endowed with natural resources. Typically, the institutions devoted to environmental regulation in these developing countries are so weak that they promote, in practice, an excessive use of these environmental resources. From the demand side, this use is encouraged because the resources are not paid for at their true social cost (Chichilnisky 1991).

In the advanced countries the awareness of the social costs entailed by overuse of environmental resources has led to the development of institutions and policies that internalize the social costs into real costs—at least more so than in the less-developed countries. Also, a cultural modification has taken place in consumer preferences, which now express a willingness to pay more for environment-friendly goods and processes. One can say that this has been largely due to the increase in the real income per capita experienced by the populations living in the mature economies. In any case, this has not happened in the developing countries. On the contrary, the desire to imitate consumers in developed countries and the low initial per capita income tend to promote a structure of preferences that does not care much for the environmental quality of production processes and consumer goods. Without reforms in the economic institutions that oversee the conditions of environmental resources in the developing countries, the enlargement of the world growth process to encompass these countries poses a real threat to the sustainability of the process itself.

Price equalization of environmental factors will not be reached simply through the international trade of produced goods, as traditional international trade theory may suggest, because technological conditions are very different in developed and developing countries (Chichilnisky 1991). In practice, the economic growth process in developing countries depends largely on technological progress in the developed economies, but there is always a gap between the technological structures of the two kinds of countries.

The role of technology developed in advanced countries is the crucial factor, because this technology will be transferred to the industrialization processes of the developing world. Without technological changes allowing for a savings of environmental factors per unit of output and per unit of consumption, a worldwide sustainable development—using nature without using it up—will not be feasible (Brundtland 1987). Technological progress in the developed economies must therefore be oriented to minimize the trade-off between the growth of man-made capital and the use of environmental capital (Barbier et al. 1989). This must concern production processes, aiming at a reduction of polluting emissions per unit of output and at the recycling of wastes and scrap materials, but it must also concern finite goods, taking into account their destination after their strict economic life.

Sustainable development has been defined as a problem of intergenerational efficiency (Brundtland 1987) because it must guarantee future generations' opportunities without impairing those of the present ones. Sustainable development is also a problem of intragenerational equity, however, because it must also guarantee opportunities for populations in developing countries; and this implies important modifications in development patterns in the more advanced economies. The problem is to shape the technological pattern in such a way that these modifications avoid a trade-off between intragenerational and intergenerational equity objectives.

It is in the ultimate interest of the developed countries themselves to prevent an excessive preoccupation with the quality of life of their own present generations from worsening the quality of life of the present generations of the developing countries. This focus has led, for example, to a relocation of the most polluting industrial processes from the rich to the poor countries. A short-term efficiency reason might claim that the less-developed countries are generally more endowed with environmental resources and are better able to absorb pollutants. In the long run, however, this would not only be contrary to an objective of distributive justice, it would also prevent a sustainable development path for the advanced countries themselves. Pollution generated by industrial processes in developing countries will sooner or later affect the quality of life in the developed countries through the damage to the earth's atmosphere, oceans, and biodiversity.

The developing countries are well aware both of the qualitative problems that must be solved in their economic growth model to minimize its impact on the natural and environmental resources with which they are endowed, and of the ultimate threat to the world environment arising from the advanced countries' strategy of protecting their own exclusive interests. This means that any effort to reach international agreements in global environmental issues embodies an element of bargaining between developing and developed countries. It is clearly not possible to discuss the problems of international cooperation for preserving global environmental resources without taking into account the constraints set by the issue of a balanced equilibrium in the world development process.

International Environment as a Public Good and a Common Property Resource

The fundamental feature of global environmental problems is the fact that they affect many countries at the same time and in an interdependent way: the countries are linked in a network of reciprocal externalities (Maler 1990). The lack of an institution that can perform the role of international environmental regulator and implement an appropriate environmental policy requires that these problems be addressed through voluntary agreements among the interested countries. Until recently, economic theory, based on an extrapolation to an international level of results derived from the theory of public goods and common property resources, accepted the conclusion that most countries would not find it in their interest to adhere to these agreements.

It seems quite natural that an agreement for voluntary environmental conservation as a public good would be particularly difficult to reach. The difficulty lies in the possibility of a community, even for those not committed to this agreement, to enjoy the advantage of environmental conservation (a public good), given its consumption indivisibility and full accessibility (Cornes and Sandler 1987). Moreover, any signed agreement would not be stable because everybody would be strongly tempted to defect, hoping to continue to receive the benefits of the agreement through the permanent commitment of the others. The obvious conclusion is that although managing global environmental externalities requires international cooperation in principle, the incentives for cooperation in the different countries would work in the opposite direction.

International Environmental Policies in Noncooperative and Cooperative Frameworks

The reality of environmental policy seems to be more complex. First, a number of international treaties already exist to deal with problems such as marine pollution, management of endangered fish populations, international river basin water resource management, and protection of animal species (Barrett 1990). Some of these treaties are ineffective; some lack carefully designed enforcement procedures; but these treaties do exist, and they can be improved and made more effective in terms of reciprocal commitments among participants.

Second, even without explicit international cooperation, individual countries undertake actions to preserve a common environment only on the basis of their own self-interest. Therefore, the absence of cooperation need not lead to an exhaustion of the environment as a common property resource or to its destruction as a public good; in other words, the absence of cooperation would not necessarily lead to the well-known "tragedy of the commons" (Carraro and Siniscalco 1991).

It is, of course, possible that the unilateral action of a country to reduce damaging emissions, undertaken in the hope of generating imitation, might cause a higher global level of pollution because the other countries do not imitate the virtuous behavior of the first country. Instead, they might feel themselves even less constrained to pursue corrective policies (Hoel 1991). Again, however, this does not necessarily mean a "tragic" outcome.

In order to examine this point more closely, it may be worthwhile to present briefly the theoretical scheme normally used by economists to analyze this kind of problem. This scheme has different versions, but I believe the most appropriate is the following one.

Each country benefits from a policy of emission reduction (*emission* is a term used here to mean the exploitation of any environmental resource potentially usable by a number of countries). This benefit may be measured by the damage that would be caused if pollution were not reduced. Moreover, each country takes advantage of the actions of the other countries to improve the environment; the intensity of this advantage depends on the physical-ecological model that defines the interdependence among the various nations. Turning things around, one can say that each country is damaged by pollution produced in other countries and by their failure to take actions to reduce this pollution. Therefore, the benefit that each nation receives depends not only on its own emission reduction but also on other nations' actions to reduce their emissions. This is what is meant by the statement that environmental protection may be considered an international public good. On the other hand, each nation bears some costs to sustain its actions devoted to pollution abatement and to the improvement of environmental quality. These costs depend only on the extent to which emissions are reduced by the individual country.

Without agreements for a common policy of emission reduction, and assuming that each country considers the abatement by the other nations as given, each country will try to maximize the net benefit from an action of abatement unilaterally undertaken, the net benefit being the difference between the benefit of emission reduction and the cost of abatement. A standard result of this noncooperative model is that each nation will abate its own emissions until the point above which the marginal abatement cost overcomes the marginal benefit that is expected from the abatement policy (Barrett 1990).

It is possible, and even likely, if nations are not very different in size and structure, that actions unilaterally undertaken to abate emissions may turn out to be mutually compatible, in the sense that no nation wishes to change its position after the abatement policies have been implemented. This is an international noncooperative equilibrium.

The noncooperative equilibrium may be characterized by a considerable reduction in emissions when the net benefit of the noncooperative abatement policy is high for each country. Moreover, in a noncooperative equilibrium, the lower the intensity of the positive reciprocal externality, the higher the emission abatement. In other words, if the abatement in the other countries has little influence on the benefit of the country that must decide the abatement policy, each country will choose a higher abatement level than it would choose if the benefits derived from the other countries' abatement were higher (Cornes and Sandler 1987; Carraro and Siniscalco 1991).

The higher the interdependence among abatement policies, the stronger the need for cooperative policies, because less intense unilateral actions tend to be taken in this situation. In this case, however, international cooperation will be more difficult to obtain even if it is more necessary. As we shall see in a moment, this has to do with a sort of "free ride" behavior, because in the case of a strong interdependence among abatement policies, each country tends to exploit the benefit from the abatement undertaken by the other countries, reducing considerably its own abatement when the others increase theirs (Cornes and Sandler 1987).

The minimum benefit necessary to undertake an effective policy of environmental improvement plays an important role in deciding the intensity of cooperative abatement policies. Often this policy requires considerable fixed costs in terms of technology and equipment transformation (Heal 1991). Only a small number of countries can afford these costs and ensure a minimum benefit to the environmental quality improvement. These countries therefore will form the minimum coalition required to cover the fixed costs necessary to start an abatement project. Below the minimum level of effort required, no unilateral abatement will take place; on the other hand, above this level, a cooperative policy will be made easier by the existence of a coalition, although a partial one.

Difficulties in Cooperation

When a number of countries decide to coordinate their policies, they must consider the interdependence of the benefits derived from emission abatement. The international environment being considered as an international public good, the rule that guides cooperating countries in implementing the chosen policy should be one that would lead to a socially efficient management of a public good. This is a well-known rule, a consequence of the fact that environmental improvement benefits different countries simultaneously, and none exclusively. It states that the abatement in each nation should reach that level above which the sum of the incremental benefit of a further action by the cooperating nations would be overtaken by the incremental abatement cost for any individual nation (Samuelson 1954; Feldman 1980).

If the size and structure of the cooperating countries do not differ too much, each country will obtain a net benefit greater than the benefit obtainable with a noncooperative equilibrium solution. The larger the degree of interdependence among the abatement policies (the greater the effect of the abatement policy in one country as perceived by another country), the greater will be the difference between the cooperative and the noncooperative abatement levels for each nation. This means that the larger the interdependence, the greater the social advantage of a cooperative environmental policy.

The cooperative solution is not easily implemented, however. Every country must act on some assumption about the likely behavior of the other countries. If the others commit themselves to a policy of environmental improvement following the strategy of the cooperative agreement, an individual country may be tempted to follow a noncooperative strategy in the hope of gaining from the others' virtuous behavior while at the same time reducing the cost of its own commitment. On the other hand, if an individual country thinks that the others might follow a noncooperative strategy with lower emission abatement, it can deduce that it is not worthwhile to follow a cooperative strategy given its minimum role in obtaining the outcome, particularly relative to the cost that it should bear.

The conclusion is that each country, whatever the strategy chosen by the others, may eventually prefer the noncooperative strategy, which therefore becomes the equilibrium solution.

This conclusion suggests that signing international environmental agreements should be almost impossible, or at least very difficult, and that once an agreement has been signed, it will be precarious and unstable because each country will be tempted to cheat, taking advantage of the good faith of the others. This, however, seems to be an excessively pessimistic view. In international environmental problems, interdependence among nations is not an episodical fact but a continuous relation. In these conditions one can imagine rules that give reciprocal guarantees of cooperative behavior. For example, one can imagine that if some country starts following a noncooperative policy and abrogates an agreement already signed, the other signatory countries would react by also moving to noncooperation, and eventually this would destroy the agreement, leaving every country worse off. Therefore, any country that wants to behave in a noncooperative way in the hope of gain must know that it has to discount the future losses resulting from the other countries following its lead and defecting (Taylor 1987). Every country must compare the short-term benefits of a noncooperative policy, when the other countries continue to follow the agreement, with the future losses it will suffer when the other countries react by abandoning the agreement. In this "repeated game" approach, if the rate of intertemporal preference is low enough to give a sufficiently heavy weight to the future losses resulting from the agreement's failure, countries will be discouraged from adopting defecting behaviors; therefore the agreement will become more stable (Ordeshook 1986; Moulin 1988).

The need to consider the role of the intertemporal rate of preference clearly brings into the analysis an ethical concept related to the acknowledged right of future generations to enjoy an improved environment. It is also clear that market rates of interest do not necessarily reflect future-oriented preferences in environmental issues. Assuming a low rate of time preference would lead to the optimistic conclusion that agreements that deal with international environmental problems are easy to conclude and stable—exactly the opposite of the conclusion reached above (Taylor 1987). This would also be a hasty and superficial conclusion, and not only because the assumption itself could be overoptimistic. Historical experience shows us a very complex reality. Agreements are sometimes successful and sometimes not; some are signed by partial coalitions of countries; sometimes the prolonged bargaining process makes agreement very difficult.

If, for example, we consider the increasing concentration of CO_2 in the atmosphere, we realize that dealing with this problem requires a minimum effort that can be sustained only by a group of countries. In other words, if ensuring global climate stability and avoiding global warming are valued as an international public good, we are not facing a problem of variable quantities of a public good among which we can select the optimal one. Rather, it is a problem of a minimum threshold below which no amount of public good will be produced. In this case we can imagine different cooperative equilibria in international environmental relations. In each equilibrium there exists a coalition with a number of countries equal to or greater than the necessary minimum, while the other countries do not sign the agreement and continue to follow a noncooperative behavior.

The possible existence of multiple equilibria, each charcterized by a group of countries that forms a coalition and by another group that is not required to cooperate, raises some relevant issues (Sugden 1986). Clearly, in a situation of this kind, each country would prefer to be in the set of noncooperating countries, leaving to the others the burden of cooperation while enjoying the benefits of it. Although the need to "produce" the public good is recognized, there is a resistance to cooperation. A situation of indeterminacy in the process of coalition formation is created, and we cannot exclude the possibility that this situation leads to no environmental agreement.

Other outcomes are possible, however. Some countries could assume a commitment to noncooperation in order to push the other countries to sign an agreement (Taylor 1987). Therefore, only those countries with less endurance will eventually cooperate. For example, developing countries could announce that they will not sign any agreement on CO_2 reduction in order to push developed countries toward a commitment to cooperate. Another possibility is a coalition formed by those countries (in this case, the more economically advanced ones) that perceive the common environmental problem with greater intensity.

Cooperation and Bargaining

The common awareness of the importance of what is at stake suggests that the interesting problem is not the contrast between cooperation and ecological disaster but the kind of cooperation required if the agreement is to be successful and stable. Reciprocal frictions, which are part of the bargaining process aimed at signing an agreement, must not be allowed to prevent the conclusion of the agreement itself. It is natural that each contracting party should try to gain the best conditions for itself in the agreement, but the common need to sign an agreement is a strong incentive to reach a positive conclusion.

If trying to solve a global environmental problem or to avoid global environmental disasters is a positive-sum game, the problem is essentially that of exploiting any space and possibility to improve simultaneously the positions of the potentially cooperating countries. The problem is similar to the situation when a minimal coalition of countries has been created and this coalition wants to expand to include other countries in order to address the common environmental issue more effectively.

Ethical and cultural factors are extremely important in favoring the conclusion of environmental agreements among countries with different levels and forms of development. If the process leading to an international environmental agreement is a bargaining process starting from a noncooperative equilibrium solution (Harsany and Selten 1988; Myerson 1991), the coalition signing the agreement may have good reasons to ask for a fair distribution of aggregate benefits on the basis of an accepted ethical criterion.

International agencies are very important in performing the arbitrage and mediation aimed at finding a "focal point" (Fudenberg and Tirole 1991) in the process of agreement conclusion. These institutions could create and maintain pressure to promote a set of norms of behavior so that countries not complying with these norms would feel very uneasy in the face of international public opinion (Sugden 1986).

Asymmetrical information and lack of communication among the parties, both in the process of agreement building and in the actions of an international agency constituted to enforce the agreement, may result in problems. When benefits and costs are not directly observable and uniquely definable, each country finds it convenient to declare a cost of the environmental policy greater than the real one, thus laying the burden of emission abatement on the other participants in the coalition.

Given the difficulty of implementing an efficient international environmental policy, it has been suggested that policies of symmetric proportional reduction in emissions in the various countries be adopted. From the economist's point of view, however, this would not be an efficient solution because social cost minimization requires that those countries that can cut back their emissions at lower cost bear a larger share of the reductions.

Besides the incentives to reduce emissions, another set of incentives would then be necessary to induce countries to reveal their true abatement cost function. This could make things so complicated that a second-best solution, like the uniform emission abatement policy, might be preferable (Spulber 1987). An alternative might be conceiving the international environmental agency as a mediator helping the bargaining countries to solve their "announcement" problem by taking confidential reports from the parties but also producing an incentive-compatible rule, known to every party, so that the expected payoff to each country reporting honestly is higher than the payoff it would obtain by lying.

International Cooperation in Solving Current Global Environmental Issues

It may be useful to discuss briefly the international cooperation problems related to some of the more important current global environmental problems. In some cases an agreement has been signed and the prospects of enforcing it are encouraging; in other cases the process of reaching an agreement seems to present more difficulties.

The Montreal Protocol and the Ozone Layer

One problem that has been dealt with rather successfully, at least in terms of the process leading to the signing of an agreement and its extension to a larger number of countries, is ozone depletion. The agreement, known as the Montreal Protocol, was signed in 1987; further refinements were signed in London in 1990.

The Montreal Protocol asks for a reduction in consumption and production of chlorofluorocarbons (CFCs), organic compounds widely used in air conditioners, refrigerants, and aerosols that are largely responsible for the damage to the stratospheric ozone layer. There is extensive scientific evidence of the damage this depletion has effected on human health, animal life, and the environment (Kemp 1990).

Essentially, the agreement was reached in such a relatively short time because a few multinational corporations such as Du Pont in the United States and ICI in the United Kingdom were able to show that substitutes for ozone layer–damaging gases could be produced at a reasonable cost. The protocol was originally signed by thirty-six countries, accounting for more than 80 percent of the total CFC consumption, but future development prospects made it necessary to widen the number of signatories to include important developing countries such as India and China.

The reduction in CFC consumption proposed by the protocol is not uniform for developed and developing countries: developed countries must reduce their 1986 consumption by 85 percent by 1998; developing countries must reach that target only ten years later. Production targets for developing countries are also more lax than those for advanced countries. Such concessions were not considered sufficient by nonsignatory developing countries, though. These countries raised the problem of burden sharing as they explicitly argued for assistance with the required change of technology along the lines of article 5 of the Montreal Protocol, which commits parties to "facilitating access to environmentally safe alternative substances and technology" and "facilitating bilaterally or multilaterally the provision of subsidies, aid credits, guarantees or insurance programmes."

The refined agreement, reached in London in 1990, provides for a multilateral fund and a number of studies to decide the best model of assistance to meet the higher costs of CFC substitutes. These decisions have been welcomed by the developing countries. An important problem from this point of view is whether a developing country should manufacture CFC substitutes or import them. The second solution seems to be more appropriate, particularly for a small developing country, at least until the production of substitutes achieves substantial scale returns. The likelihood of future cost reductions due to increasing returns to scale is also a reason to recommend a delay in the time required to comply with CFC consumption and production reduction by the developing countries.

Global Warming and Climate Change

Reaching an agreement on less immediately threatening global environmental problems such as global warming and global climate change—or, more modestly, on a problem such as pollution of the world's atmosphere—will be much more difficult.

The first source of difficulty is the uncertainty about the extent of global warming that should be considered dangerous. David Pearce suggests that targets should avoid a zone of unknown risk on the grounds that the unknown includes potentially catastrophic impacts (Pearce 1991). The threshold should be a rate of warming of 0.1°C per decade. To keep within this rate of warming, CO_2 concentrations should be stabilized at 400–500 ppm in 2030; to reach this target the emission rate would have to begin falling before that year. Pearce's conclusion is that stabilization at current levels of emission must be introduced immediately if we are to avoid the zone of ignorance. But negotiators are not talking about immediate stabilization: current discussions are about stabilizing CO_2 emissions at the 1990 level by 2000 or by 2005 with further reductions thereafter.

Another source of difficulties is the lack of agreement about the impacts of global warming and related climate changes. The evaluations by various countries differ because of the geographical nonuniformity of the impacts (negative effects of global warming are likely to be stronger in semiarid irrigated areas; climate change will probably produce destructive flooding in the vast delta networks of tropical Asia; the impact in terms of sea level rise will affect coastal areas in particular; cold northern latitudes may even benefit by global warming, etc.) (Barbier et al. 1989). Each country gives a different weight to the ratio between negative global warming impacts and their target of increasing their economic growth rate. This difference of relative weights may be very high between economically advanced and developing countries.

The economic costs of dealing with global warming will inevitably, for some countries at least (such as the oil-exporting countries of the Middle East), exceed the gains. Russia is not only a large source of CO_2, but it will be one of the countries gaining from a warmer climate as it will be able to grow more food in its northern area. China has one-fifth of the world's population and one-third of the coal reserves. None of these countries, and none of the large majority of the developing countries is likely to take seriously a climate treaty unless other countries pay it to do so.

These uncertainties and nonuniformity of vision explain why governments have increasingly pushed toward embracing an adaptive rather than a preventive approach to global warming. Adaptive policies will be needed only after the precise effects of the warming become clear; however, any adaptive approach will delay a global warming agreement.

An international agreement must point to preventive policies. The least ambitious task would be that of coordinating some partial national policies (reducing subsidies to coal-using plants and increasing taxes on fuel and electricity in advanced countries, price liberalization of energy and electricity in developing countries). A more ambitious task would be to construct an international agency that uses economic instruments to promote appropriate behavior in the participating countries. This agency should also be given powers to guide a policy of compensatory transfers to the more reluctant developing countries. It is clear that the energy production scenario is the principal factor in dealing with global warming; even if the perception of the problem is stronger in the advanced countries, it cannot be negotiated without involving the developing countries, particularly the largest in terms of population such as India and China.

There will be a bargaining process between the developed and the developing countries in which issues other than environmental protection may be discussed. As it is likely that in the short term, and possibly even in the near future, the advanced countries will benefit more from the environmental agreement, these countries should be willing both to put some order in their own houses as far as energy production and utilization are concerned and to transfer at least some of their benefits to the developing countries to induce them to stay in the coalition.

It will not be only a problem of monetary transfers; technology transfers may be more important to allow developing countries to choose a growth path more compatible with environmental protection. It is, of course, a road much different from that currently followed, whereby many advanced countries declare that international environmental agreements favoring developing countries are necessary at the same time they use these countries as waste deposits or as the location of polluting industrial processes.

Even if an agreement could be reached so that an international agency would be allowed to use economic incentives, a number of problems would arise relative to the implementation of the chosen policies. One economic instrument might be the introduction of a carbon tax. It is clear that a decision regarding the power to impose such a tax will affect the negotiations for the international treaty. Developing countries will be favored if the tax is decided by the international agency and the collected money is redistributed to nations on the basis of their populations: high-income countries that consume more energy will pay higher taxes, and the developing countries will also be favored by the redistribution of the collected sum (Barrett 1991).

Analogous problems would be created by a decision to allocate a stock of tradable emission permits among nations. An initial allocation based on current emissions would favor the rich countries, while an allocation based on population would favor the developing countries. Without some commitment to an ethical criterion of justice, neither criterion would be accepted in an international agreement.

Conservation of Biological Diversity

One of the points on the agenda of the Rio de Janeiro conference on environment and development was the proposal of an international convention for the conservation of biological diversity. Biological diversity is crucial to maintaining natural habitats: when the rate of extinction of species far exceeds the rate of creation, there is a potential threat to global ecosystems. Some scholars believe that at the current rates of exploitation, the entire remaining unprotected natural habitat will be subject to some form of development within a few decades. The problem is not necessarily that there is conflict between natural habitat exploitation and development prospects; rather the problem lies in designing development practices compatible with the maintenance of an adequate stock of natural habitat.

The ever-increasing human pressure for a greater share of the earth's products is the main cause of natural habitat decline. The way humans appropriate the products, aiming primarily at productivity gains, replaces species' variety with species' specialization. Thus, of the thousands of species of plants edible and adequate for human consumption, only twenty now produce the vast majority of the world's food (Swanson 1991). The process of conversion of natural habitats continues at a rapid pace in developing countries, with negative effects on natural habitats and decreasing value returns. On the other hand, the declining stock of natural habitats increases the comparative advantage of their use as public consumption goods (e.g., tourism, recreation activities).

There is also an increasing awareness that a productive use of natural habitats to provide food, energy, and building materials should be made less harmful to natural ecosystems. It should entail less indirect usage (not in the form of consumption, but of waste created by production systems) of the earth's products. Judicious direct productive use of natural habitats for recreational purposes can combine development with maintenance of the precious stock of natural habitats.

Moreover, adequate account must be taken of the "informational" value of biological diversity: there are at present around 120 plant-derived drugs in use throughout the world, obtained from less than a hundred species of plants. The stock of existing plants is an enormous pharmacopoeia that may be very helpful to future generations (Swanson 1991).

Finally, natural habitats are valuable because they play a role in fixing the carbon from the atmosphere and maintaining stocks—such as animal populations on the way to extinction—that have by themselves an existence value.

There is no doubt that convincing the world's nations to subscribe to an international convention for the protection of biological diversity would play a great role in saving and improving the opportunities of choice for future generations. We are facing a problem whose solution is itself fraught with difficulties, and only a strong ethical motivation can turn the attention of the international community toward seeking a solution rather than avoiding the problem.

In the three global environmental problems briefly discussed above, the development model used by developing countries will play an essential role. Any effort to build international environmental agreements cannot avoid the issue of the relations between advanced and developing countries and their patterns of development.

From this point of view, the problem of international environmental cooperation is a part of the broader problem of international cooperation for development: any development process, to be sustainable, must consider the objective of environmental resource preservation.

At the level of the international community, this effort to promote development not in conflict with the environment can take many forms. First, environmental agreements should be organized to include compensatory money, technology transfer clauses, and periods of delay to comply with established quantitative targets in pollutant emissions.

Second, international financial institutions such as the International Monetary Fund and the World Bank should extend their financial support for appropriate environmental policies in the developing countries: economic incentives to deal with environmental externalities should be a part of the required strategy of "economic reform."

Third, a comprehensive restructuring of international trade will be necessary. We have seen how developing countries have a growing comparative advantage in pollution-intensive industries because they have more untapped natural resources and because they lack environmental regulatory institutions. Further, the need for foreign exchange, along with low commodity prices, compels many developing countries to use their natural resources at a rate higher than the regeneration rate. Since prices in developing countries do not reflect environmental externalities, we can say that these countries are virtually subsidizing industries and consumers of the advanced countries.

If the prices in developing countries reflected the true social costs of environmental damage, these countries could change their production structure and technology and use less-damaging production techniques. Therefore, not only are appropriate international environmental agreements needed, but also reforms in international trade—particularly in international commodity negotiations—to promote a premium price for commodities produced in ways more compatible with environmental preservation and to cover the costs of alternative production techniques or environmental reconstruction expenses.

The premium could be either a commodity-specific export tax levied by the exporting countries or a commodity-specific import duty collected by the importing countries. In both cases, funds from the surcharges should be used for environmental reconstruction and preservation; this would be best supervised by an international financial agency (Kox 1991).

This does not necessarily mean imposing further restrictions on international trade. There are many examples showing that liberalizing international trade can promote environmental protection. Consider the case of the highly protective European agricultural policy, which is currently producing harmful effects on the environment because the incentive embodied in high agricultural prices has led to overuse of fertilizers and pesticides. If the Uruguay Round of the General Agreement on Tariffs and Trade should succeed in allowing more free trade in agricultural products, this would mean more agricultural production in countries where the cost structure requires lower environmental degradation.

To summarize, appropriate international institutions will be necessary to address the pressing environmental problems of our time. These institutions should consider the promotion of development at a world scale as an unavoidable constraint in their environmental policy. We have seen that there are difficulties and forces acting against a world development model able to integrate principles of intergenerational and intragenerational distributive justice. As Paul Streeten (1989) points out, however, excessive preoccupation with "the feasible" tends to reinforce the status quo, favoring in negotiations those who oppose any changes and frustrating attempts at reform. On the other hand, actions that promote an ethic motivation in international public opinion that stresses the importance of intergenerational and intragenerational distributive justice are bound to be powerful factors pushing countries toward international cooperation for sustainable world development.

REFERENCES

Barbier, E., D. Pearce, and A. Markandya. 1989. *Blueprint for a Green Economy.* London: Earthscan.

Barrett, S. 1990. "The Problem of Global Environmental Protection." *Oxford Review of Economic Policy,* pp. 68–79, n. 1.

————. 1991. "Global Warming: Economic of a Carbon Tax." In *Greening the World Economy,* ed. D. Pearce et al., 31–52. London: Earthscan.

Brundtland, G. 1987. *Our Common Future.* Oxford: Oxford University Press.

Carraro, C., and D. Siniscalco. 1991. "The International Protection of the Environment." Fondazione ENI Enrico Mattei, Milan. Mimeo.

Chichilnisky, G. 1991. "Global Environment and North-South Trade." Columbia University, New York. Mimeo.

Cornes, R., and T. Sandler. 1987. *The Theory of Externalities, Public Goods and Club Goods.* Cambridge: Cambridge University Press.

Feldman, A. 1980. *Welfare Economics and Social Choice Theory.* Boston: Martinus Nijhoff.

Fudenberg, D., and J. Tirole. 1991. *Game Theory.* Cambridge: MIT Press.

Hardin, G. 1968. "The Tragedy of the Commons." *Science* 162:1243–48.

Harsany, J., and R. Selten. 1988. *A General Theory of Equilibrium Selection in Games.* Cambridge: MIT Press.

Heal, G. 1991. "International Negotiations on Emission Control." Columbia University, New York. Mimeo.

Hoel, M. 1991. "How Should International Greenhouse Gas Agreements Be Designed?" Oslo University. Mimeo.

Kemp, D. 1990. *Global Environmental Issues.* New York: Routledge.

Kox, H. 1991. "Integration of Environmental Externalities in International Commodity Agreements." *World Development,* pp. 933–43.

Maler, K. G. 1990. "International Environmental Problems." *Oxford Review of Economic Policy,* pp. 80–108, n. 1.

Markandya, A. 1991a. "Economics and the Ozone Layer." In *Greening the World Economy,* ed. D. Pearce et al., 63–74. London: Earthscan.

————. 1991b. "Global Warming: The Economics of Tradeable Permits." In *Greening the World Economy,* 53–62.

Moulin, H. 1988. *Axioms of Cooperative Decision Making.* Cambridge: Cambridge University Press.

Myerson, R. 1991. *Game Theory.* Cambridge: Harvard University Press.

Ordeshook, P. 1986. *Game Theory and Political Theory.* Cambridge: Cambridge University Press.

Pearce, D. 1991. "The Global Commons." In *Greening the World Economy,* ed. D. Pearce et al., 11–30. London: Earthscan.

Samuelson, P. 1954. "The Pure Theory of Public Expenditure." *Review of Economics and Statistics,* pp. 387–89.

Spulber, D. 1987. *Regulation and Markets.* Cambridge: MIT Press.

Streeten, P. 1989. "International Cooperation." In *Handbook of Development Economics,* ed. H. Chenery and T. Srinivasan, 1153–86. Amsterdam: Elsevier.

Sugden, R. 1986. *The Economics of Rights, Cooperation and Welfare.* Oxford: Basil Blackwell.

Swanson, T. 1991. "Conserving Biological Diversity." In *Greening the World Economy,* ed. D. Pearce et al., 181–208. London: Earthscan.

Taylor, M. 1987. *The Possibility of Cooperation.* Cambridge: Cambridge University Press.

UDO E. SIMONIS

Toward a
"Houston Protocol"

How to Allocate CO_2
Emission Reductions
Between North and South

The major problems in the world today are the result of
the difference between the way nature works and the
way man thinks.—Gregory Bateson

The effort to negotiate a global climate convention
is one of humankind's great endeavors—and a challenge to economists,
development planners, diplomats, and politicians alike. The inherent linkages between climate and the habitability of the Earth are increasingly well
recognized, and a climate protocol could help to ensure that conserving
the environment and developing the economy in the future go hand in
hand. Growing environmental concern and increasing evidence have led
the United Nations General Assembly to set into motion an international
negotiating process for implementing a convention on climate change. One
of the specific tasks in these negotiations is deciding how to share the duties
in reducing climate-relevant gases, particularly carbon dioxide (CO_2), between the industrial and the developing countries. The respective proposals
could be among the most far-reaching ever made for socioeconomic development; indeed, for global security and survival itself. Although the nego-

I choose Houston, Texas, as a symbol of a wasteful use of energy in modern times. It may
be unfair to the Houstonians, but I want to indicate that it is the highly developed United
States, the most material- and energy-intensive economy in the world, that must take the
initiative to save the world from the anthropogenic greenhouse effect.

106

tiations are about climate and protection of the atmosphere, they could lead to fundamental changes in energy, forestry, transport, and technology policies, and to future development pathways with low greenhouse gas emissions. Some of these aspects of a climate convention and a real CO$_2$ agreement, the "Houston Protocol," are addressed in this essay.

Preliminary Assessment

In the future, economists, planners, diplomats, and politicians will not only have to deal with growth and development processes, they will also have to pay increasingly more attention to reduction and redistribution processes. This is particularly true with regard to the most important global environmental problem so far, climate change. Up to the present, this problem has been caused mainly by the industrial countries, and the debate is about how much the North should give up in climate-relevant emissions. The developing countries might, however, follow suit in their pollutant production if they keep to the "standard development path." Ecologically, the developing countries will suffer most from the effects of climate change. Economically, the costs will depend on the kind of preventive or adaptive measures taken, the institutional arrangements made, and the wisdom of global environmental diplomacy.

Greenhouse Gas Emissions

Three categories of emissions are important in analyzing global climate change and formulating a corresponding policy (global climate policy): absolute emissions, per capita emissions, and emissions per unit of gross domestic product (or gross national product).

Although the basic statistical data on emissions of CO$_2$, methane (CH$_4$), and chlorofluorocarbons (CFCs), the major greenhouse gases, are few and still weak, it is clear that the reduction of, or adaptation to, climate change will present a formidable task to the world in general, and to industrial and developing countries, respectively. Negotiations on reductions are presently under way; concrete results, however, are still lacking. Some points of orientation have emerged, but a final solution is not yet in sight.

Ideally, all greenhouse gases should be included in any international agreement on their reduction (climate convention and respective protocols). This, however, is quite unrealistic. Technical, economic, social, and political aspects of emission reductions for individual gases differ greatly from country to country. While the industrial countries are responsible for approximately 80 percent of the global CO_2 emissions (among them the United States, with its rather inefficient energy and transport structures), the developing countries are mainly responsible for CH_4 emissions (from rice paddies and cattle ranches). Although some greenhouse gas emissions can be easily controlled (captured), others can be controlled only through adjustments of the product mix and production technology. For some gases (e.g., CFCs) a quick and complete phasing out seems necessary and possible; for others (e.g., CH_4, NOx), reduction is conceivable only as a slow step-by-step process.

Accordingly, in drafts for a convention on global warming (climate convention), the problems involved are being described, the necessary actions are being acknowledged, and further research and monitoring programs are being initiated. Such a convention will have to be implemented by one or several protocols specifying targets and measures for the reduction of the respective greenhouse gas emissions, the protection of the tropical rain forests, and the large-scale introduction of renewable energy. It is only then that the work on details can begin, including the distribution of costs and benefits, finance and technology transfer, and the employment of suitable economic and regulatory instruments such as charges and taxes or norms and standards.

Global Environmental Policy: Experiences

What can the discussion on a global climate convention and its corresponding protocols build on? What experience do we have with regard to agreements on environmental protection involving both industrial and developing countries?

The number of effective international agreements on environmental protection for more than a single region (for example, river basins), and for more than individual projects (like debt-for-nature swaps or the tropical forest action plan), that have been signed by both industrial and developing countries is rather limited. Only five come to mind: the London Dumping Convention (1972), the Convention for the Prevention of Sea Pollution by Ships (1973 and 1978), the United Nations Conference on the Law of the Sea (1973–82), the Vienna Convention (1985; these listed in Hartje 1989), and the Montreal Protocol on the Protection of the Ozone Layer (1987).

These agreements contain innovative regulations and instruments, including not only technical provisions but also fiscal incentives and quota systems. The Montreal Protocol (with four revisions) is even considered a model blueprint regarding international environmental regimes (Gehring 1990), an example of intelligent "ozone diplomacy" (Benedick 1991).

These agreements have been of only minor significance for the developing countries, which have had to meet hardly any strict obligations for the reduction of harmful emissions. In this respect, too, the Montreal Protocol is a new beginning—modified, though, by a ten-year grace period and provisions for information and technology transfer. The global climate convention, by contrast, will mean significant economic adjustments by the developing countries with regard to production as well as technology.

Theoretically speaking, a relative or absolute reduction of all the greenhouse gases is desired, and all conceivable mechanisms and instruments should be used to achieve this: negative lists (London Dumping Convention), technical provisions (Marpol Agreement), property rights (the Law of the Sea Conference), and rates of reductions or phasing out of production (Vienna Convention, Montreal Protocol). With continuing high population growth in the developing countries, on the one hand, and urgent economic needs, on the other hand, relative limitations (with regard to population or gross domestic product) and absolute limitations of greenhouse gases would generate quite different consequences. These consequences will influence the readiness of countries to cooperate or oppose in the process of negotiating the climate convention and the respective protocols. Taking into account only the major greenhouse gases, these are probably the most important measures to be considered:

Relative or absolute limitation of CO$_2$ emissions resulting from the
    combustion of fossil fuels
Conversion of the trends of CO$_2$ emissions from biotic sources (i.e.,
    reduced deforestation and increased reforestation, respectively)
Phasing out consumption and/or not taking up production of CFCs
Relative or absolute limitation of CH$_4$ emissions
Relative or absolute limitation of the use of nitrogen fertilizers

Taking the formulation of the CFC reduction plan (not its implementation) as solved, further negotiations will focus on protocols for CO$_2$, CH$_4$, and N$_2$O, or a combination of these, and their supplementation by other protocols (on reforestation and biodiversity). Apart from CFCs, only CO$_2$ has been discussed seriously on the international level. I shall therefore focus on CO$_2$, which presently causes more than 50 percent of the anthropogenic greenhouse effect.

Reduction and Redistribution Processes: Theoretical Considerations

In the Montreal process, three steps or targets emerged: freeze, reduction, and phasing out. The endeavors centered on rules to reach quantitative restrictions, and a solution via fiscal disincentives (CFC tax) was not seriously pursued. The volume of funds made available (CFC Reduction Fund) was and still is rather modest, sufficient at best to cover the costs of information transfer. With regard to CO_2, however, only freezing and reduction seem technically feasible; phasing out is not possible.

Global solutions that employ price and quantitative regulations are possible as far as mechanisms of stimulation or sanctioning are concerned (Bonus 1991). At the very start of all environment policy, the market mechanism is changed. There are two approaches: (1) fix prices for environmental services and leave it to the market mechanism to decide how much emission is economical (price solution); or (2) fix a quota for the quantity of emissions allowed, while the prices for using the environment are left to develop in the market (quantity solution). These two basic approaches are symmetrical with one another, but they are not equivalent. One parameter, price or quantity, is fixed while the other is left to the market mechanism. The real question is which of these parameters should be fixed with regard to which environmental problem!

The crucial problem with price solutions (taxes, charges) is to determine the correct level of the price to be fixed (shadow price). With quantity solutions, the crucial problem is to determine the appropriate ceiling (quota) of emissions of a certain type to be permitted. In either case, if the determination is wrong, permitted emissions may exceed the absorption capacity of the ecological system (in our case, the climate system). Price as well as quantity solutions may therefore miss the actual target (i.e., conservation, stabilization, or restoration of the ecological system).

With regard to a CO_2 protocol, it is to be expected that both types of solutions will be introduced in the course of the negotiations. To date, quantity solutions are in the foreground, while the discussion on price solutions (global resource tax, national CO_2 charge, "climate tax") has only just begun.

Moreover, with regard to quantity solutions, legal rules (reduction duties) do prevail; however, the use of market-based instruments (certificates or tradable permits) seems to be gaining ground. This suggests implementing certain parameters (e.g., a specified rise in temperature) by using emission quotas (see Tietenberg 1985). These systems would have to be transformed into specific certificates that entitle the holder (country or group of countries) to an (annual) emission of a certain amount of CO_2. These certificates (or tradable permits) could be regionally or globally transferable (exchanged). They would be exchanged in the market at prices corresponding to their scarcity, and the resulting revenue might then be used to substitute low emission products and technologies for high emission products and technologies. The certificates would add up to the set framework parameters (global emission limit). The certificates traded could thus be interpreted as compensation for partial renunciation of production or use.

It appears, then, that CO_2 emissions qualify for a quantity solution, in the sense of certificates to be traded at the local, national, regional, and even the international levels. However, specific conditions would have to be met to implement this theoretical option smoothly in actual practice. There are also alternative instruments of global climate policy to be considered, such as a tax on fossil fuels or a CO_2 charge. The related questions of these solutions are, however, beyond the scope of this essay.

Global CO₂ Emission Reductions: Three Scenarios

Let us briefly compare three global emission-reduction scenarios (Table 1). They include all the important greenhouse gases, but for reasons of clarity only the CO_2 data are considered in detail.

Bach derives drastic reduction duties from the (catastrophic) projections of climate models, whereas Mintzer and the Environmental Protection Agency (EPA) define the emission reductions from possible changes of relevant parameters (e.g., energy intensity, mileage efficiency, or energy tax). Accordingly, the three scenarios differ quite significantly.

Bach's scenario can be called a strict preventative strategy. It calls for a drastic reduction of CO_2 emissions from the burning of fossil fuels and also from biotic sources (clearing of forests, burnings, losses of vegetation).

The EPA's scenario occupies a middle position. A reduction of CO_2 emissions from fossil fuels of about 40 percent is expected, and an active reforestation policy (enlargement of the CO_2 sinks) is envisaged, leading to negative net emissions.

Mintzer's scenario may be regarded as a modest policy. Prevention fails,

Table 1. Three scenarios for CO_2 reduction based on current (1975–85) and future (2075–2100) emissions (billions of tons of CO_2).

	Current emissions	Future emissions
Preventative strategy (Bach 1988)		
Fossil fuels	18.0	< 0.1
Land use	4.0	< 0.1
Total	22.0	< 0.1
Intermediate position (EPA 1989)		
Fossil fuels	19.4	12.2
Land use	3.0	−0.4
Total	22.4	11.8
Modest policy (Mintzer 1987)		
Fossil fuels	17.1	34.6
Land use	3.8	2.5
Total	20.9	37.1

Sources: Bach and Jain 1991; EPA 1989; and Mintzer 1987.

emissions from the burning of fossil fuels double, and changes in land use have only minor relieving effects. The resulting increase in the average temperature (2.3–7°) makes far-reaching adaptation necessary.

Of course, it is difficult to predict which scenario will be taken as a reference for the global climate convention and the respective protocols. Results from recent climate conferences attended by scientists and politicians indicate that a limitation of average global warming to less than 2°C might develop as a reference point.

The implied mixed strategy of precaution (prevention) and adaptation (cure) actually will be determined by three major factors: (1) the real or supposed costs and benefits of the corresponding measures, (2) the perception of the irreversibility of damage induced by climate change, and (3) the institutional and instrumental measures that can be agreed on in the north-south context.

The current discourse over the reduction of CO_2 emissions is, I think, an indicator of an already existing common interest in a sustainable future industrial society. At the same time, the discourse recognizes the need for further economic growth in the developing countries. There are interesting (and surprisingly coincidental) plans, summarized in the following section.

CO$_2$ Emission-Reduction Plans:
Three Examples

At the Second World Climate Conference in Geneva in 1990, two plans on CO$_2$ emission reduction for the period before 2050 were presented: the IPCC proposal and the ministers' proposal. The International Panel on Climate Change (IPCC) called for drastic and rapid reductions of CO$_2$ emissions in the Organization for Economic Cooperation and Development member countries, whereby global emissions would decrease only after the year 2005 and then fall by 46 percent until 2050, ending below the level of 1987 (Table 2).

The ministers' proposal was less drastic and incorporated some temporary delay. The ministers, however, followed the scientists' notion, whereupon a further increase of CO$_2$ emissions should be accorded to the developing countries.

The plan of the Enquête-Kommission of the German Parliament is the

Table 2. Three CO$_2$ emission plans for the years 1990–2050 (percentage change from 1987).

	1990	1995	2000	2005	2020	2050
IPCC proposal						
Industrial countries						
OECD	5	7	−4	−20	−50	−80
Others	5	8	5	−10	−30	−70
Total	5	7	−1	−16	43	−76
Developing countries	11	24	37	50	60	70
World total	6	11	7	−3	−21	−46
Ministers' proposal						
Industrial countries	5	8	5	0	−20	−60
Developing countries	11	24	37	50	60	70
World total	6	11	12	10	−4	−33
German Enquête-Kommission						
Industrial countries						
Economically strong	5	5	−10	−30	−50	−80
Economically less strong	5	7	−4	−15	−35	−80
Economically weak	5	8	5	−5	−25	−80
Developing countries	11	24	37	50	60	70
World total	6	10	4	−5	−20	−50

third possible reference case. The proposal differentiates the industrial countries according to their gross domestic product and suggests that reductions of CO_2 emissions be realized more quickly and thoroughly. Again, a preference is accorded to the developing countries.

Implicit criteria for the allocation of reduction duties and the related redistribution goals between industrial and developing countries, the North and the South, can be inferred from the three plans. The next section addresses special features of these sensitive issues for a global CO_2 protocol more explicitly.

Possible Criteria for the Distribution of CO_2 Emission Reductions Between North and South

The allocation of the duties of the climate convention and its accompanying protocols between industrial and developing countries depends on various factors, especially the degree to which one greenhouse gas should be reduced in relation to other gases, and what criteria should be applied for the reduction.

A strategy for reducing all greenhouse gases would probably focus on their relative importance for climate change with respect to the global benefits of a climate stabilization. A partial strategy for one single greenhouse gas would probably focus less on possible benefits and more on the technical options, the costs of emissions reduction, and the substitution of the reduction duties vis-à-vis other gases. For example, a total phasing out of CFC production in the industrial countries theoretically allows for a less strict reduction of CH_4 or N_2O, which is technically difficult to achieve in the developing countries. At this stage, however, there is no need to go deeper into this potentially complex substitution dispute.

Possible and realistic criteria for CO_2 emission reductions are included in two successful international environmental agreements: the Economic Commission for Europe (ECE) Convention on Long-Range Transboundary Air Pollution (1979) and the Montreal Protocol (1987). With the signing of the ECE convention, a small number of European Community (EC) countries joined a "30 Percent Club" with regard to the reduction of sulfur dioxide (SO_2). Other EC countries subsequently joined the club. Contributing to this successful beginning of acid rain control were not only the pressure from damage to the forest ecosystems (the so-called *Waldsterben*), the formation of the electorate, and the generation of technical and financial solutions, but also the consensus achieved by the club over a simple distribution criterion: Every country must reduce its SO$_2$ emissions by the same rate of 30 percent! (This consensus was reached only after an intense discussion of whether the current or the accumulated emissions and the size of the country and its emission export/import situation should be taken into account, etc.) In this way, the given departure point was legitimized; prior accomplishments or geographic and other peculiarities were not considered.

Thus, this case exemplifies allocation criterion 1: *A proportionally equal reduction rate for all countries referring to the starting point (a base year).* The Montreal Protocol not only requires a proportionally equal reduction rate (50 percent at first, 100 percent later on), it permits a temporary limited exemption from this rule for developing countries, which were relieved from the reduction duty because they judged it as being unfair: it was the industrial countries that had caused the damage to the ozone layer with their accumulated CFC emissions. Thus, the developing countries could not be expected to assume a proportional part of the duties. They might even have a right to emit in the future.

On this line of argument is founded allocation criterion 2: *A proportionally equal reduction rate for one group of countries (industrial countries), and fixation of a limited permissible increase of emissions for the other group (developing countries).* The Montreal Protocol concedes the developing countries a CFC production of up to 0.3 kilogram per capita for ten years, and then requires a reduction to 50 percent. In comparison with CO$_2$ emissions, the reduction of CFC emissions needs only slight adjustment measures because of oligopolistic production and low initial production level; not millions of tons but thousands. By contrast, the adjustments necessary for a CO$_2$ protocol will be much more extensive because many technologies, products, and economic branches are at stake. The industrial countries may therefore bargain their own absolute reduction duties against the relative reduction duties (rate of growth of CO$_2$ emissions) of the developing countries. Apart from disparities in current emissions, the developing countries instead might point at the historical emissions accumulated in the earth's atmosphere. The more such allocation arguments (and others) are brought into the arena, the higher the probability that no common (mutual) reduction formula can be agreed on. This makes a criterion of equal treatment attractive. One that could be accepted as fair by the developing countries is equal CO$_2$ emissions per capita of population.

This is allocation criterion 3: *Every country has a right to emit, re-*

sulting from the set (reduced) global limit of emissions per capita of the world's population, multiplied by the country's population. According to this criterion, countries exceeding the fixed limit of emissions per capita (the industrial countries) would have to reduce emissions drastically; countries falling below this limit (the developing countries) could emit increased amounts. This criterion is geared to fairness, does not legitimize the present emissions situation, and requires huge redistribution in the north-south context.

The differences between the contracted emission rights (limits) and the current emissions would lead to different rates of emission reduction in the case of industrial countries, or growth of emissions in the case of developing countries. By introducing this criterion, peculiarities such as geographic situation, size of the country, resource endowment, and differences in costs would not be taken into consideration. This, again, might open corridors for bargaining in the negotiation of a CO_2 protocol.

Applying allocation criteria 1–3 to the three scenarios presented in Table 1 reveals quite different magnitudes of the reduction duties and, respectively, the resulting redistribution between industrial and developing countries (Table 3).

Technically speaking, there exists a wide range of possible measures to reach a reduction of current CO_2 emissions (see Goldemberg et al. 1987; Kats 1990; Enquête-Kommission 1991); the most important are probably the following:

Reduction in the use of fossil fuels by way of energy saving or increase in the efficiency of energy use, especially with regard to transport, electricity, and heating

Substitution of low-emission fuels for high-emission fuels

Installation of new power-generating technologies such as cogeneration, district heating, district cooling, and gas turbines

Substitution of renewable energy such as wind energy, photovoltaics, and solar hydrogen for fossil fuels

Technical improvement or refitting of fossil fuel–based power plants and engines

That is to say, more is needed than just a relative decoupling of energy consumption from economic growth, which actually has occurred in several industrial countries. For ecological reasons, economic growth in the medium and long terms should be possible only if the reduction in energy consumption and environmental damage is absolute.

Up to now, I have discussed only CO_2 emissions from fossil fuels. In

Table 3. Distribution of CO_2 emissions from fossil fuels (in billions of tons) between industrial and developing countries according to three criteria. Criteria 1, 2, and 3 allocate, respectively, approximately 72, 56, and 25% of the world's total CO_2 emissions to industrial countries. (The 72% is based on the percentage of CO_2 emitted by industrial countries in 1982.)

	1982 emissions	Allocation in 2075 or 2100 according to		
		Criterion 1	*Criterion 2*	*Criterion 3*
Preventative strategy (Bach 1988)				
Industrial countries	12.6	< 0.1	< 0.1	< 0.1
Developing countries	4.8	< 0.1	< 0.1	< 0.1
Total	17.4	< 0.1	< 0.1	< 0.1
Intermediate position (EPA 1989)				
Industrial countries	12.6	8.8	6.9	3.1
Developing countries	4.8	3.4	5.3	9.1
Total	17.4	12.2	12.2	12.2
Modest policy (Mintzer 1987)				
Industrial countries	12.6	25.1	19.0	8.7
Developing countries	4.8	9.5	15.6	25.9
Total	17.4	34.6	34.6	34.6

Sources: Bach and Jain 1991; EPA 1989; and Mintzer 1987.

their case, freezing and reduction are the only issues. With CO_2 emissions from biotic sources, however, phasing out and a reversal of trends (i.e., negative growth rates) come into the picture. To strive only for a reduction in emissions would be too modest in view of a possible net assimilation of carbon into the biomass. Even the introduction of allocation criterion 3 does not make sense here, as positive emissions fall very much behind the possibility of negative per capita emissions (by enlarging carbon sinks).

An additional criterion might therefore consist in linking the obligation to stop deforestation in the developing countries with the obligation of reforestation in the industrial countries. Another possibility consists in a direct link with the right to CO_2 emissions from fossil sources: biotic emissions (resulting from slash-and-burn agriculture, deforestation, changes in land use) reduce the right to per capita emissions of CO_2 from fossil sources, and vice versa; reforestation increases it.

Another allocation criterion might also come into prominence in the process of negotiating the CO_2 protocol, an age criterion (see Grubb 1989). It is well known that the population structure of the developing countries differs widely from that of the industrial countries.

In view of the fact that the population of the developing countries is generally rather young, an equal per capita emission right might prove ecologically counterproductive (i.e., might give an incentive to keep a high rate of population growth). Therefore, the industrial countries might tend to introduce a minimum age criterion (adults' emission rights), by which their CO_2 reduction duties could be reduced or their per capita emissions be increased. When age is considered in a CO_2 protocol between the North and the South, however, there are dramatic consequences for all concerned. If fewer people are counted, per capita emissions will be higher. Nations with a comparatively high number of adults would thus have a significant advantage over nations with a larger proportion of children, who would not count.

Of course, questions of allocation are questions of power. The problem of climate change is so complex that debates on allocation may be perpetuated. Therefore it seems to me that a guiding criterion has to be postulated. It should be both simple and generally convincing. The respective options have been presented above. Some of them seem easier to implement than others. But how to get from here to there?

From Here to There: Confrontation or Cooperation?

With regard to global environmental problems Peter M. Haas recently formulated a theory of "epistemic consensus" (Haas 1990). According to his (and my) view, substantial changes have occurred in the process of negotiating international agreements. This evolution of competence in environmental policy can be understood as a collective learning process, an evolution that might refute Hardin's thesis of the "tragedy of the commons" (Hardin 1968).

Within this learning process, epistemic communities have formed transnational networks that are politically relevant because of their authoritative knowledge. If such networks develop, and if they get and maintain access to policymakers, global conventions and protocols might have an "efficiency guarantee." Common interests per se (on which the Brandt Report [1980] was based), the notion of sustainable development (Brundtland Report 1987), or responsibility for the future (Nyerere Report 1990) alone will not sufficiently enlarge the chances for international cooperation. Cooperation depends also on the kind and strength of the consensus within the epistemic community, and that consensus can be strengthened through improved cooperation among the community members.

This theory, it seems, has been verified by the Montreal process: political action was prompted by an ecological crisis (ozone hole); international experts established the scope of political alternatives, then diplomats negotiated the terms of agreement; and when the members of this negotiations community had consolidated their position with the national governments, the latter supported the agreements.

Whether this theory will hold true for the anthropogenic greenhouse effect and can be verified by the formulation and implementation of a CO$_2$ agreement—the "Houston Protocol"—remains to be seen. While a loosely cohering epistemic community does exist, the internal consensus is not (at least not yet) as strong as in the ozone case. There is a rift within the greenhouse community. Preventionists are pleading for immediate action in order to avoid or at least confine climate change while adaptionists are arguing for slow and gradual adaptation to a climate change that cannot be avoided anyway.

There is also a rift between ethics and praxis. From an ideal ethical perspective, each person on earth should have equal emission rights. But this would be revolutionary! It would imply that we of the industrial North would have to reduce our excessive consumption in favor of the poor South. How likely is it, in that case, that such radical principles and norms will be established as international rules? How many conferences, how many books on ethics and environmental policy, will be needed to get that message across—and widely accepted? Only a professional optimist could answer such questions without hesitation, or even dismay. But the issues are too urgent, and history too unpredictable, to warrant despair. We need not be shallow optimists to continue, within the crucial epistemic community and beyond, to speak out on behalf of wider popular understanding and a more virtuous public will.

REFERENCES

Arrhenius, E. A., and T. W. Waltz. 1990. "The Greenhouse Effect: Implications for Economic Development." World Bank Discussion Paper 78, Washington, D.C.

Atmospheric Pollution and Climate Change Ministerial Conference. 1989. *The Nordwijk Declaration on Climate Change*. Nordwijk, Netherlands.

Ayres, R. U. 1989. *Energy Efficiency in the U.S. Economy: A New Case for Conservation.* Laxenburg: IIASA Publications.

Bach, W., and A. K. Jain. 1991. *Von der Klimakrise zum Klimaschutz.* Münster: Institut für Geographie (extension of a 1988 manuscript).

Bateson, Gregory. [1972] 1987. *Steps to an Ecology of Mind.* Northvale, N.J.: Jason Aronson.

Benedick, R. E. 1991. *Ozone Diplomacy: New Directions in Safeguarding the Planet.* Cambridge: Harvard University Press.

Bergen Ministerial Declaration on Sustainable Development in the ECE Region. 1990. Bergen.

Bolin, J., et al., eds. 1986. *The Greenhouse Effect, Climate Change, and Ecosystems.* New York: Scope 29.

Bonus, H. 1991. "Umweltpolitik in der Sozialen Marktwirtschaft." *Aus Politik und Zeitgeschichte* 1 March 37–46.

Brandt Report. *See* Independent Commission on International Development Issues.

Brown, L., et al. 1985. *State of the World.* New York: Worldwatch Institute Report on Progress Towards a Sustainable Society.

Brown-Weiss, E. 1989. *In Fairness to Future Generations: International Law, Common Patrimony, and Intergenerational Equity.* Tokyo: Transnational Publishers.

Brundtland Report. *See* World Commission on Environment and Development.

Burgess, J. C. 1990. "The Contribution of Efficient Energy Pricing to Reducing Carbon Dioxide Emissions." *Energy Policy* (June): 449–55.

Burtraw, D., and M. A. Toman. 1991. "Equity and International Agreements for CO_2 Containment." RFF Discussion Paper, Washington, D.C.

Carrol, J., ed. 1988. *International Environmental Diplomacy.* Cambridge: Cambridge University Press.

Chandler, W. U., ed. 1990. *Carbon Emission Control Strategies: Case Studies in International Cooperation.* Baltimore: World Wildlife Fund and the Conservation Foundation.

Committee on Science, Engineering, and Public Policy. 1991. *Policy Implications of Greenhouse Warming.* Washington, D.C.: National Academy of Sciences.

Council of the European Communities. 1988. "Directive on the Limitation of Emissions on Certain Pollutants into the Air from Large Combustion Plants." 88/609/EEC.

Daly, G., P. R. Ehrlich, H. A. Mooney, and A. H. Ehrlich. 1991. "Greenhouse Economics: Learn Before You Leap." *Ecological Economics* 4:1–10.

Enquête-Kommission. 1990a. "Vorsorge zum Schutz der Erdatmosphäre des Deutschen Bundestages." In *Schutz der Erdatmosphäre: Eine internationale Herausforderung.* 3d ed. Bonn: Deutscher Bundestag, Referat für Öffentlichkeitsarbeit. [Also in English.]

―――. 1990b. *Schutz der Tropenwälder: Eine internationale Schwerpunktaufgabe.* [Also in English.]

————. 1991. *Schutz der Erde: Eine Bestandaufnahme mit Vorschlaegen zu einer neuen Energiepolitik.* Vol. 1 and 2. [Also in English.]

EPA. 1989. "Policy Options for Stabilizing Global Climate." Draft Report to Congress, Executive Summary, Washington, D.C., February.

Flavin, C. 1988. "Slowing Global Warming: A Worldwide Strategy." Worldwatch Paper 91, Washington, D.C.

Gehring, T. 1990. "Das internationale Regime zum Schutz der Ozonschicht." *Europa Archiv* 23:703–12.

Glantz, M., ed. 1988. *Forecasting by Analogy: Societal Responses to Regional Climate Change.* Boulder: National Center for Atmospheric Research.

Goldemberg, J., et al. 1987. *Energy for a Sustainable World.* Washington, D.C.: World Resources Institute.

Grubb, M. 1989. *The Greenhouse Effect.* London: Royal Institute of International Affairs.

Haas, P. M. 1990. "Obtaining International Environmental Protection Through Epistemic Consensus." *Millennium Journal of International Studies* 19:347–63.

Hahn, R. W., and G. L. Hester. 1989. "Marketable Permits: Lessons for Theory and Practice." *Ecology Law Quarterly* 16:361–406.

Hardin, G. 1968. "The Tragedy of the Commons." *Science* 162:1243–48.

Hartje, V. J. 1989. Studienbericht E9a. "Verteilung der Reduktionspflichten: Problematik der Dritte-Welt-Staaten." MS. Enquête-Kommission, "Vorsorge zum Schutz der Erdatmosphäre." Berlin.

Hckstra, G. P. 1989. "Global Warming and Rising Sea Levels: The Policy Implications." *Ecologist* 19:4–15.

Hoeller, P., A. Dean, and J. Nicolaiscn. 1990. "A Survey of Studies of the Costs of Reducing Greenhouse Gas Emissions." OECD, Department of Economics and Statistics, Working Paper no. 89. Paris.

Independent Commission on International Development Issues. 1980. *North-South. A Programme for Survival.* Cambridge: MIT Press. [Brandt Report.]

Intergovernmental Panel on Climate Change [IPCC]. 1990. "Policymakers' Summary of the Scientific Assessment of Climate Change." Report prepared for IPCC by Working Group I, June 1990; "Policymakers' Summary of the Potential Impacts of Climate Change." Report prepared for IPCC by Working Group II, June 1990; "Policymakers' Summary of the Formulation of Response Strategies." Report prepared for IPCC by Working Group III, June 1990, ed. J. T. Houghton, G. J. Jenkins, and J. J. Ephraums. Cambridge.

Japanese Council of Ministers for Global Environment Conservation. 1990. Formulation of the Government's Policy on Global Warming. Tokyo.

Jochem, E. 1991. "Reducing CO$_2$ Emissions: The West German Plan." *Energy Policy* (March): 119–26.

Juda, L. 1979. "International Environmental Concern: Perspectives and Implications for the Developing States." In *The Global Predicament: Ecological Perspec-*

tives on World Order, ed. D. W. Orr and M. S. Soroos. Chapel Hill: University of North Carolina Press.

Kats, G. H. 1990. "Slowing Global Warming and Sustaining Development." *Energy Policy* 18:25–33.

Keepin, W., and G. H. Kats. 1988. "Greenhouse Warming: Comparative Assessment of Nuclear and Efficiency Abatement." *Energy Policy* 16:538–61.

Kelly, M., et al. 1990. *Cities at Risk.* Norwich: School of Environmental Sciences, University of East Anglia.

Lashof, D. A., and D. Tirpak, eds. 1990. *Policy Options for Stabilizing Global Climate.* Washington, D.C.: U.S. Environmental Protection Agency.

Manne, A. S., and R. G. Richels. 1990. "CO$_2$ Emission Reductions: An Economic Cost Analysis for the USA." *Energy Journal* 11:51–74.

―――. 1991. "International Trade in Carbon Emission Rights: A Decomposition Procedure." *American Economic Review* 81:146–50.

Mathews, J. T., ed. 1991. *Greenhouse Warming: Negotiating a Global Regime.* Baltimore: WRI Publications.

Maumoon Abdul Gayoom [President of the Republic of the Maldives]. 1987. Address to the Forty-second Session of the UN General Assembly on the Issues of Environment and Development, New York, 19 October.

Mintzer, I. M. 1987. *A Matter of Degrees: The Potential for Controlling the Greenhouse Effect.* Washington, D.C.: World Resources Institute.

Morgenstern, R. D. 1991. "Towards a Comprehensive Approach to Global Climate Change Mitigation." *American Economic Review* 81:140–45.

Morrisette, P. 1989. "The Evolution of Policy Responses to Stratospheric Ozone Depletion." *Natural Resources Journal* 29:793–820.

Morrisette, P., and A. J. Plantinga. 1991. "How the CO$_2$ Issue Is Viewed in Different Countries." RFF Discussion Paper, Washington, D.C.

Nitze, W. A. 1990. *The Greenhouse Effect: Formulating a Convention.* London: Royal Institute of International Affairs.

Nordhaus, W. D. 1990. "Greenhouse Economics: Count Before You Leap." *Economist* 7 July, 19–22.

Nyerere Report. 1990. *The Challenge to the South: The Report of the South Commission.* Oxford: Oxford University Press.

Oates, W. E., and P. R. Portney. 1991. "Policies for the Regulation of Global Carbon Emissions." RFF Discussion Paper, Washington, D.C.

Ogawa, Y. 1991. "Economic Activity and the Greenhouse Effect." *Energy Journal* 12:23–36.

Okken, P. A., R. J. Sorart, and S. Zwerver. 1989. *Climate and Energy: The Feasibility of Controlling CO$_2$ Emissions.* Dordrecht: Kluwer Academic Publishers.

Ominde, S. H., and C. Juma, eds. 1991. *A Change in the Weather: African Perspectives on Climatic Chance.* Nairobi: African Centre for Technology Studies.

"Princeton Protocol on Factors That Contribute to Global Warming." MS, Princeton University, December 15, 1988.

Reid, W. V. C., and M. C. Trexler. 1991. *Drowning the National Heritage: Climate Change and Coastal Biodiversity in the United States.* Baltimore: WRI Publications.

Robertson, D. 1990. "The Global Environment: Are International Treaties a Distraction?" *World Economy* 13:111–27.

Rosenberg, N. J., et al. 1989. *Greenhouse Warming: Abatement and Adaptation.* Washington, D.C.: RFD Proceedings.

Sand, P. H. 1990. *Lessons Learned in Global Environmental Governance.* Baltimore: World Resources Institute.

Schipper, L. 1991. "Improved Energy Efficiency in the Industrialized Countries: Past Achievements, CO$_2$ Emission Prospects." *Energy Policy* (March): 127–37.

Schneider, S. H. 1989. "The Greenhouse Effect: Science and Policy." *Science* 243:771–81.

Sedjo, R. A. 1990. "Forests to Offset the Greenhouse Effect." *Journal of Forestry* (July): 12–15.

Simonis, U. E. 1990. *Beyond Growth: Elements of Sustainable Development.* Berlin: Edition Sigma.

Skolnikoff, E. B. 1990. "The Policy Gridlock on Global Warming." *Foreign Policy* 79:88.

Smith, D. A., and K. Vodden. 1989. "Global Environmental Policy: The Case of Ozone Depletion." *Canadian Public Policy* 15:413–23.

Smith, J., and D. Tirpak, eds. 1988. *Potential Effects of Global Climate Change on the United States.* Washington, D.C.: U.S. Environmental Protection Agency.

Solomon, B. D., and D. R. Ahuja. 1991. "International Reductions of Greenhouse-Gas Emissions." *Global Environmental Change* (December): 343–50.

Speth, J. G. 1989. *Coming to Terms: Towards a North-South Bargain for the Environment.* Washington, D.C.: World Resources Institute.

Streeten, P. P. 1989. "Global Institutions for an Interdependent World." *World Development* 17:1349–59.

Tietenberg, T. H. 1985. *Emissions Trading: An Exercise in Reforming Pollution Policy.* Baltimore: Resources for the Future.

Tolba, M. K. 1990. "A Step-by-Step Approach to Protection of the Atmosphere." *International Environmental Affairs* 1:304–9.

Topping, J. 1991. *Global Warming: Impact on Developing Countries.* Washington, D.C.: Overseas Development Council.

Trexler, M. C. 1991. *Minding the Carbon Store: Weighing U.S. Forestry Strategies to Slow Global Warming.* Baltimore: WRI Publications, 1991.

Tyson, J. L. 1989. "Why China Says Ozone Must Take Back Seat in Drive to Prosperity." *Christian Science Monitor* 23 March.

UNEP. 1985. Vienna Convention for the Protection of the Ozone Layer. Vienna, 22 March.

———. 1987. Montreal Protocol on Substances That Deplete the Ozone Layer. Montreal, 16 September.

United Nations. 1983. Conference on the Law of the Sea. New York.

United Nations. Economic Commission for Europe (ECE). 1979. Convention on Long-Range Transboundary Air Pollution. Geneva, 13 November.

———. 1985. Protocol to the 1979 Convention on Long-Range Transboundary Air Pollution on the Reduction of Sulphur Emissions or Their Transboundary Fluxes by at Least 30 Per Cent. Helsinki, 8 July.

———. 1988. Protocol to the 1979 Convention on Long-Range Transboundary Air Pollution Concerning the Control of Emissions of Nitrogen Oxides or Their Transboundary Movements of Hazardous Fluxes. Sofia, 31 October.

———. 1990. Energy Efficiency: Action for a Common Future. Geneva, 8–16 May.

Usher, P. 1989. "Climate Change and the Developing World." *Southern Illinois University Law Journal* 14:257–64.

Williams, R. H. 1990. "Low-Cost Strategies for Coping with CO_2 Emission Limits." *Energy Journal* 11:35–59.

WMO/UNEP. 1990. IPCC Response Strategies Working Group, Emissions Scenarios. Geneva.

World Commission on Environment and Development. 1987. *Our Common Future*. Oxford: Oxford University Press. [Brundtland Report.]

World Resources Institute. 1990. *World Resources 1990–91*. New York and London.

CORRADO POLI

The Political Consequences
of an Environmental
Question

The title of this essay refers to the initiatory part of a program of studies and research called "Ethics and Environmental Policies" that the Fondazione Lanza has been developing for the last few years at the national and international levels. At the first international conference, held in Borca di Cadore, Italy, in 1990, an interdisciplinary approach was adopted in three seminars. The first dealt mostly with theological and philosophical themes, the second with arguments related to the political and social sciences, and the third with the ethical aspects of economic behavior (Poli and Timmerman, 1991).

It cannot be said that the Borca conference, or the research program of the foundation, met the challenge, culturally speaking, of being truly interdisciplinary. Nor was this the intention. Dialogue was occasionally difficult, although there was never the sensation of speaking to the deaf, since everyone demonstrated great willingness to understand the problems and to look for new ideas to fuel action. But it is precisely this openness that today is characteristic of the "cultural anthropology" of those who are concerned with environmental problems, or better yet, with environmental policies.

The area of environmental studies exhibits a moral tension that is slackening in other fields of political action; we feel the lack of cultural means and commonly shared scientific approaches to define the way environmental problems and their consequent solutions should be understood. The very definitions and notions of the terms *economic development* and *social justice* (even *freedom* and *democracy*) are becoming more and more confused and disputed, although they still hold a central position in the political language. The increasing lack of consensus on their definitions and on how to achieve them has resulted in a loss of ethical-political tension in these fields, at least in the Western countries. In this situation, environmental issues can become the center of the political debate, or a proxy battlefield for political competition. Therefore the emphasis of the program of the Fondazione Lanza is not environmental ethics but rather ethics in environmental policies.

In this area, the foundation's research program and conferences are making an original contribution by entering into little-explored territory. The lack of an established ethics, especially in Europe, is the reason why it has proved more difficult to deal with the environment in social, political, and economic terms than in theological and philosophical terms. In the latter area there exists a consolidated tradition of investigating the underpinnings of philosophical discourse. Nonetheless, there is no obstacle to believing that the moment is near—if it has not already arrived—when the elaboration and systematization of the philosophical and theological principles of environmental ethics must be carried out simultaneously with (instead of before) social and political evaluations. Above all, the basic principles of environmental ethics must be accepted and entered into the mainstream of the political and cultural debate and must become part of environmental decision-making processes.

One of the main points that emerged from the conference in Borca was that there is an increasing tendency for environmental issues to assume an epistemological content. Furthermore, these epistemological issues, because they are interwoven with the structure of modern society, currently bear a solid political content. The way we perceive and represent reality often ends up being the last point in question in discussions of environmental issues. In order to understand environmental problems in their entirety and to respond effectively to the challenge they offer contemporary culture, it is necessary to analyze their roots. The epistemological question has to be faced by questioning the validity of various approaches to knowledge and, in particular, by questioning contemporary culture's paradigms of rationality. Even if the traditional paradigm of rationality were considered worth conserving and developing, its reconsideration and comparison with possible alternative approaches to knowledge could not be avoided. Thus, the need for a new epistemological approach emerges, one that clarifies the role of science and the ethical, political, and economic consequences stemming from the change—or, in other words, the way in which our knowledge is formed.

Naturally, it is still possible to face environmental problems in a more neutral manner; that is, as economic and decision-making problems, and therefore without either changing or discussing society's final ends. This approach certainly maintains force, but it can no longer be critically accepted.

The following paragraphs do not deal directly with the epistemological aspects of the environmental question. An attempt is made, however, to clarify the role the environmental question, depending on how it is understood, may play in the process of modern society's change.

It is possible to distinguish between widespread concern for a number of environmental problems and the recognition of the existence of an environmental question. Moreover, it is possible to deny the very existence of both the environmental *problems* and the environmental *question*.

Therefore, four positions are possible:

A. Denial of the existence of environmental problems.
B. Recognition of the existence of environmental problems, which are, however, marginal to or separated from the core of society. (In other words, they rank at the same level or at a lower level than other problems.)
C. Denial of the existence of a specific "environmental question," although environmental problems rank high, and even first, among society's other problems.
D. Recognition of the existence of an environmental question.

In case A, problems such as noise pollution, the greenhouse effect, water and air pollution, and the enlargement of the hole in the ozone layer, which are often collectively grouped as environmental problems, could probably be included on other lists if different criteria of aggregation were used. These problems are cataloged as environmental on the basis of two implicit assumptions: (1) they belong to a common and meaningful field of investigation, and (2) close connections exist among them. Theoretically, such a hypothesis can be denied or replaced by others that use different categorization criteria. There is no logical impediment to assigning problems that nowadays are defined as environmental to other categories instead. Prima facie we assume that environmental problems are earth, air, and water pollution, depletion of nonrenewable resources, and permanent alterations of the earth and its atmosphere. In a broader sense, we can also list as environmental problems the consequences of bioengineering and cultural change when centuries-old ways of life are destroyed by modernization. Issues such as excessive noise in the cities, the progressive broadening of the hole in the ozone layer, water pollution, and global warming might just as validly be considered unrelated and placed on different lists of problems—as was, in fact, the case until recently. A specific grouping is selected, obviously, because reality is observed, perceived, and managed through the filter of current opinions derived from contingent historical and cultural factors.

The opportuneness of formulating a single list that includes all the so-defined environmental problems seems to be a generally accepted praxis. There is an extensive consensus on the items belonging on such a list. This approach, however, concerns exclusively the political and cultural debate; at best we can argue that some social scientists have adopted the environmental problems list to define a specific field for their analysis. In the natural sciences and in technology, on the contrary, the epistemological foundations of these fields—their analytical methods, and the organizational structure of scientific knowledge itself—are still derived from and defined by tradition rather than by any list of environmental problems. In other words, scientists refuse the list of environmental problems when it is used to define a field of inquiry.

As a matter of fact, from the viewpoint of their mere assessment, noise pollution and water pollution are completely different phenomena. The same can be said of air and soil pollution, although in this case more relations certainly exist between them, since the two are closely associated. The assessment methods adopted in each case, however, are profoundly different, and specialists in these phenomena belong to different scientific disciplines and different professional associations. Insofar as we accept a scientific method that founds truth on the assessment of phenomena (operationalism), this approach may be reasonable. If not, the relation between soil pollution and noise pollution, for example, is exclusively based on a judgment pronounced on a variation of the natural state.

A solution internal to this framework of knowledge could be to replace the object of observation and assessment. For example, instead of assessing rain acidity, the noise level, the rate of soil depletion, and so on, one might use methods able to assess, say, the public health level, the quality of life, or the pace of genetic and cultural change. These assessment methods already exist, but they have not received the widespread consensus enjoyed in the other fields. Actually, such a replacement implies a real cultural and political revolution, a contingency probably feared by many. Such a cultural revolution would generate at least psychological insecurity in the people, while a political revolution might alter the balance of powers and produce a different kind of knowledge promoted by different political or professional groups.

Clearly, as soon as we consider it worthwhile to group environmental problems together, we admit their importance. Moreover, we endorse a distinctive identification and configuration of the problem that cannot help but affect the way it is handled. Before offering answers one must formulate questions; any question contains a part of the answer.

Regardless of the current debate, it is possible to argue that a certain number of problems have first been defined and grouped together, and only afterward have they been described as environmental problems rather than the contrary; that is, first a topic or an analytical field has been assumed— in this case the environment—and then its problems have been identified. Likewise *environment* is too broad and vague a term to be defined with rigor. As a matter of fact, a group of phenomena has been identified, and, for a number of reasons, they are listed as *environmental problems*. This recent but now conventional classification is considered a product of the present times; it is meaningless applied to other historical periods.

When environmental problems are effectively recognized, their location on the scale of priorities becomes an important issue. Environmental problems are only one of the concerns of this era. They may be considered less important, or at most equal to, other issues on which the future of humanity depends. Their solution remains in the domain of contemporary science and the existing social, economic, and political orders. The environment might be taken to represent a new challenge among other more traditional ones such as social justice, the development of backward economies, and civil rights.

Even if environmental problems are put at the top of the list of priorities, this still does not mean that there exists an "environmental question" that must be faced by society as a whole. If we believe that we are dealing with an environmental question, then we assume that it affects society at all levels, both in its basic nature and in its consequences. The grouping together of these problems as environmental problems may indicate a growing awareness of a situation that needs to be faced in the same way as other social problems. It does not imply that it is necessary to understand all the linkages that exist within the whole society in order to overcome these problems. This line of reasoning may be paralleled with the Marxist thesis, which maintained that recurring economic recession and unemployment could not be handled by antitrend intervention but rather denoted a structural crisis whose solution could not help but imply a profound change in the system of production and in the overall society.

For some decades it has been clear that the production and consumption systems exported by the industrialized nations to the rest of the world are responsible for pollution, resource depletion, and irreversible global change. Moreover, these systems generate permanent transformations that either are unwelcome to the majority of the world's population or infringe some inviolable rights of minorities, future generations, and even animals and things. For this reason they must be considered unjust, notwithstanding any possible benefit that the majority presumes to secure for itself.

Now we move to the recognition that an environmental question exists. Such an awareness logically leads to the compilation of a list of environmental problems. It may generate two ultimate outcomes: (1) the existing social structure and its philosophical underpinnings are approved of; or (2) the existing social structure and its philosophical underpinnings are questioned.

The first outcome, resulting from an exclusively taxonomic approach, presumes that it is possible to solve individual environmental problems without having to express an overall judgment on society, the system of production, and models of scientific knowledge. That is, environmental problems are not perceived as being strictly interconnected, nor are they studied in relation to a series of political and social considerations. The fundamental epistemological hypothesis, analytical methods, and, primarily, society's (and humankind's) goals—as well as the means to pursue them—are not discussed; or, if they are, the discussion concludes with a positive judgment on the traditional approaches, the main characteristic of which is the fragmentary structure of knowledge and its provisions.

Of course, such a grouping resumes the identification and structuring of the problem in a fashion that cannot help but influence the way it is treated. In this case we have singled out a group of problems and consequently defined them as environmental, and this automatically favors the opportunity of facing them coordinately. Nonetheless, such a prospect does not always need to be stressed or explicitly declared. Moreover, the need for broad political, philosophical, and sociological studies on decision-making methods and on cause-and-effect linkages is not perceived as crucial. In other words, the resolution of environmental problems is not linked to a project for the reform of society that extends to its epistemological and ethical foundations. Consequently, it seems important to stress that we do not necessarily proclaim the existence of an environmental problem that might challenge the entire global political and economic system as well as the methodology of scientific knowledge that has been developed during the modern age; the methodology of scientific knowledge is intended to be related to the development of the political and economic system. Thus it is possible to argue that solving numerous environmental problems does not require a sweeping restructuring of the economic and political system, and that it is not essential to review traditional scientific paradigms.

The now commonly accepted classification of a number of issues as environmental springs from the protests against environmental deterioration that began in the late 1970s. Most of these protests were expressed in catastrophic terms in order to capture public attention, among other reasons. Their publication had a certain influence in creating the groundwork necessary to achieve the second possible outcome mentioned above.

Nonetheless, there does not yet exist a sufficiently exhaustive theory that has a broad consensus. Such a theory is needed to explain the long-term planned and unplanned results of the environmental solution. In the short term, it does not seem possible to formulate such a theory, given that the present cultural circumstances do not favor efforts in this direction. Rather there is a tendency to make the best of a bad situation by theorizing on fragmentation, deconstructionism, experimentalism, *petite histoire,* and the like. The result is that efforts made to find an overall solution are often not very convincing; or if they are, they are not taken seriously in many cultural milieux, so that to continue in these efforts becomes almost a heroic enterprise.

Theorizing underlines the need to carefully evaluate the political and ideological consequences of problem classifications and the empirical approaches to the study of the phenomena in question.

Those who approve of the existing social structure are inspired by modern science and by Western democratic society's way of thinking and acting. This manner represents the political and institutional form closest to the ideal type of modernity. Those who question the current social structure can be divided into two groups: the postmoderns, who are in some way still linked to the idea of modernity although they emphasize its feature of fragmentation while deemphasizing the role of the modern project; and the theoreticians of nonmodern alternative ethics (somewhat confused at the moment), which range from technocratic aspirations to elitism, from the ideology of an ethical state to the rediscovery and reelaboration of nontraditional ethics that sometimes are applied outside the cultural framework in which they were originally elaborated. Here it should be specified that Christian religion and ethics are considered a part of modern thought, or at least of postmodern evolution.

I have used the terms *modernity* and *postmodernity* in a rather undefined way. A preliminary definition is now required. According to A. Giddens, "modernity refers to modes of social life or organization which emerged in Europe from about the seventeenth century onwards" (1990:45–46). In modern society, science also plays a crucial role. Postmodernity is even more difficult to define. The notion of postmodernity refers to something other than modernity: it "means that the trajectory of social development is taking us away from the institutions of modernity towards a new and distinct type of social order. Postmodernism, if it exists in a cogent form, might express an awareness of such a transition" (Giddens 1990:45–46).

The problem is that in a period of transition during which the past is considered "different" from what we are moving toward, the modern institutions still exist and predominate; they are likely to react to the challenge of postmodernity as well as to develop their own programs, which may be antithetical to the postmodern ecological movements. We do not know which is worse: a reaction against or a further implementation of the modern program. What is certainly important is that new ethics tend to widen the breach between the old (i.e., the modern) tradition and the new approach (i.e., the postmodern).

Modern thought and the modern project constitute the historical and ideological basis on which most current political, economic, and social institutions are founded. The principles of justice, democracy, individual liberty, and human rights are closely tied to the technological and productive evolution undergone by society. A feature of modern development is the desire and need to continuously change the world and society. In other words, there is a desire to create a world in which man, understood as the supreme being, can realize the goal of artificially creating whatever he needs. Emblematic of modern thought is Marx's famous phrase that "all that is solid melts into air"; or Shumpeter's entrepreneur with his "creative destruction"; or even Goethe's Faust, who tries to re-create the world by performing great works that substitute the artificial for the natural. According to Jürgen Habermas, the implementation of the modern project began in the seventeenth century. The intellectual effort of the Enlightenment consisted of the elaboration of an objective science, a morality, a universal law, and an art—all autonomous entities, each according to its own internal logic. Humankind's emancipation was to be achieved through the dominion of science over nature. In the modern project, it is often implicitly assumed that every question has only one answer (Habermas 1983:9). For example, Condorcet maintains that "a good law must be good for everyone in exactly the same way that a true proposition is true for all" (Condorcet 1988:286). In other words, nature can be controlled and rationally ordered only if it is correctly represented; but this presumes that there is only one correct representation.

Modern thought, or, better, the hope of realizing the modern project, is increasingly criticized by those who form the postmodern archipelago. In fact, although society works as a whole, cultural, political, and artistic groups form that reflect a reality so fragmented that it cannot be unified. Even if these groups have a project, it is, either by choice or by necessity, limited to the partial or the temporary—to the individual group. The geographer David Harvey proposes the interesting idea that social theory has traditionally faced the problem of progress only in its temporal dimension: today, however, in relation to understanding environmental problems, there should be a new discussion of the different conceptions of space and time held by the social groups that form postmodern society (Harvey 1989). The fundamental feature of the postmodern condition is the lack of a comprehensive project, represented by the individual islands of the archipelago, which will never be unified into a continent. The only possible answer to the environmental question, according to the postmodern approach, seems to be an evolution toward the reduction of the projects' dimensions and the decomposition of the modern project into a series of small projects—small communities, small cities, small states—and, as proposed by economist Herman Daly, a financial system that operates only on the local level (Daly and Cobb 1989:315–22). Each community presents remarkable internal homogeneity. Tolerance for diversity, an essential (if ambiguous) value of modernity, is expressed by the acceptance of the existence of other communities, about which no judgment is expressed.

These positions find common ground in the disbelief that modern society can solve the problems it has created. Naturally this implies the need for something more than society's reform; as a matter of fact, many movements that were once revolutionary meet in the variegated group of the postmoderns. Nonetheless, this subversive element is never too evident, both because of the disintegration of postmodern thought into numerous contradictory positions and because of its own confused state. At times this confusion results in a failure to reject some of the principles typical of modernity, such as the methodology of scientific knowledge or the ideals of justice and democracy, for which acceptable alternatives have not yet been proposed. The postmoderns, although they do not pursue any "great" design, in a certain sense carry some characteristics of modern thought to the extreme; these include tolerance for alternative opinions and approval of constant change, which by now has exploded into a lust for the ephemeral and the piecemeal.

The postmoderns should not be confused with the antimoderns and the nonmoderns. The postmoderns declare the end, the failure, and/or the limits of the modern project and believe that the environmental question represents the final expression of the unsuitableness, or even the immorality, of the project. They envision nature's revenge against humans and against their effrontery in modifying it and making everything artificial. But they do not propose comprehensive alternatives, or at least they have not up to now.

On the other hand are those who, taking the same consideration as their starting point, propose various types of alternative projects; for example, authoritarian and technocratic proposals that twist the concept of rationality. In commenting on these tendencies, R. Bernstein (1985:9), referring to Horkheimer and Adorno's observations on the relation between Enlightenment thought and Nazism and Stalinism, argues that the Enlightenment's desire to dominate nature was transformed into an attempt to dominate humankind. Although triggered by different events, this same mechanism could come into action again.

Bernstein believes that nature's reaction against the oppressive power of this exclusively "instrumental rationality" is manifested by a revolt of human nature leading to the liberation of culture and the personality. Others aspire to the emergence of a new comprehensive system of ethics, either religious or secular, that is more sensitive to the problems of the relationship between human beings and nature. Today it is difficult, but more necessary than ever, to succeed in distinguishing between the two since the language spoken by both groups is ambiguous and little codified.

In the current environmental debate, the critique of the modern project is often vague. Some critics seem to believe that industrial and technological development meet an insurmountable impediment in the limited availability of environmental resources. On the basis of what has been asserted above, however, the question should be formulated in a more appropriate way in order to successfully cope with the problem. One possible thesis is this: The environmental question is not an external threat to the structure of modern society but is itself a result of modern society's crisis. The adoption of one or the other of the two viewpoints I described earlier carries crucial repercussions for the way individual problems are encountered. In fact, if the environmental question is assumed to be the fundamental issue, on whose solution human survival on earth depends, it is easier to justify radical changes in social and political relations, and consequently "renunciations," in fields like democracy, social justice, human rights, and so on. On the contrary, if it is assumed that modern society lacks the capacity to cope with the problems it has created—the environmental question being simply a projection of such a deficiency—the required reforms can be envisaged within and according to current values.

In other words, the new perception of the environment represents an evolution in contemporary thought that can lead to its own overthrow. Nonetheless, the environmental problem is generated and is identified in a different manner.

Natural limits did not cause the environmental question that arrests progress toward modernity. Rather, because of an ongoing organizational crisis, modern society, which until now theoretically and practically resolved many of the problems it assumed, fails to accept new challenges. The seriousness of the situation is demonstrated by a new challenge that is clearly of a very general kind. It is to be understood as an internal, rather than external, threat to society's traditional organization.

It would not even be completely absurd to argue that the environmental question might be taken as society's fundamental problem by those who control the political and the economic systems in order to favor their totalitarian designs. As a matter of fact, precisely because of the revolutionary potential of the environmentalist movements, it is possible to imagine the most powerful lobbies trying to defend themselves by gradually accepting these movements' theses in order to defuse their subversive tendencies. Once the situation is dramatized enough, authoritarian measures could be proposed for an economic restructuring that would probably be more attentive to environmental conditions but less observant of democratic principles.

The recognition that the environmental question is the result of modern society's internal crisis need not necessarily lead to a totalitarian solution. An alternative consequence might be the nondramatization of the situation. People would thus be encouraged to rely on the system and on modern values. The inversion of great historical processes is not an easy task, and the resulting erosion of modern society's institutions is certainly a major historical event. If, lacking a valid alternative, we concede that the modern project is credible, a less disruptive transition is likely and it would be possible to defend the existing system from those who want to overthrow the established social and political institutions in attempting to answer an incorrectly formulated question.

The Christian tradition is considered part of the modern tradition. Symbolic of this is its openly declared anthropocentrism, even though this element is not carried to the extreme because humans who respect basic religious principles accept a responsibility to care for nature. Humankind, nonetheless, is believed to have the right to modify the natural environment. The problem must not be stated only in philosophical or theological terms, however. It is crucial to take into consideration the elaboration of the Catholic church's social doctrine as well. The Christian tradition, with its reevaluation of the individual and its consequent anthropocentrism, became part of the modern theories of society and democracy mostly by passing through the social and economic consequences of the Reformation. Some of the fundamental principles that the Reformation promoted are now part of Western culture, including Roman Catholicism. In a certain sense it is possible to identify or link reformed Christianity to the development of modern society, the principles of which were later extended to Catholicism and to other non-Christian religions and traditions. Twentieth-century Roman Catholic social doctrine is inspired by the principles of modernity, even though it rejects extreme forms of secularization. In referring to the religious principles from which individual and collective ethics are derived, it tempers the desire to tend toward the complete realization of the modern ideal type.

Today, some Christians denounce modernization vis-à-vis the need for religious values. Non-Christians meet this need in a different way. Instead of emulating modern society's ideal by thinking in a positivist, utilitarian, and functionalist manner, non-Christians refer to contractualist approaches and to the discovery of a system of public ethics. In this case, the ethical limit of modern behavior is determined by a set of legitimate and shared values rather than by positive laws or utilitarian ethics. These shared principles and values belong to a tradition inspired by the Christian cultural background of Western society.

If the thrust toward ceaseless and radical change typical of modernity is a characteristic of the Western tradition, to what religious aspect is due the coincidence between Christianity and modernity? A. Autiero (1991) proposes an environmentalist reading of hope as a theological virtue. Humankind's activity cannot be inhibited by fear and desperation for the future. It can be limited by moral principles, but these are intended as religious limits to action, not as an encouragement to inactivity.

The interpretation of the role that environmental problems will have in shaping society's structure in the future depends on how they are interpreted and located in the cultural and ideological milieu. The crisis of ideologies, and in general the current cultural climate, has not encouraged the attempt to systematize the ideological framework of the environmental question in order to combine its study with other aspects of the social crisis and models of knowledge. If, in the future, the environmental question is commonly accepted, it will become convenient and compulsory to study its ties with issues such as social justice, democracy, and freedom.

Often, and not unexpectedly, the terms *environment* and *environmentalism* evoke a radical political approach in public opinion because many scholars and political activists assert the need to change the most common modern scientific paradigms in order to effectively handle the so-called complexity of environmental problems. The increasing opposition of the systemic approach to Cartesian logic has been an essential epistemological turning point in environmental studies. Though I do not pretend to propose a comprehensive dissertation on this subject, I want to start from this statement to propose some hints on the close and mutual relationships existing between these scientific approaches and their possible political consequences. As a scholar, I consider more research in this area crucial in order to offer citizens and decision makers more unclouded and articulated alternatives from which to choose.

Briefly, Cartesian and systems theory logic are based on four conflicting principles. The first principle asserted by the Cartesians is *evidence;* to this, systemic logic opposes the principle of *pertinence.* According to the principle of evidence, every subject is true if it obviously appears as such. We have to accept only what is clear and well defined. Systemic logic advances a different concept: every subject is definable only according to the goals of the analyzer, be they explicit or implied. When goals are modified, the observed object also changes. Consequently, we can maintain that to know is the same as to act, and that if we change our minds, the world changes as well.

The second Cartesian principle is *reductionism,* to which systemic logic opposes the principle of *holism.* According to Descartes, reality must be separated into a number of parts in order to facilitate the solution of a problem. On the contrary, according to the principle of holism, the object is perceived as a part that actively belongs to a broader situation. The object is to be perceived globally in its relations with the environment in which it is located without paying too much attention to the problem of defining its internal structure, the existence and uniqueness of which we will never be able to comprehend.

The third Cartesian principle is *causality,* to which systemic logic opposes the principle of *teleology.* According to Descartes, knowledge must derive from the simplest objects and ascend to the most elaborate ones, assuming that a logical order exists also among those objects that are not arranged in natural sequences. Systemic logic studies the object on the basis of its behavior without trying to explain a priori such behavior through laws governing its possible structure. Behavior is to be intended in relation to the goals that the observer assigns to the object.

The fourth Cartesian principle is *exhaustiveness,* according to which it is always necessary to produce complete classifications and lists: nothing can be overlooked. Systemic logic opposes with the principle of *aggregation,* meaning that every representation of reality is per se biased. Consequently it is necessary to design methods apt to select groups of elements that are meaningful instead of believing in the unprejudiced objectivity of an exhaustive classification including all the elements worth being considered.

One of the reasons that decision making in environmental matters is difficult is the partial delegitimation of the basic principles of the Cartesian scientific method. Moreover, the generalized adoption of Cartesian principles represented a long-term project aimed at an unabridged knowledge of a given reality. Actually, it can be considered a goal itself: though unreachable, the process of pursuing exhaustive knowledge is itself a project.

Assuming that knowledge is based on the ends of the observer means denying the possibility of knowledge that is unprejudiced and politically neutral. If there is consensus on the development process and on the desired model of society, the problem is not important, and it is not even raised. The adoption of Cartesian principles eases interpretations, eases the projects and the consequent decisions, as far as the implicit ends and the methods to pursue them are shared. The project of modern science, based on the principles of the Cartesian method, was primarily an attempt to achieve total knowledge. Once faith in this project—a revolutionary one when it was conceived—dwindled, as it has in our time, anxiety spread due to fear of the unknown and disorder, notions that Cartesian logic does not consider. Systemic logic sought and found a place for such notions using rational principles.

When faced with the onset of a scientific revolution, the political establishment may react. It may use the legitimacy and the consensus with which it is endowed by the people—who may fear change—to implement a political-scientific program aimed at putting an end to this spreading and destabilizing revolution, which is itself justified by ideological reasons or by the necessity to face new problems. In such a situation, the strategy of the political establishment might be to capture or strengthen consensus by exploiting widespread anxiety. Environmental dilemmas could be resolved by yielding to those who eliminate concerns, although they curb some rights that are considered essential in traditional democratic systems. The people might give consensus to a government of technocrats—based on traditional science—who claim that they can resolve environmental problems according to more understandable and convincing programs.

The contemporary hurriedness in making decisions concerning environmental affairs also derives from the lack of consensus on how society should develop. It is difficult to rely both on a science that claims to be politically neutral and on teleologically oriented systemic logic. The misfortune of the first derives from the increasing questioning of the goals that were identified in the once-shared project of modernization. According to the systemic method, insofar as one maintains that teleologically oriented knowledge is tenable, and insofar as one does not deny the ideological pluralism distinctive of democratic societies, many decisions can be logically acceptable, although their selection becomes more difficult.

A typical example of the difficulties in reconciling the widespread Cartesian mentality with the systemic method is evident in the many cases in which environmental impact assessment techniques are adopted without paying enough attention to their profound philosophical implications. From a political point of view, the environmental crisis elicits anxiety among the population. Such emotional attitudes are positive when they prime changes capable of solving the problems; however, they can have a negative impact on decision-making when they provoke reactions whose goal is primarily the removal of the most superficial aspects of the problems. These attitudes inhibit the discovery of the real causes and their deepest mechanisms. To a certain extent, Cartesian logic provides scholars and decision makers with some confidence: describing objects in terms of cause and effect, dividing the structures into independent elements, and obtaining a complete description constitutes a safe approach. It provides a shield from the possible doubt that reality might have black holes that cannot be explained. Cartesian logic provides the confidence that permits decisions that allow nature to be separated into many self-contained parts.

Nonetheless, when the method is questioned, the anxiety of the unknown definitely shows up again. Systemic logic tries to give a rational location to the flaws in knowledge, but to accomplish this it must structure the method on the basis of the anticipated definition of the objectives. The choice of the goals is discretional, while Cartesian logic claims to be objective, at least when it does not challenge the general framework in which it is adopted. It is important to emphasize that only if there exists a diffused consensus on goals is it likely that the anxiety produced by a lack of knowledge can be overcome. When we are facing a critical fragmentation of preferences and ways of thinking—and ultimately of goals—anxiety for the future and uncertainty about what are right actions become dramatic. The undesirable outcome of this circumstance could be that some political elites might exploit the situation in order to create consensus around an unquestioned goal, even though this behavior denies the plurality of political ideas and of knowledge itself, which is a contradictory and counterintuitive effect of the systemic approach. The elites could cope with ignorance by offering noncontestable positions to the people, who always face ignorance with anxiety. The political problem of the systems theory and of complex approaches to the environmental question resides in the possibility of engendering too wide a consensus—fostered by widespread anxiety—on one objective whose pursuit is imposed by political elites that do not give dissent a chance.

REFERENCES

Autiero, A. 1991. "Una 'speranza' per il nostro pianeta," in *L'etica nelle politiche ambientali,* ed. C. Poli and P. Timmerman. Padua: Gregoriana Editrice.
Bernstein, R. 1985. *Habermas and Modernity.* Cambridge: MIT Press.

Condorcet. 1988. *Esquisse d'un tableau historique des progrès de l'esprit humain.* Paris: Flammarion.

Daly, H., and J. Cobb. 1989. *For the Common Good.* Boston: Beacon Press.

Foster, H., ed. 1983. *The Anti-aesthetic: Essays on Postmodern Culture.* Port Townsend, Wash.: Bay Press.

Giddens, A. 1990. *The Consequences of Modernity.* Stanford: Stanford University Press.

Habermas, J. 1983. "Modernity: An Incomplete Project." In *The Anti-aesthetic: Essays on Postmodern Culture.* Ed. H. Foster. Port Townsend, Wash.: Bay Press.

Harvey, D. 1989. *The Condition of Postmodernity.* Oxford: Basil Blackwell.

Poli, C., and P. Timmerman, eds. 1991. *L'etica nelle politiche ambientali.* Padua: Gregoriana Editrice.

GARY E. VARNER

Environmental Law and
the Eclipse of Land
as Private Property

In a 1965 article titled "Property, Production and
Revolution,"[1] Adolph A. Berle observes that in the first two-thirds of the
twentieth century, the ownership of industrial (or, as Berle puts it, "productive") property changed in a way that would legitimize increased public
interference with what had previously been regarded as private property.

Berle argues that increasingly, the infrastructure on which a corporation
depends is the product of public investment. This is so both in the relatively mundane case of publicly funded highway systems and in the more
dramatic case of the television and radio frequencies owned by broadcast
corporations. The state is, in effect, a major investor in both cases. "Without its activity, the enterprise, if it could exist at all, would be [spending] or
would [be] compelled to spend money and effort to create position, maintain access to market, and build technical development it currently takes
for granted."[2] On this basis Berle argues for high tax rates for corporations: "Under these circumstances, there is little reason or justification for
assuming that *all* profits should automatically accrue to stockholders."[3]
And he notes that a similar argument could be used to justify government
constraints on hiring practices and to ensure equal access to public ac-
commodations.[4] Berle concludes that a "revolution" in productive (i.e.,

industrial) property was well under way in the first two-thirds of this century, and that productive corporations would increasingly be treated like "statist" enterprises, beholden to all the same constitutional restrictions as the state.[5]

My thesis is that in the final third of the twentieth century, a different but in some ways parallel revolution is well under way. As environmental laws and regulations proliferate, we increasingly treat land as a public resource owned in common and held by individuals only in a stewardship (or trust) capacity.[6] My aim in this essay is to clarify how and why this is so.

While resisting my natural inclination to wallow in the interpretational details of United States common law, I will discuss in some detail the well-publicized case of *Lucas v. South Carolina Coastal Commission,* on appeal to the U.S. Supreme Court as I write this. It nicely illustrates what I see as the crucial philosophical point about the growth of environmental regulation in relation to land as private property. The case therefore warrants direct attention, but I have kept the discussion of relevant precedents to a minimum and I focus on the ways these precedents frame the takings issue as it faces any legal system.

Certainly there are striking differences between the common law tradition of the English-speaking nations and the civil law tradition of western Europe and Latin America. The most striking differences are the absence of the doctrine of *stare decisis* and the power of judgments in equity from the civil law tradition. Above all else, civil law judges are not supposed to make law, only to apply it. Precedent therefore carries no authority, and judges may not bend the rules even in isolated cases to prevent miscarriages of justice. The relative stature of judges in the two traditions reflects this. Common law judges are respected and studied as individuals whose opinions shape the course of law. A civil law judge is seen as a kind of expert clerk.

Behind this fundamental difference in ideology, however, lies a striking similarity in practice. There will always be cases where legislative enactments have no "plain meaning," and there will always be lacunae, cases not covered by any explicit legislative enactment. Despite the fact that judges are not supposed to legislate in such cases, modern civil law judges turn to three sources, in the following order: (1) ascertaining the intention of the legislature from the legislative history of relevant enactments, (2) reasoning by analogy, and (3) appeals to natural law or a constitution.[7] The first is a familiar feature of the common law tradition. The requirement of reasoning by analogy arguably approximates the doctrine of *stare decisis,* and the appeal to natural law corresponds roughly to a judgment in equity in common law.

More important, both legal traditions have tended to treat private property and liberty of contract as fundamental institutions that should be limited as little as possible. The question addressed in this essay therefore arises in both kinds of systems. Whether we take the agent of reform to be the legislature alone, as would the civil law tradition, or both the legislature and the courts, as would the common law tradition, the same question arises: To what extent is the current growth in environmental regulation compatible with respecting land as private property?

The Concept of Land as Private Property

What does it mean to think of land as private property? The intuitive answer is something like this: owning something, in the sense of holding it as one's *private* property, means being legally permitted to do with it as one will, independently of others' wishes. This is the *fee simple* concept of ownership, borrowing the term that surfaces all the time in wills and land transfers. It usually is reflected in legal dictionaries' definitions of private property. For instance, *Black's Law Dictionary,* probably the most widely used English-language legal reference dictionary, defines *property* as "the exclusive right of possessing, enjoying, and disposing of a thing . . . which [in] no way depends on another man's courtesy," and *private property* as "protected from being taken for public uses, . . . [which] belongs absolutely to an individual, and of which he has the exclusive right of disposition."[8] A toaster and money honestly earned would seem to be paradigm examples of private property in this sense: I may do as I wish with my toaster, even destroy it; and I may do as I wish with my money, even spend it frivolously while refusing aid to the hungry.

Yet it is not true that I may do *anything* I want, even with these paradigm examples of private property. I may not destroy my toaster by throwing it through your window; I may not burn my money (at least not literally), and I am required to pay some of my honestly earned money in taxes.

Acknowledging constraints on the use of such paradigm cases of private property moves us in the direction of a looser conception of property as "an aggregate of rights which are guaranteed and protected by the government," which *Black's* characterizes as property "in the strict legal sense."[9] This is the *legal positivist* conception of private property, legal positivism being the view that there is no "law of the land" apart from whatever has actually been enacted by the governing authorities. As David Hume, one of the forerunners of general philosophical positivism, puts it, property is "nothing but those goods, whose constant possession is establish'd by the laws of society." [10]

At first glance, the positivist conception of private property has greater intuitive appeal than the fee simple conception because, as we have just seen, even where the paradigm cases of private property are concerned, control is not absolute in the way suggested by the fee simple conception. The metaphor of sticks in a bundle that is commonly used to describe property rights lends itself to the positivist conception: bundles can be larger or smaller, and at any time a stick may be added to or subtracted from a bundle.

At the same time, however, the fee simple concept's emphasis on unfettered control of, or personal fiat over, one's property seems crucial to the concept of land as *private* property. Suppose that automobiles were held in common and our legal system guaranteed the use of each automobile to whoever claimed it first on a given day. If we took the positivist conception of private property literally, there would still be private property under these conditions because each individual would still have "an aggregate of rights which are guaranteed and protected by the government," namely, the right to claim a car under certain conditions and (having exercised that right under appropriate conditions) the right to use that car for the day. But I could *not* say that the car is mine, that it is my private property, even for that day that I have the right to use it. What is missing is the emphasis on unfettered control, or personal fiat, that is at the heart of the fee simple concept of ownership. I can neither destroy the car nor determine to whom the right to use it accrues next, and it is for precisely these reasons that there is no private property in properly socialist and communist systems. Hume may have sensed something like this, leading him to include "constant" in his otherwise positivistic definition of property (as "those goods, whose *constant* possession is establish'd by the laws of society," quoted above).

So our intuitive concept of private property lies somewhere between the fee simple and positivist concepts. Something is not held as private property unless the "aggregate of rights which are guaranteed and protected by the government" includes substantially unfettered control of, or personal fiat over, that thing.

Turning to land specifically, three areas of unilateral control have always been recognized in both the common law and civil law traditions: possession, disposition, and use. The element of possession would actually be more accurately described (as it often is) as a right of *exclusive* possession, since it consists of the right to exclude others from land that is one's private property. The right of disposition includes not only the right to sell one's land to a willing buyer but a right of noninterference by others in one's dealings with any prospective buyer. Although there are cases in which environmental regulation affects exclusive possession and the right to disposition, environmental regulation most often threatens to interfere with the right to use one's land in various ways.

It is impossible to say precisely how much unilateral control one must retain over a piece of land for that land to count as one's private property, but, as a general rule, the more the law wrests unilateral control from the hands of a landowner, the more it chips away at the concept of land as private property. To return to the bundle metaphor, the greater the number of sticks government removes from the bundle of rights landowners hold, the closer it comes to eclipsing land as private property. At some (admittedly unspecifiable) point, the individual retains so little unilateral control over land as to make the appellation "*private* property" meaningless, or at least unnatural.

Preventing Nuisances and Harms

With this admittedly rough and approximate conception of private property in hand, we can now proceed to the question, How does the proliferation of environmental regulation in the last third of the twentieth century threaten to eclipse the notion of land as private property? Environmental laws and regulations have undoubtedly had an enormous impact on land use; however, some of the most important and far-reaching forms of environmental law cannot be said to have diminished at all the bundle of rights that owners have in land.

Air and water pollution standards are a clear case in point. Although these laws have had dramatic impacts on corporations' behavior, and conformance has cost them considerable amounts of money, it would be incorrect to say that in such cases the bundle of rights held by landowners has been diminished. The reason is that the general presupposition that no one has the right to use his or her property in any way that causes harm to others has always been recognized in both the civil and common law traditions.

Pollution standards are becoming more restrictive as our ability to detect pollutants at lower concentrations improves. If a pollutant is harmful at a concentration of one part per billion but we can only detect it at one part per million, then it is impossible to craft enforceable regulations that will eliminate all the harms involved. That does not mean there is no harm, however, and so when we do develop the ability to detect the pollutant at a concentration of one part per billion, we can further restrict land uses without restricting the landowner's right to use his or her land, even if the newer, more restrictive regulations force the landowner to abandon a previously permitted use of the land.

A perfect analogy is the situation in which it is discovered that a substance or a practice (e.g., of dealing with a substance in a specific way) previously thought to be safe is dangerous and is on that basis regulated for the first time or even outlawed. Consider, for example, bans on the use of chlorofluorocarbons (CFCs). Not long ago, "waste" CFCs were simply vented into the atmosphere. Today, elaborate measures are taken to recycle CFCs when refrigeration systems are retired, but growing evidence that the earth's ozone layer is developing holes that pose serious health hazards to human beings (as well as less well understood hazards to plant life) has led at least thirteen nations (the twelve European Community nations plus the United States) to ban all use of the chemicals by 1996. The cost of the changeover to new refrigeration technologies will be enormous, and it is not just air conditioning that is at stake—one refrigeration company spokesperson estimates that "forty percent of the world's food would spoil if it was not refrigerated." [11] The costs are high, yes, but by the spring of 1992 dangerous depletions were thought to be developing over Britain, Europe, and Canada, in addition to South America. [12] It is increasingly clear that users of CFCs are using their property in ways that harm others, even if it is impossible to say who precisely is being harmed.

In both examples, the regulation is justified by the general principle that landowners do not have the right to use their land in ways that harm others. But how are we to describe what happens in such cases, if not as taking certain rights from the bundle they hold? Since a landowner never has the right to use his or her land in a way that harms others, and since the previously permitted uses in fact did harm others, what we must say is this: previously, we *thought* that landowners had the right to do X with their land, but now we see that we were mistaken. We *thought* you had the right to do X, *but we were wrong*. The harm was there all along, and therefore the activity in question should have been restricted all along, although the agent, the victims, and the government were all ignorant of this. There is no taking of rights from the landowner's bundle, only the discovery that certain rights that we previously believed were part of the bundle were never there in the first place.[13]

The examples discussed in this section show that some of the most restrictive categories of environmental regulation do not in any way strip landowners of their rights. In general, air and water pollution standards merely codify our evolving understanding of which uses of land in fact harm others, and which may therefore be restricted or prohibited without taking any rights from the bundle a landowner holds.

These examples also suggest that the best places to look for actual restrictions in landowners' bundles are cases where the landowners try to claim compensation when their uses of lands are restricted by regulation. Any society that professes to take private property seriously must address the question of when public use of private property requires compensation.

The Takings Controversy

Understanding the requirement of just compensation is crucial to answering the central question of this essay, for if the commitment to private property entails that every time government takes a stick from a landowner's bundle of rights it must compensate him or her, then environmental regulation will be prohibitively expensive. If we must pay for every restriction imposed on an owner's use of private land, then the practice of holding land as private property stands squarely in the way of progress toward ecological sustainability.

A case entered the U.S. court system in January 1989 and brought this question into dramatic focus. The case concerns South Carolinian David Lucas, who bought two beachfront lots for about a million dollars, planning to build a house on one lot and to sell the other to another home builder. The state subsequently passed the Beachfront Management Act, which prohibited building in the area.[14] The trial court awarded Lucas $1.2 million in compensation, but the state supreme court reversed. It cited the U.S. Supreme Court's most recent decision on this issue, *Keystone Bituminous Coal Association v. DeBenedictis,* quoting the court's dictum that where property is taken to prevent public harm, no compensation is called for. The South Carolina Supreme Court denied Lucas any compensation because he did not contest the state's claim that the relevant legislation was necessary to prevent "serious public harm." Lucas appealed to the U.S. Supreme Court, which heard oral arguments on March 2, 1992.

Where the U.S. Supreme Court will come down on this case is unclear, because takings jurisprudence is one of the more inchoate areas of United States constitutional law. The Fifth Amendment to the Constitution states (among other things) that "private property [shall not] be taken for public use, without just compensation." There is dramatic disagreement among justices and legal scholars about the implications of the clause, however, as well as inconsistencies in the use of the key terms in this area: *taking, eminent domain,* and *police power.*

One of the most influential scholars in this field is conservative legal theorist Richard Epstein, whose 1985 book *Takings: Private Property and the Power of Eminent Domain* inspired President Ronald Reagan to issue an executive order stating that all "governmental officials should be sensitive to, anticipate, and account for, the obligations imposed by the Just Compensation Clause of the Fifth Amendment in planning and carrying out governmental actions so that they do not result in the imposition of unanticipated or undue additional burdens on the public fisc." [15] While couched in terms of avoiding unanticipated suits for compensation, the order clearly signaled the administration's sympathy with Epstein's view that "the eminent domain clause and parallel clauses in the constitution render constitutionally infirm or suspect many of the heralded reforms and institutions of the twentieth century: [including] zoning, rent control, workers' compensation laws, transfer payments, [and] progressive taxation." [16] Although Epstein was not concerned exclusively or even primarily with environmental regulation, his argument, if accepted, would render much or most environmental regulation exorbitantly expensive by requiring government to pay landowners for any value their property loses as a result of regulation. [17]

While disagreeing with his conclusions, I admire Epstein's conceptual clarity. He distinguishes more clearly than have most jurists among the terms *taking, police power,* and *eminent domain,* and I will follow his usage here. Epstein uses *taking* to describe any case in which government action causes an owner to lose one or more of the rights in the bundle representing his or her property, regardless of whether or not the taking requires compensation. He then distinguishes between takings pursuant to the police power and those pursuant to the power of eminent domain: the state exercises its police power when it acts to prevent one individual's use of his or her property from causing harm or becoming a nuisance to another individual; it exercises its power of eminent domain when it seizes or prevents a use of an individual's property in order to secure a public good.

Epstein's distinctions can be used to clearly and succinctly describe four possible formulations of the just compensation requirement. On the first interpretation, a taking requires no compensation so long as it substantially advances a legitimate public purpose. It certainly would be inconsistent with respect for private property to allow government to take private property at any time for any public purpose without requiring compensation, and there is no precedent for this interpretation in United States common law. In an early case, *Mugler v. Kansas* (1887), the Court did hold that property may be taken without compensation whenever doing so bears a "real or substantial relation" to the ends of protecting "the public morals, the public health, or the public safety." [18] But in the same decision the Court clearly distinguished the police power from the power of eminent domain, and it identified the exercise of police power with the pursuit of these ends. [19]

In subsequent cases the Court claimed to be departing from *Mugler* by introducing the caveat that if regulation "goes too far" it requires compensation, [20] and sixty years later, in *Agins v. Tiburon,* the Court explained that a regulation "goes too far" if it "denies an owner [all] economically viable use of his land." [21] In these cases the Court did not explicitly limit compensation to the exercise of eminent domain. So a second interpretation of the takings clause is that it requires compensation whenever the government "goes too far" in the exercise of either the police power or the power of eminent domain.

There is good reason for limiting the compensation requirement to the exercise of eminent domain, because when the state acts to prevent a use of property that causes harm, it does not take from the owner any of the sticks in his or her bundle of rights. The Supreme Court has implicitly acknowledged this. In the 1987 case of *Keystone Bituminous Coal Association v. DeBenedictis,* the Court observed in a footnote that "since no individual has a right to use his property so as to create a nuisance or otherwise harm others, the state has not 'taken' anything when it asserts its power to enjoin the nuisance-like activity." [22] This is the dictum cited by the South Carolina Supreme Court in its *Lucas* ruling. Epstein uses this same argument and observes that the reference to "public use" in the Fifth Amendment clearly suggests that the amendment is about the exercise of eminent domain rather than the police power. So a third interpretation would be that (a) compensation is never required for an exercise of police power, but (b) compensation is required for an exercise of eminent domain (when property is "taken for public use") if the taking "goes too far" by depriving an owner of all economically viable use of his land.

Epstein's view is different in one very significant way. He argues that if compensation is required when regulation denies an owner *all* economically viable uses of his or her land, then compensation must also be required when regulation denies an owner *any particular* economically viable use. He reasons as follows. Suppose that B holds all the possible sticks in a bundle of property rights save one (for instance, in the context of mining law, the mineral estate and the "support estate," but not the surface estate), whereas A holds only one of those sticks (the surface estate). Epstein writes: "Does it make the slightest difference if A sells [the surface estate] to B before the government acts? To be sure, the sale converts what was a complete taking from A into a partial taking from B, but it cannot alter the characterization of the underlying rights or of the government action, even if a different person is now entitled to compensation."[23] So a fourth interpretation (Epstein's) is that (a) compensation is never required for an exercise of police power, but (b) compensation is required for an exercise of eminent domain (when property is "taken for public use") whenever the taking deprives an owner of any particular economically viable use of his or her land.[24]

Lucas provides the U.S. Supreme Court with an opportunity to choose among these options (or some variation thereon), which I summarize below.

Formulations of the Just Compensation Requirement

1 A taking requires no compensation so long as it substantially advances a legitimate public purpose.
2 Compensation is due whenever government "goes too far" in the exercise of either the police power or the power of eminent domain by depriving an owner of all economically viable use of his or her land.
3 Compensation is never required for an exercise of police power. It is required for an exercise of eminent domain if the taking "goes too far" by depriving an owner of all economically viable use of his or her land.
4 Compensation is never required for an exercise of police power. It is required for an exercise of eminent domain whenever the taking deprives an owner of any particular economically viable use of his or her land.

Where the Court will come down is unclear. It could very well choose interpretation 2, ruling that compensation is required even for an exercise of police power if the taking deprives the owner of all economically viable use of his or her land. This is not an unlikely outcome, because the substantial minority in the Court's 1987 *Keystone* decision held precisely this, and the Court's composition has shifted to the right since then. The minority opinion was written by Chief Justice William Rehnquist and joined by Richard Nixon appointee Justice Lewis Powell and Reagan appointees Justices Sandra Day O'Connor and Antonin Scalia. The opinion reviews the major takings cases and notes that "though nuisance regulations have been sustained despite a substantial reduction in value, we have not accepted the proposition that the State may completely extinguish a property interest or prohibit all use without providing compensation."[25] Since *Keystone,* Powell has resigned, but Presidents Reagan and George Bush have added Justices Anthony Kennedy, David Souter, and Clarence Thomas to the Court, suggesting that a majority could overrule *Keystone* by siding with the second interpretation of the Fifth Amendment.

Such a holding would make many forms of environmental legislation too expensive to maintain. Zoning regulations prohibiting development of beachfront properties or wetlands would suddenly be held to have worked a taking, and federal and state governments would be required to pay many millions of dollars to affected property owners. Similarly, where endangered species provisions prohibit development, governments would be liable. A floodgate of astronomically expensive litigation would be opened on many fronts.

Luckily, despite their commitment to protecting private property, the civil and common law traditions have both recognized that no individual has the right to use his or her property in a way that harms others; a government deeply committed to protecting private property need not compensate individuals affected by its exercise of police power. Because this general principle is so deeply entrenched in our major legal traditions, we may hope that even if today's Supreme Court sides with the second version of the just compensation requirement, courts in other common law nations, and legislatures in the civil law nations, will stick to something more like the third interpretation.[26]

The third interpretation, however, leaves room for environmental regulation only if such regulation can be construed as preventing harm, as an exercise of police power not requiring compensation. Epstein doubts that they can, and for this reason, combined with his belief (discussed earlier) that compensation is required whenever lands are deprived of a particular economically viable use, he concludes that most forms of environmental regulation amount to regulatory takings for which compensation is required.

Although much environmental legislation is couched in terms of avoiding harm and would therefore qualify as an exercise of police power for which no compensation is required, Epstein argues that it is usually implausible to hold that regulations are designed to prevent harm rather than to secure a public benefit. Discussing *Just v. Marinette,* a celebrated takings case in which the Wisconsin Supreme Court upheld regulations prohibiting the filling of wetlands even though they lay entirely on private property, Epstein writes:

> The opinion fails to bring the case within the confines of the anti-nuisance doctrine. Although the development may pollute the lands owned by the Justs, there is no *tort,* because harm, to be actionable, must be *to another,* not to "the citizen's own property." Yet when the opinion speaks of harm to others, it speaks not of pollution, but solely of the economic and aesthetic losses resulting from removing private land from the general ecological balance. There is no physical invasion created by the landowner's use of the property, but only a desire by the state to use that property as part of an extended wildlife sanctuary. It is impossible to conceive of a successful action that any private owner of real estate or wildlife could maintain if the Justs decided not to use their property in its natural state. The normal bundle of property rights contains no priority for land in its natural condition; it regards use, including development, as one of the standard incidents of ownership.
>
> Stripped of its rhetoric, *Just* is a condemnation of these development rights [i.e., it is an exercise of eminent domain], and compensation is thus required.[27]

Epstein concludes that many or most forms of environmental regulation are exercises of eminent domain that require compensation. He explicitly mentions restrictions on building on floodplains and prohibitions on the sale of feathers from endangered birds, each of which could arguably be said to deny an owner all economically viable use of his or her property, and as such would be compensable on the second interpretation of the just compensation requirement. But Epstein would go further and require compensation whenever any particular economically viable use is denied. He mentions, for example, strip mine reclamation requirements, regulations prohibiting unlimited fishing, and even "regulations [which] require owners to allow others to gain access and entry to their property," none of which could be said to deny an owner all economically viable use of his or her property.[28]

So, to follow Epstein would be even more devastating for conservation efforts than to side with the second interpretation of the takings provision. If a government must pay mining companies to restore their land, if it must pay fishing companies for their lost catch when it restricts fishing to sustainable levels, and if it must pay landowners merely to gain access to their land for environmental monitoring (of water quality or an endangered species's biological status, for instance), then virtually all effective environmental legislation will be too expensive to implement.

It is not inconceivable that a majority of today's U.S. Supreme Court would adopt a stance in some ways analogous to Epstein's. In *Keystone,* the four-justice minority held that a taking can require compensation when it denies all economically viable use to identifiable parts of a larger parcel, and the same minority was skeptical of attempts to construe some forms of environmental regulations as preventing public harm. The issue in *Keystone* was whether or not a regulation worked a taking by requiring mining companies to leave in place 50 percent of the coal underlying property where others held surface rights that might be affected by subsidence. The majority held that " 'taking' jurisprudence does not divide a single parcel into discrete segments and attempt to determine whether rights in a particular segment have been entirely abrogated. . . . [T]he destruction of one 'strand' of the bundle is not a taking because the aggregate must be viewed in its entirety."[29] The minority held, however, that "there is no question that this coal is an identifiable and separable property interest" and would have required compensation on that ground.[30] Further, the *Keystone* minority characterized the nuisance provision as "a narrow exception" to the just compensation clause and added: "The Subsidence Act . . . is much more than a nuisance statute. The central purposes of the Act, though including public safety, reflect a concern for the preservation of buildings, economic development, and maintenance of property values to sustain the Commonwealth's tax base. We should hesitate to allow a regulation based on essentially economic concerns to be insulated from the dictates of the Fifth Amendment by labeling it nuisance regulation."

The *Mugler* Court construed very broadly the class of harms that may be prevented through the exercise of police power. It held that property may be taken without compensation whenever doing so bears a "real or substantial relation" to the ends of protecting "the public morals, the public health, or the public safety." In the passage just quoted, the *Keystone* minority observes that, even on this very broad construal of the harms police power may be applied to prevent, the regulation in question is designed to secure public benefits as much or more than it is designed to prevent public harms.

It is somewhat unclear whether Epstein and the *Keystone* minority believe that regulations like those at issue in *Just* and *Keystone* violate the just compensation requirement because they are designed to secure public benefits as well as to avoid harm to individuals, or because, "stripped of their rhetoric," they are actually directed only to the former. But if the argument were that they do both, then there would be good reason for thinking that they should be treated under the law of police power rather than that governing eminent domain. If my action causes (or would cause) harm to others, government exercise of police power is justified and no compensation is due me. The fact that the government's exercise of police power simultaneously secures some public benefit does not change that.

So, the real question is, Can a regulation like that at issue in *Just*—one that prohibits filling wetlands even when the wetlands lie entirely on private property—plausibly be claimed to cause harms of a kind that a government may legitimately use its police power to enjoin? I think it surely can, but if we are to see clearly why this is so, we must have a better grasp of what kinds of harms fall within the purview of the police power.

Harm in the strongest sense occurs only when your act or omission physically impairs me. Physical assaults—stabbing me or kidnapping me—are the paradigm cases of harm in the strongest sense, and clearly such harms fall within the scope of the police power. There is also a very weak sense of the term, however, in which any forgoing of a benefit constitutes a harm. In this sense, your acts or omissions harm me whenever they cause me to forgo a benefit I did not previously enjoy, even when I had no right to that benefit. For instance, when you buy the house that I had my heart set on, you cause me to forgo a benefit (ownership of that particular house). Although it would sometimes be plausible to say that I suffer harm when I am caused to forgo a benefit to which I had no right, these kinds of harms do not fall within the purview of the police power. However devastated I am that you bought the house I wanted, the government cannot legitimately intervene to prevent this harm to me.

If these were the only two kinds of harm, then it would be difficult to see how the Justs harmed anyone by filling their wetland. In between these extremes, however, lies another kind of harm that *is* still covered by the police power. I have in mind cases where you deprive me of a benefit I previously enjoyed and to which I *did* have a right. Although not tantamount to physical invasion, such harms still constitute a tort and can be prevented by the state without compensation being due. For instance, if I have vested water rights senior to yours and your water use diminishes streamflow to the point that I cannot use all of the water to which I am entitled, you harm me by depriving me of a benefit I previously enjoyed as a matter of legal right. This is a clear case in which the state can exercise police power and your use of your land can be enjoined without compensation being due.

Does harm of this kind occur when landowners fill wetlands lying entirely on their own property? If we concentrate on the actions of individual landowners, it is difficult to see how it does. The filling of their wetland in Wisconsin by the Justs, taken of and by itself, does not, for instance, affect waterfowl populations anywhere off their land in any appreciable way. One landowner filling a wetland would not harm anyone. But the same could be said of CFC use. Venting one refrigerator's worth of CFCs into the atmosphere will not cause an ozone hole over anybody's land. In both cases the harm occurs because many people are doing the same thing— venting CFCs, on the one hand; filling wetlands, on the other. Bans on the relevant behaviors are justified by the harm being caused, and no exceptions are allowed because there is no fair way of deciding who should be the free rider.

In the wetlands case, there is the additional difficulty that if we concentrate on harms to individual landowners, then the restrictions on land use look draconian. In the case of CFCs, we can point to serious harms to individuals: skin cancer and retinal damage. But all the filling of wetlands that has occurred to date has not made it impossible for me to shoot ducks on my land, nor has it given me skin cancer; at most it has reduced appreciably the number of ducks I get. Such diffuse impacts on individuals may not even amount to a nuisance. Epstein may be right that (as I quoted earlier) "it is impossible to conceive of a successful action that any private owner of real estate or wildlife could maintain" against a jurisdiction that allowed landowners to fill their wetlands. But if we stop focusing on harms to individuals and focus instead on what Joseph Sax calls "public rights," the harms approach actionable magnitude.

In a widely cited article published in 1971,[31] Sax advocates using the concept of "public rights" to gather up and make visible the diffuse harms that many landowners suffer when legally protected uses of their property are adversely affected by the activity on other owners' lands. An appeal to "public rights" in the justification of a regulation would be analogous to filing a class action civil lawsuit. In both cases, diffuse but no less real harms exist, and we need a way to make them visible to the legal system. It is somewhat more than that, however. Describing the harm in terms of a public *right* implies that the many individuals were deprived of a benefit *to which they were entitled as a matter of legal right.*

The Continental and Anglo-American legal traditions have always recognized that certain things cannot be reduced to private property but are inherently public property, which individual landowners have the right to use. In Roman law, wildlife, air, and the oceans were recognized as things no one could own, although it was recognized that one could "reduce individual animals to one's possession" and thus acquire a property right to an individual animal as a chattel. Air and the oceans, however, could not be captured and thus could not even be "reduced to one's possession." This treatment of wildlife carried over into Anglo-American law and the public trust doctrine, which grew up around tidal lands and then (in the United States) all navigable waters; it reflects the Roman law tenet that certain resources are held in common. (The public trust doctrine is stronger, however, because it requires the state to administer the trust for the benefit of the public and prohibits the state from alienating the property held in trust.)[32]

Wetlands do much more than provide us with ducks to shoot. They help reduce flooding by slowing the runoff of heavy rains and cycling nutrients, among other things. Such ecological processes are paradigm cases of things that, if they can be said to be owned at all, are inherently public property. They cannot be captured or reduced to possession; they can only be used. And as no individual can own them, they are by right available to all.

So Joseph Sax's term, "public rights," is quite apropos. It serves simultaneously to gather up diffuse harms and make their aggregate magnitude visible to the legal system and to emphasize that the harms in question consist in depriving individuals of benefits to which they are entitled as a matter of legal right.

The Status of Land as Private Property in the Age of Ecology

In this essay I have not questioned the validity of our legal traditions. I have simply tried to show that although the civil and common law traditions share a profound commitment to the protection of private property, each has resources on which it can draw to justify strict environmental regulations. In the preceding section I discussed four formulations of the just compensation requirement. Any country that professes to take property rights seriously must adopt some variation on these formulations, only two of which (the third and the fourth) are, I argue, plausible. On either of these plausible formulations, however, much or most environmental regulation would be prohibitively expensive unless it could be construed as an exercise of police power. Unless we can plausibly construe an act like filling a wetland on private property or building among beach dunes as causing harm to others, there is a deep tension between the civil and common law traditions and the current groundswell of support for ecological sustainability.

The notion that ecological processes ought to be regarded as public goods like air, oceans, and wildlife, which all individuals have a right to use, allows us to construe environmental regulation as an exercise of police power, as designed to prevent harm. But what really is left of the concept of land as private property once we have done this? Increasingly, taking an ecological view of land forces us to treat it as a public resource that individuals hold only in a stewardship (or trust) capacity. Any and every piece of land is involved in diverse ecological processes, and any and every form of land use affects these processes to some extent. So any stick in the bundle of rights held by a landowner would, under the right circumstances, be subject to taking without compensation.

My conclusion is that the eclipse of land as private property is near at hand. Just as Adolphe Berle could observe, in 1965, that industrial properties had come to depend so heavily on a public infrastructure as to be hardly "private" any more, in this age of ecological literacy we have discovered that land uses depend so heavily on an ecological infrastructure—on processes that, if they are property at all, are inherently *public* property—that it hardly makes sense to conceive of land as private property. The proliferation of environmental regulation thus threatens to wrest unilateral control of land from the landowner to such an extent that the appellation "private property" no longer naturally applies. The situation regarding land is beginning to approximate the example I gave earlier in which automobiles were held in common and only their temporary use was secured to individuals. In that society, I noted, we would *not* say that automobiles are private property. In interpreting the just compensation requirement in a way that allows aggressive environmental regulation, we arrive at a similar point in regard to land.

NOTES

1 Adolph A. Berle, "Property, Production and Revolution," *Columbia Law Review* 65 (1965): 1–20.
2 Berle, "Property," 9.
3 Berle, "Property," 9.

4 Berle, "Property," 10–11.

5 Berle, "Property," 19.

6 Throughout, my intention is to construe the term *environmental law* broadly, so as to include both statute and (in the common law tradition) case law, but also regulations promulgated to enforce statute and case law.

7 Modern codes tend to appeal to something more like "general principles of legal order of the State" (as the Italian Civil Code of 1942), in contrast to older codes that made explicit reference to natural law (as the Austrian Civil Code of 1811), but I take it that the more contemporary language comes to roughly the same thing. See John Henry Merryman, *The Civil Law Tradition*, 2d ed. (Stanford: Stanford University Press, 1985), 44–45.

8 *Black's Law Dictionary* (1979), 1095, 1096.

9 *Black's*, 1095.

10 David Hume, *A Treatise of Human Nature*, book 3, sec. 2, ed. L. A. Selby-Bigge and P. H. Nidditch (Oxford: Oxford University Press, 1978).

11 Marlise Simons, "Europeans Worry about Ozone-eating Chemicals," *New York Times*, 3 March 1992.

12 Simons, "Ozone-eating Chemicals."

13 Note, by the way, how this stresses the positivist conception of property rights. It is not clear how a positivist could coherently say that the law clearly and explicitly said one thing but nevertheless should have said something else at that same point in time.

14 Existing homes in the affected area were grandfathered in.

15 Executive Order 12630, 15 March 1988, *Federal Register* 53 (1988): 8859–62, at 8860.

16 Richard Epstein, *Takings: Private Property and the Power of Eminent Domain* (Cambridge: Harvard University Press, 1985), x.

17 The only exceptions are the exercise of police power, which Epstein admits does not require compensation, and cases in which the benefits of the taking are distributed on a pro rata basis reflecting the relative contributions of various individuals. He offers no argument for this tenet while laying out his theoretical framework in the first three chapters of the book, but much later he says the following: "This pro rata distribution has . . . an important allocative function because it does not skew the incentives of private parties in the choice between public and private control over human affairs. For example, if each person received an equal portion of the general gain, there would be an incentive for persons with smaller shares to force matters into the public arena, where they would be relative gainers. . . . The political situation is more stable if each person receives the same rate of return from an investment in social governance" (163). Or, more directly, perhaps, the goal of government (to secure individuals in the exclusive posession, use, and disposition of their private property) is more effectively achieved if individuals have no incentive to force matters

into the public arena, and pro rata distribution of the public good derived from condemnations reduces this incentive.

18 *Mugler v. Kansas,* 123 U.S. 623 (1887), at 661.

19 Compare *Mugler,* at 661 and 669. Unfortunately, Supreme Court justices have subsequently blurred the distinction between "police power" and "eminent domain" by holding that the "scope of the 'public use' requirement of the Takings Clause is 'coterminous with the scope of a sovereign's police powers,' " in *Ruckelshaus v. Monsanto Co.,* 467 U.S. 986 (1984), at 1014 (quoting *Hawaii Housing Authority v. Midkiff,* 467 U.S. 229 [1984], at 240).

20 *Pennsylvania Coal v. Mahon,* 260 U.S. 393 (1922), at 415.

21 *Agins v. Tiburon,* 447 U.S. 255 (1980), at 260.

22 *Keystone Bituminous Coal Association v. DeBenedictis,* 17 ELR 20440, at 20445, n. 20.

23 *Keystone,* 57–58.

24 In this case a bit of formal logic helps to make the point more clearly. Where $Ex = x$ is an economically viable use of one's land, $Tx = x$ is a taking, $Dxy = x$ denies an owner of y, and $Cx = x$ requires compensation, the third interpretation of the Fifth Amendment is that $(x) [\{Tx \& (y) [Ey > Dxy]\} > Cx]$, whereas Epstein's view is that $(x) (y) [\{(Tx \& Ey) \& Dxy\} > Cx]$.

25 *Keystone,* 17 ELR 20440, at 20451.

26 On June 30, 1992, the Court issued a narrowly drawn decision remanding the case for retrial in a manner consistent with the third interpretation of the just compensation requirement. The majority opinion, while admitting that " 'harmful or noxious uses' of property may be proscribed by government regulations without the requirement of compensation" (60 LW 4842, at 4847), held that a state must do more than assert that legislation is designed to prevent harm—it bears the burden of showing how this is so (60 LW 4842, at 4849).

27 Epstein, *Takings,* 123.

28 Epstein, *Takings,* 101, 124, and 125.

29 *Keystone,* 17 ELR 20440, at 20447, quoting *Penn Central,* 438 U.S. 104 (1979), at 130–31; and *Andrus v. Allard,* 444 U.S. 51 (1979), at 65–66.

30 *Keystone,* 17 ELR 20440, at 20452.

31 Joseph Sax, "Takings, Private Property and Public Rights," *Yale Law Journal* 81 (1971): 149–86.

32 I am, of course, simplifying a great deal here. Among other things, there is controversy over the degree to which trusteeship constrains the actions of state and federal governments in the United States. See Charles F. Wilkinson, "The Public Trust Doctrine in Public Land Law," in *The Public Trust Doctrine in Natural Resources Law and Management: Conference Proceedings,* ed. Harrison C. Dunning (Davis: Regents of the University of California, 1981), 169–202.

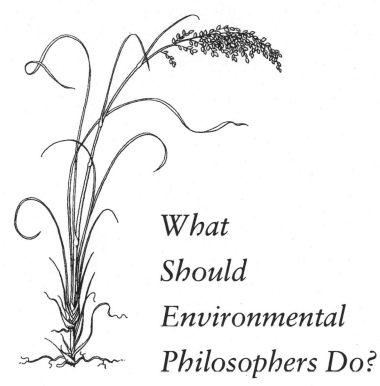

*What
Should
Environmental
Philosophers Do?*

ERAZIM KOHÁK

Red War,
Green Peace

For all the futility of efforts to design an ecofriendly high explosive, I do not think a reflection on the ecological aspects of organized warfare love's labor lost. The point is not that if only we try harder we will yet invent a rubber tank tread for use in fragile ecosystems or a solar-powered battleship to prevent oil spills. The point is just the opposite: that try as we might, such efforts are futile. There are no technological solutions for the environmental problems of war because the problem is not technological. It is a cultural problem and as such calls not just for a technological quick fix—though God knows our technology could stand fixing—but rather for a basic cultural reorientation. It is what we do that endangers the earth, not how we do it.

That crucial point is easily lost—or perhaps repressed—in the case of less dramatic activities such as driving about on our lawful activities or trawling for fish. Those are such innocuous activities, such pure Norman Rockwell! It is distressing to discover that, technologically enhanced by a factor of seventy and multiplied by five billion, they can become as deadly as warfare. We love our motorcars and our sushi—or our tuna-noodle casserole. We are eager to believe that if only we could invent a solar-powered motorcar with biodegradable tires we could go on dreaming the

American dream of infinite expansion without running into the reality of a finite earth.

The hope of a technological quick fix that would not require a cultural reorientation has, in fact, guided most of the efforts of the various ministries of the environment—and it may be rather fortunate that it has. Europe is a tight little continent, and European intellectuals tend to be notoriously verbose and ineffectual. Left alone, we might still be discussing the deep meaning of *dwelling* while our rivers burned and forests died. The dirty triangle formed by the former DDR, Czechoslovakia, and Poland shows what an industrial country looks like without the benefits of environmental technology. Fortunately, in most of Europe the engineers got into the act, as ferociously efficient as European intellectuals are ineffectual—and thank God for it. If both nature and humankind are to survive, we need to make the fullest use of the most appropriate technology, including the very highest.

Unfortunately, the very success of our technology, welcome though it is, masks the fundamental contradiction in our efforts. It tends to make our exploitation of nature more efficient and less polluting, not to reduce it, creating the illusion that we can conserve without slowing down the expansion of our individual consumption. Even the most affluent countries remain committed to a policy of expanding consumption. Ecofriendly technology seems to make that policy sustainable.

Perusing the various well-intended lists of thirty-seven and a half things people can do for the environment through Second World eyes is instructive. We are bade to cluster our errands so that we do not have to drive our cars to the store six separate times in a day. A good idea, surely—for someone who has a car. But we travel by streetcar and on foot, a shopping bag in each hand. If the author is so concerned for the environment, why does he drive a car? We are told to save and recycle aluminum cans—but we buy our beverages in returnable bottles; or to compost our food scraps . . . but why cook such gargantuan servings in the first place? Altogether, it is difficult to avoid the impression that those lists are designed to salve the consciences of obscenely opulent countries. They make us feel incredibly virtuous . . . until we look at our Second World consumption through Third World eyes.

The great ecological virtue of war is that it cuts through all such illusion. There are no technological quick fixes when it comes to organized warfare. Certainly it is crucial to hold our various armies to the same ecological standard as other enterprises. Certainly it is necessary to make military technology as ecofriendly as possible; there is no reason and no excuse for military vehicles to pollute any more than civilian ones. But nothing can change the fact that a bomb is an immensely destructive device and is supposed to be. The problem is cultural, not technological—and much as we try, we cannot resolve it technologically.

That conclusion, alas, gives rather less validity to various alternative approaches to matters ecological, whether "deep" or "environmental," than might at first seem to be the case. Unquestionably we badly need a far greater sensitivity both to the living nature around us and to the deep nature we are. Undoubtedly Aldo Leopold's reflections on Sand County and Annie Dillard at her creek have a great deal to offer. So do Morris Berman and Gary Snyder. It is only as a quick fix that their deep ecology fails like its technological counterpart.

People who commune with mountains and talk to trees—and I speak as one of them—would find it distressing to have their deep appreciation of the autonomy of nature described as just another quick fix. Their concern long antedates the age of fixes—or even the recognition that nature might need fixing. They can count among their predecessors the Renaissance poet Petrarch and even the Roman poet Virgil with his Bucolics, and more recently Henry David Thoreau, John Muir, and Aldo Leopold. Their motivation is not technological, economic, or even "ecological" in the more recent sense of that word. At the root of their concern is an empathy for living nature, a mute horror at its devastation at the hands of human greed, and a longing for a restored harmony, both with the nature around us and with the nature we are.

It is the sense of harmony disrupted that such alternative approaches to ecology share. Morris Berman borrows a term from Friedrich Schiller and speaks of a "disenchantment" of the world. Modernity, he claims, is less a state than a process of a gradual reduction of all reality, humans included, to mechanisms. He uses the painful metaphor of the experimental animal whose vocal cord the vivisectionist cut so that its screams would not interfere with his activities. The Czech thinker Emanuel Rádl had used the metaphor of the anatomist a generation earlier. The point is that the moderns, eager to exploit the world as a resource, have lost all sense of it as kin, denying it any meaning, value, or purpose. To salve their consciences as they set about plundering nature, they taught themselves to think of the world as material and mechanical.

In a world so conceived, purposeful, valuing, and feeling humans inevitably experience themselves as alienated amid a wasteland. The most obvious sense of alienation is the obvious disharmony between the life of humans and the life of the rest of nature. We have, literally, placed a layer of technology between ourselves and the natural world. We walk on asphalt, not on the good earth; we touch plastic, not good, living wood; we look up at neon and smog, not at the starry heavens. We have lost the rhythm of day and night, the rhythm of the seasons, the rightness of our lives. In Neil Evernden's words, we have become the natural aliens. For a long line of naturalist writers from Thoreau to Michael Pollan and beyond, that is the basic alienation—and a return to Walden or Cornwall the basic strategy.

For writers such as Berman or Arne Naess, the alienation from nature is as much a reality as it is a metaphor of our alienation from the nature within us, from the depths of our being. Some will use metaphors borrowed explicitly from depth psychology, such as Jung's collective unconscious; others, such as Gary Snyder, draw on Eastern thought; still others draw on the West's own hermetic tradition. Harmony with nature then acquires a Renaissance sense of a harmony with our own nature, with the depth of our being. We moderns are said to be the disconnected generation, out of touch with the rich psychic ground of our own being. Alternately, we are said to be isolated in our dry and brittle "reason," cut off from and denying our "emotions." Or again, we are said to be caught up in our "masculine" side, cut off from or denying the rich "feminine" aspect of our being.

Some of these metaphors are, admittedly, somewhat unfortunate. Thus the polarity of "reason" and "emotions" draws on a primitive conceptual apparatus borrowed from faulty psychology and ignores both the passion of reason and the reasons of the heart. Similarly, the metaphor of the "masculine" and the "feminine" can be accused of perpetuating a naive—and rather sexist—stereotyping.

Still, such criticisms miss the profound insight that the "deep" ecologists seek to express—the sense of a disharmony within us, a loss of sense for the deep rhythm and rightness of life and of our own being and an alienation from it. The turning point may have been the Industrial Revolution, when humans literally lost their hands-on contact with the living world and locked themselves inside a world of artifacts. Or it may have been the trauma of the Thirty Years' War, which led Europe to retreat from the labyrinth of the world to the self-certifying certitude of the *ego cogito*. It might even have been the mythical moment in the Garden when humans yielded to the temptation to be like the gods, deciding what will be good and what evil. Or, less mythically, it may be the inadequate human instinctual apparatus and the need to make up for it—human freedom—that lie at the root of that alienation. The basic insight behind all such metaphors, though, is the sense of alienation from the sources that nourish and sustain human being.

That is also where the various philosophical ecologies encounter the temptation to look for a quick fix of their own in a literal return to nature at Walden Pond or in a figurative return to it at the *centrum securitatis* in dream or myth. Thoreau and his various successors—sensitive to the rhythms of nature, cherishing the communal ways of our nonhuman kin, or appreciative of the putative antelapsarian virtues of Native Americans— are convinced that we could resolve our ills by returning to a more direct, pretechnological contact with living nature. The various "deep" ecologists appear no less convinced that if only we could "reconnect" with our emo- tions, with our unconscious, or perhaps with our femininity, our ecological problems would either disappear or yield to the new harmony.

The diagnosis is intuitively immensely appealing. Clearly we would be far happier with a greater sensitivity to nature and to our own nature. I can think of no privilege more precious and more restorative than being able to live for several seasons away from the power line and the paved road, deep in the woods, between the embers and the stars. Thoreau's Walden and Annie Dillard's Tinker Creek—or my own New Hampshire home- stead years ago—or, for that matter, the gardens of Epicurus and Michael Pollan, are places of special healing power and beauty. Nor is the rediscov- ery of our own depth in myths and poems, dreams and emotion any less important. This is clearly a civilization out of contact with its own depth and distorted thereby. The rediscovery of nature and of our own nature may well prove the most important side effect of the environmental crisis.

It is, however, rather problematic whether it is also a quick fix—or even a slow one. Our civilization is unnatural and out of contact with its depth . . . but is that the root of its problems? It does not seem to be so in the case of war. Making war is as natural as making love: indeed, the two activities have traditionally gone hand in hand. Only the brave, we have been told, deserve the fair—and the fair have not exactly shown an aversion to the brave. The Native Americans, surely the most natural of peoples, made war incessantly and enthusiastically long before being contaminated by Euro- peans. The Serbs and the Croats, in their latest lapse into barbarism, did only what they have been doing for centuries and what their various neigh- bors in the former Soviet Union are probably about to go and do. With the global arms market flooded with secondhand ordnance at bargain prices, war, once the sport of kings, has come within the reach of the common man. And, let us note, not only on the scruffier margins of civilization, as in the Balkans or the Caucasus. The Americans, too, loved their war in the Persian Gulf. A year later, they still thrilled to the memories of their victory, like Twin Cities' fans remembering the 1991 World Series. A great little war, as Theodore Roosevelt described it, is a natural.

Nor is the warrior "disconnected" from his or her unconscious depth. Myths and dreams alike show that depth to be a turbulent and violent one. A man—the downtrodden, disciplined, little-civilized man—is seldom as profoundly at one with his deepest emotions as when he yanks the lanyard of a howitzer and sends a 155-mm shell sailing into a faraway slope. Ah . . . it is an immense release, a surge of the suppressed depth. There is no reason to suppose that a civilization fully connected with the depth of its unconscious would be any less warlike. If anything, the opposite seems likely. Reason counsels peace and tolerance; it is the primitive tribal passions, once invoked by the Nazis and now by their direct nationalist heirs, that stir humans to war.

The problem, finally, is not psychological just as it is not simply technical. Unquestionably, we badly need to rediscover the integrity of living nature and the depth of our own being just as we need to design environmentally friendly technology. We should not, though, expect that doing so will remove our environmental crisis. The roots of that crisis lie elsewhere: in the self-perception of our culture—in what it sees as what makes life worthwhile, its purpose and goal, its fulfillment. For centuries we have let our goals just happen to us, making love and war indiscriminately as the spirit moved us, confident that Nature would guide us and, in any case, that it would clean up after us, heal the wounds inflicted by our activities. That we can no longer do. As Hans Jonas argues cogently—and many others with him—our numbers and our demands have risen so much that we can no longer rely on nature to guide our doings and make good our damage. We have become responsible not only for the means and mores of our doings but for the aims and goals to which we orient our culture. We need not only a scientific and philosophical ecology but also a cultural ecology.

Here a terminological excursus may be in order. I use the term *ecology* to designate the study of a functioning—or malfunctioning—system, with special attention to the interaction of cultural (human-generated) and "natural" (extracultural) systems.

A great part of such study assumes that human aims and goals, individual and cultural, are nonproblematic, whether because they are determined by "nature" or by God or are simply too intangible to study. Ecology focuses all its attention on the means and rules of that interaction. What humans strive for is a given. Our task is simply to devise the means of making such striving compatible with sustainable functioning of the system. For that I generally use the term *scientific ecology*. Its basic assumption is that what humans do is not a problem; the problem is how they do it.

Within the whole area of scientific ecology, much beloved by ministries of environment, one trend tends to believe that the problem with what we do is that we do it with wasteful and polluting technology. So, *that* we consume ever more energy is simply a fact; the problem is that the technology we use to generate it wastes and pollutes. Ecology here is perceived as a search for ecofriendly technologies. For this I use the term *technological ecology*.

A second, compatible trend notes that the problem with what we do is also that we do it chaotically, with little consideration for the morrow or for the environment today. So, for instance, commercial fishing is a fact; the problem is that we fish with no system of quotas or any consideration of long-range sustainability. Ecology here tends to mean a search for the rules of encounter between humans and the rest of the natural world to ensure sustainable development. For that, I use the term *ethical ecology*, recalling Aldo Leopold's definition of ethics.

A rather different approach, which I call *philosophical*, as against scientific ecology, starts with the assumption that the problem is not simply "objective" but involves also the way humans as subjects relate to the rest of nature or perhaps to their own nature, the depth of their being.

For that part of philosophical ecology which sees the problem in the alienation between humans and the rest of living nature I use the term *naturalistic* or *environmental ecology*, which is concerned with reestablishing the harmony between humans and the rest of nature.

For that part of philosophical ecology which sees the problem in the alienation between humans and their own nature—their unconscious, their emotions, their repressed feminine side—and the solution in the reconnecting with such alienated aspect, the conventional label is *deep ecology*.

When I speak of *cultural ecology* I have in mind an inquiry not into how the system functions or malfunctions but rather into what the system seeks to accomplish. In a more traditional terminology, I could speak of it as *moral* ecology—as I have in Czech—invoking the archaic eighteenth-century sense of the term *moral* as pertaining to the works of human freedom in general and to their goal, the summum bonum in particular.

The labels finally do not matter greatly as long as we can establish conventions sufficient for communication.

The levels of concern do matter. We love to use our motorcars, but they pollute dreadfully. What questions ought we to ask about them? Should we ask simply how to build a nonpolluting motorcar? Or under what conditions to use them—say, for pleasure trips but not for commuting or expressway travel? Should we be asking how motorcars affect our coexistence with other species? Or should we be asking how hurtling through space at 120 kilometers per hour affects the soul of a being whose body and senses are designed to function optimally at a fraction of that speed? Or do we need to be asking the difficult moral (or "cultural") question, What is the good we as persons and we as a culture seek? And how good is that good?

Though my personal predilections are for environmental ecology, for seeking the lost harmony between the lives of other species and my own life as a human in a clearing in the woods of New Hampshire—between the embers and the stars—living as I now do in a crowded postcommunist city in central Europe amid the festering hatreds and the environmental devastation of past neglect and present greed, I have to turn to cultural ecology of the culture of which I am a part—and which in two centuries brought the planet to the verge of an environmental breakdown.

This is the second global culture to reach out from Europe. The first European culture was a Mediterranean one. It grew out of Greek and Roman roots and extended its power throughout the region, until by the second century of our era it could consider itself truly global. It was an urban culture with a high degree of social organization and a highly developed technology, but with limited sources of energy: the chief source of energy was still the slave. It was a culture so reminiscent of ours that it is difficult to identify significant differences between third-century Rome and late twentieth-century America. Its attitude toward nature was rather similar to ours, too, exploiting it ruthlessly while extolling its virtues, as in Virgil's *Bucolica*. Perhaps the only difference is that Rome failed to devise an efficient means of releasing energy or to reach a sense of responsibility for the earth, which our civilization just might be reaching. It was also a civilization that perished so utterly that its successors told tales of a race of giants to account for the ruined buildings amid which they lived.

The second European civilization emerged a thousand years later, less on the ruins of the first than among the forests north of the Alps. The church, a latecomer on the Roman scene (it was established in A.D. 391 by

Theodosius; the Visigoths sacked Rome only nineteen years later, in 410), preserved some echoes of the first civilization, though for the most part Europe was built anew. The foundations were in part Gothic and Germanic, in part Christian, with fragments of Greco-Roman culture absorbed only very gradually. It took four hundred years to build up rudiments of social organization—Pope Leo III crowned Charlemagne emperor of the Holy Roman Empire in 800; he was the first emperor since the deposition of Romulus Augustulus in 476. It took some four hundred more years to build up a culture: the church reached the zenith of its power during the reign of Pope Innocent III (1198–1216). During the next four hundred years that culture flowered in Scholasticism, including the reformation within and without the church, and in attempts to revive the fervor of the Middle Ages. In the first half of the seventeenth century, the Thirty Years' War brought that age to an end as surely as the sack of Rome put an end to the Roman Empire. Only then, with Descartes, Galileo, and Newton, began the "modern age" which in three hundred years spread the second European culture over the entire globe.

What was the motivation that drove that incredible expansion and goes on driving us, hell-bent for leather, to what might well be our destruction? It was not technology. The Egyptians and the Chinese, with whom the Romans had contact (a Roman embassy reached the Han court in 112), had the technology needed to build a culture as "modern" as ours but lacked all desire to do so. What makes the second European culture—the Atlantic culture—so different? Or, to switch metaphors for the moment, what is the deep program that drove Europe to expansion and is today driving the world to its doom?

On the level on which cultures are built, one of the crucial components in the European cultural makeup may well be the idea of evil as something that requires redress. In our European awareness, evil is not simply a fact; it is a challenge: something should be done about it.

That view is a part of our Judeo-Christian heritage, reinforced by the Reformation. Ancient Greeks perceived evil differently. To them, evil— sorrow, woe, suffering, ill intent—was the human lot. To revolt against it was *hubris,* the undue pride punished less by individual gods than by *ananke,* the built-in necessity of the system. One might feel an infinite compassion for the sufferer—though a wise man, mindful of his peace of mind, would avoid doing so—but one had to accept it. Evil was an intrinsic and irreducible component of the cosmos.

So the Greeks believed—but so we do not. Deep within, we believe that evil *should not be,* and if it exists, we should do something about it. Though most of us no longer use the imagery, we remain convinced that God created this world as good and that evil has no place in it, that evil is something that happened to the world somewhere along the way. It does not matter whether we imagine it as miscegenation of the sons of the gods and the daughters of humans, as a serpent offering Eve a pomegranate, as the invention of private property, or as the publication of *Mein Kampf.* The point is that evil is something that happened and so can be made to *unhappen.* Things can be other than they are: the actual is not the inevitable; the real is not the rational. Hunger, disease, oppression, and, yes, environmental damage are not simply the human lot. They are a challenge, something to be undone. In its Judeo-Christian roots, the West is profoundly and essentially meliorist, unwilling to leave bad enough alone. Whether it is a matter of seeking to eliminate hunger by building ever more polluting factories or of saving the land by tearing them down, evil is not something to be accepted mutely; it is something against which to do battle.

This deep-rooted conviction has its counterpart, no less deeply rooted in our Western cultural heritage, that life is not just about being lived; it is about fulfillment, about salvation. Most humans at most times have lived with rather more modest expectations. For the most part, as Thomas Hobbes and the utilitarians after him noted, humans prefer pleasure to pain, but they had modest expectations with respect to that pleasure. They hoped, for the most part, for a positive balance overall, but even the Epicureans did not expect or hope for salvation, an ultimate fulfillment. We do—and we feel positively cheated by anything less. Whatever it is, we want it huge, ecstatic, overwhelming—fulfilling.

That, too, is a part of our Judeo-Christian heritage, especially as Saint Augustine formulated it for us. God created humans as good but not as self-sufficient. They remain as dependent on God's grace as a plant is dependent on moisture. When in their pride they turn away from God, they grow brittle, discontented, evil. They are not that of themselves: it is a condition in which they find themselves when they grow estranged from God. It is a condition that can be overcome when God in the fullness of His grace breaks through the estrangement and literally fulfills our being, as, according to the Christians, was done in the Christ. The point, though, is that human life is capable not only of the horizontal success of a generally positive balance of pleasure over pain. It is also capable of an ecstatic, vertical fulfillment, humans reaching up to God or God reaching down to humans, filling them with grace.

That imagery, again, has long since grown obsolete for all but a handful of us. We do not search or hope for the ecstasy of the vertical moment that cuts through the horizontal sameness of life. We say that we do not "believe in salvation"; and yet, look attentively in the faces of the contestants watching the drawing of the Massachusetts lottery. A number will be drawn—and one of these people will become fabulously rich. They watch raptly, transported by the unthinkable thought of seven million dollars. We may not believe in salvation, but we do look for an ultimate fulfillment. Americans who divorce wives or husbands of a lifetime at age sixty do not do so because the partner was not a good partner—one does not last forty years with a bad one. They do so because they feel cheated out of the great orgasm, the ultimate fulfillment.

That is the second moment: the quest for ultimate fulfillment. The third entered in during the latter half of the seventeenth century with the conviction that the ultimate fulfillment is not a matter of the intersecting vertical dimension but rather something that can be found on the horizontal line of this life. When Thomas Jefferson substituted the phrase "pursuit of happiness" for John Locke's original "pursuit of property," he was reflecting that changing attitude. Happiness cannot be pursued, to be sure: happiness is a by-product or a gift. Humans can pursue the material infrastructure of happiness, however, and can hope, not realistically, that happiness will be added unto them as a superstructure. Jefferson clearly believed that property was worth pursuing because it could make happiness possible.

A number of commentators have pointed out that this faith was really an unhappy one: no longer confident of reward in heaven, humans turned to seeking ultimate fulfillment at least on this earth. Postponing eternal reward until a putative afterlife was a recent idea in any case: Christians had traditionally looked to the coming of the Holy Spirit in *this* life. What was really new was not the idea of salvation on earth but of salvation by riches rather than by the Holy Spirit.

All that, though, matters more to a historian than to us. For us, the crucial point is that the culture that spread from Europe throughout the globe in our time carries with it at least three basic components: the conviction that evil is something we should do something about; the conviction that what we need to do about it is not just a matter of marginal amelioration but of salvation, of an ultimate fulfillment; and the conviction that ultimate fulfillment can be achieved by providing all its material counterparts. To a Westerner, the plight of orphaned child laborers in Indonesia is not just a fact, it is a call for help, a challenge. It does not call simply for marginal amelioration—perhaps stricter child labor laws—but rather for fundamental transformation: those boys should be placed in a well-financed boarding school. And, when they are, they should experience not just the contentment of a full stomach and a clean, warm bed but an ecstatic fulfillment—the happiness whose pursuit we consider an inalienable right.

It is the third component that has proved most problematic. Material security can provide the wherewithal of contentment, but it is rather tricky to look to it for ecstatic fulfillment. The reason is something the West has been fast to note but slow to acknowledge: that possession generates ecstatic fulfillment—happiness in the recent usage—only at the moment of increase. It is not owning that brings with it that tingle of excitement, it is getting. That is why in affluent societies humans invest so much more effort in acquisition than in maintenance even though, hour for hour, the latter is far more rewarding. It is also why women and men will squander energy so lavishly on the pursuit of an affair and skimp so painfully on maintaining an existing relationship. When we look to possessions for happiness, it is not owning but acquiring that matters.

That is also what has locked the second European civilization, today global, into the vicious lockstep of an expanding economy. Since it is fulfillment we seek from our possessions, not simply the contentment of a need well met but the exhilaration of fulfillment, and since that exhilaration comes only at the moment of expansion, our economy must expand. The Americans or the Germans cannot rest, content that they have achieved the highest level of individual consumption in the history of humankind. Contentment is not enough: it is exhilaration we want, and that requires expansion, *more,* no matter how hard-pressed we may be to imagine that more and no matter how many yard sales we must hold to make room for it.

That, ultimately, is our dilemma. The culture we have created and offered to the world as a model is committed to an endless expansion in a finite world. That is the contradiction we have sought to mask with our technological and psychological quick fixes, the contradiction that stands out when we turn from considering our more benign activities to considering one of the most natural activities of all, warfare.

Is there a way out of that dilemma? To speak of a "cultural reorientation" is well enough—it is what we need—but not very helpful. We need, in effect, to eliminate one of the components of our cultural consciousness.

We might, for instance, choose the path of defeat—or perhaps wizened realism—and seek to free ourselves of the conviction that evil is something to do something about, a challenge and a call to action. We might instead teach ourselves to accept evil as a part of the human lot, calling for compassion but not action. If we broke ourselves of our compulsive do-gooding, we might know at least the contentment less compulsive cultures have known since the world began, leaving nature—and history—to look after themselves.

For better or for worse, though, that is no longer an option. We have intervened too deeply; there are too many of us. Nature might have been expected to heal the damage done by two bands armed with bows and arrows, but we can hardly expect it to fix the damage that would be done if two hundred million former Soviets divided up their ex-country's nuclear arsenal and set about defending assorted national honors. The momentum of our culture is too great to let go; there are too many starving millions to leave the earth at the mercy of humankind.

We might seek to abandon the second unspoken tenet of our culture, the assumption that the point of life is not just living but transcendence, reaching above the weary horizontal concerns of need and gratification. There are billions of weary drudges, surviving on the margins of subsistence, whose hopes we activated with a vision of improvement we are hard put to fulfill. Perhaps it is time to give up the rhetoric of "advancement" and abandon the Third World and our own Third Estate to its fate.

That is certainly the message being sent out by the "me generation," but in vain. It is not rhetoric that activates the millions of the deprived, it is the fact that there is a world of humans whose great problem is their surplus. We cannot expect them to abandon their pursuit of property until we are prepared to abandon ours.

But is that possible? I think not. There might be individuals—even many individuals—willing to take to the woods with Henry David Thoreau and Louise Dickinson Rich, but the ethos of striving onward is too deeply rooted in us—and perhaps in humans as such.

It may be the third aspect of our heritage that most deserves attention: the assumption that self-fulfillment can be found in self-gratification. It is something of which we have become convinced and, in America at least, that is constantly being reinforced: it is impossible to open a magazine or turn on the radio without being told that ultimate fulfillment can be had for the price of purchasing a particular item that we had never missed before. The urgent voice seldom promises that the item in question will perform a finite task satisfactorily. Instead, it promises ultimate fulfillment, nothing short of happiness.

Yet daily experience mitigates against it. The happiness of acquisition is transient and requires ever more powerful stimuli to achieve. The satisfaction of loving someone or something, of loving and serving a cause, is lasting. After all, we have also been told, for centuries, that we should first seek what is good, and the rest will happen to us along the way.

That, finally, might prove to be the most important contribution the ecological movement can make. Not that it will help generate nonpolluting technologies, though I fervently hope it does. Not that it will restore the harmony between humans and the rest of nature, including their own—though that, too, is badly needed. Rather, the movement's significant contribution could be overcoming the narcissism that has been perhaps the most pronounced trait of modernity. Turning once again to our cultural makeup, we might point out that ours is the culture convinced that there is nothing higher than our own self-gratification. The plight of the earth—the agony of the nonhuman species, the irreversible damage to the global ecosystem—and the plight of our fellow humans is making the point that even if God were dead (a report I think rather exaggerated) there would be something higher than self-gratification: solidarity with our suffering fellow humans and our endangered world. That is the most important point I can make: there *is* something higher. If the economy is to expand, let it expand in the service of social justice and environmental renewal.

What, then, of my original topic, arms and the environment, or simply war? We cannot make war ecofriendly: military technology is supposed to be destructive. Nor can we eliminate it by restoring humankind to harmony with their nature: war is too natural. We can, though, hope to offer humankind what William James called for, a moral equivalent of war. Humans, ultimately, will serve: that is a basic need. The primary task of culture is to give humans something to serve. So far, the culture of modernity has given humans only self-gratification and collective hatred to serve. If the ecological movement can give humans the love of earth and neighbor to serve, it might yet bring about the cultural reorientation that could still save the earth.

REFERENCES

Bergen. 1990. *Action for a Common Future*. Bergen: Ministry for the Environment.
Berman, Morris. 1981. *The Reenchantment of the World*. Ithaca: Cornell University Press.

Carson, Rachel. [1962] 1987. *Silent Spring*. Boston: Houghton Mifflin.

Evernden, Neil. 1985. *The Natural Alien*. Toronto: University of Toronto Press.

Jonas, Hans. 1984. *The Imperative of Responsibility*. Chicago: University of Chicago Press.

Kohák, Erazim. 1982. *The Embers and the Stars*. Chicago: University of Chicago Press.

Leopold, Aldo. 1966. *A Sand County Almanac*. 2d ed. New York: Ballentine Books.

Naess, Arne. 1990. "Sustainable Development and Deep Ecology." In *Ethics of Environment and Development*, ed. J. R. Engel and J. G. Engel. London: Belhaven.

Pollan, Michael. 1992. *Second Nature*. New York: Dell Laurel.

Rádl, Emanuel. 1946. *U'ticha z filosofie*. Prague: Leichter.

Snyder, Gary. 1990. *The Practice of the Wild*. San Francisco: North Point Press.

KRISTIN SHRADER-FRÉCHETTE

An Apologia for Activism

Global Responsibility, Ethical Advocacy, and Environmental Problems

One of the most difficult *theoretical* problems in normative ethics is understanding and resolving conflicts over collective responsibility for global environmental crises. It is difficult both because the precise contribution of each member of a collectivity (a group, nation, or planet) in causing and alleviating planetary problems is hard to determine and because environmental goods are both public and indivisible. One of the most difficult *practical* problems in normative ethics is how to achieve authentic collective responsibility. It is problematic both because international laws and sanctions are difficult to formulate and enforce and because the tragedy of the commons and the appeal of being a "free rider" are typically more powerful motivators than ethical suasion. I shall address the second, more practical, problem.

Apart from devising legal, governmental, and institutional strategies for creating and enforcing solutions to problems of the global environmental commons, the other main strategy for environmental action (a noninstitutional strategy) is education and advocacy, especially through nongovernmental organizations. Advocacy of any kind, however, is viewed as inimical both to objectivity in general and to the academy in particular. In this essay I argue that environmental advocacy by scientists, philosophers, and other intellectuals is not only permissible but perhaps ethically mandatory. My conclusion is based on at least four premises for which I shall argue: (1) because decision making in industry, government, and the academy is highly partisan and often contrary to environmental interests and fair play, alleged neutrality (rather than advocacy) actually serves the status quo; (2) scholarly objectivity regarding environmental issues is not achieved by neutrality; (3) provided certain conditions are met, there are sound deontological arguments for scholars assuming positions of environmental advocacy; and (4) provided certain conditions are met, there are sound consequentialist arguments for scholars assuming positions of environmental advocacy.

In sum: the world has grown too small and too troubled to be served by an ivory tower, if, indeed, it ever served us. The ivory tower model of objectivity is clearly wrong, in part because there is no tower, but instead there is an academic and industrial playing field heavily tilted against environmental interests, against fair play, and against open exchange. This is illustrated easily by a recent experience of Peter Singer's.

The Playing Field Is Tilted

In May 1991, Peter Singer was standing in an auditorium at the University of Zurich, about to give a lecture on animal rights. Before he could begin, a massive group of leftists and anarchists—including a large number of disabled persons in wheelchairs—disrupted his lecture. They accused Singer, because of one chapter in his *Practical Ethics,* of advocating active euthanasia for severely disabled newborn infants. Singer said that one-third to one-fourth of the auditorium began to chant "Singer *'raus! Singer 'raus!"* in a deafening roar. As he rose and tried to speak, one of the euthanasia protesters came up from behind him, tore Singer's glasses off his face, threw them to the floor, and broke them.[1]

Part of the Singer case is similar to that of other advocates, including my own—in having my phone bugged and in being threatened, intimidated, and harassed by industry and government groups who have tried to stop some of my writing and speaking on nuclear power and hazardous waste. Although I won't discuss these experiences here, they, like Singer's, illustrate that environmental or ethical advocates, especially those who "rock the boat," are often subject both to the disapproval of the academy and to the violence of vested interests. Yet, the very violence and power of these vested interests is precisely one of the reasons why advocacy, especially environmental advocacy, is so needed in the academy if we are to solve our global environmental problems.

What is environmental advocacy? It is taking a stand, in a partisan sense, in one's professional writing or speaking; taking a stand on a specific, practical issue and defending that stance as rational and ethical rather than merely pointing out the assets and liabilities of alternative positions, rather than merely maintaining a stance of informed neutrality. Environmental advocacy might be exemplified by taking a stand in favor of a solar economy or unilateral disarmament or against commercial nuclear fission or deep geological disposal of hazardous wastes.

Because the justifiability of normative and partisan stances in one's research is proportional to the degree to which the research game is already played in an ideological and highly partisan way, it is important to know something about who controls academic research. Academia is no longer an ivory tower, if indeed it ever was. Adam Smith has co-opted it. In 1981, for example, the West German pharmaceutical company Hoechst gave $70 million to Harvard's Department of Molecular Biology in exchange for rights to market all discoveries made in the department and to exclude all funding and research that interfered with Hoechst's proprietary position. In the same year, Jack Whitehead gave MIT $125 million in exchange for MIT's relinquishing control over patent rights, finances, hiring, and choice of research at its biotechnology research center. Likewise, at Carnegie Mellon, 60 percent of the research funds are from the U.S. Department of Defense.[2] Hence, any environmentalist who takes a particular stand against certain uses of biotechnology or military technology is already speaking within a highly partisan framework created by special interest groups.

Part of the reason for the power of special interest groups, particularly those that are antienvironment, is that of all corporate monies given to United States universities, one-third is provided by only ten corporations, and one-fifth of all industry funds—millions of dollars—is provided by only two corporations.[3] Faculty in molecular biology at Harvard are indentured servants to Hoechst. MIT biotechnologists are hired hands of entrepreneur Jack Whitehead; at Carnegie Mellon, they comprise a branch of the army and the air force.

Universities appear to be selling their integrity in much the same way as medieval churches sold pardons and indulgences. Typically, they give the most power and internal support to departments that have the most corporate monies behind them. As noted Harvard biologist Richard Lewontin put it when he heard about Harvard's deal with Hoechst: "What about the rest of us who are so foolish as to study unprofitable things like poetry, Sanskrit philology, evolutionary biology and the history of the chansons? Will the dean have time to hear our pleas for space and funds between meetings

with the university's business partners?"[4] Indeed, will academic adminis-
trators even give such researchers a "fair shake" if their scholarship leads
them to question the research methods, assumptions, and politics of the
government and industry groups, typically antienvironment groups, that
funnel their money into the university?

In universities dominated by narrow technical, governmental, and industrial concerns and driven by extramural funding from corporate sources,
environmental awareness is almost nonexistent, and liberal education has
become progressively more narrow. As Nobelist Isidore Rabi warned, this
narrowness is paving the way for a repetition of what happened in Germany during the 1930s when the rise of militaristic nationalism, fueled
by the dominance of narrow technical and professional training, eroded
ethical values and liberal university education, thus laying the foundation
for Hitler's rise. Given such a restrictive conception of the university and
scholarship, it was no accident that in 1937 the Prussian Academy of Sciences condemned Albert Einstein because he criticized the violations of
civil liberties in the Nazi regime. (The academy said that he should have
remained silent, neutral, and objective.) Once an Einstein, or any disinterested academic, is condemned for speaking out in the public interest, then
the narrowing of the ivory tower begins to strangle democracy as well.
No country can survive the theft of its universities' capacity to criticize.
Democratic institutions are fed by the free flow of information and criticism, and government and science, as well as the public, require universities to provide this independent perspective. Otherwise government must
blindly choose the answers offered by individuals and corporations, who
are by nature self-interested. Because they are self-interested, they cannot
be trusted to judge what is in the common interest. Democracy needs the
Socratic gadfly, the detached observer, and the social critic. Neither society
nor the university can afford to become the whore for special interest
groups.[5] The way to avoid their domination by antienvironmental industrial or militaristic special interest groups is for scholars themselves to
take partisan stands and advocate positions that are ethically defensible,
especially when the positions run counter to those of the interest groups.

Objectivity Is Not Achieved by Neutrality

One reason why scholars so often fail to engage in
environmental advocacy through their speaking and writing is probably
that they have accepted the antiquated positivistic model of objectivity as

neutrality. A corollary of the outmoded positivist tradition of research is that whatever scholarship is not neutral is also subjective in a reprehensible way. If it makes sense for philosophers and other scholars to be advocates and partisans, however, and not merely neutral observers of society, then obviously the acceptability of advocacy presupposes that neutrality is not objectivity. Thanks to Thomas Kuhn, Michael Polanyi, Stephen Toulmin, Paul Feyerabend, and others, we now know that complete objectivity is impossible and that there is no value-free inquiry, at least not free from cognitive or methodological values.[6]

Philosophical analysis, moreover, can show that not all methodological and ethical values deserve equal respect, and therefore not all values are subjective in a reprehensible way. Not all values deserve equal respect— or disrespect, as the positivists would have it—because formulation of any scientific theory is incompatible with the avoidance of methodological values, because there is no fact-value dichotomy, and because values alone never determine all the facts or all aspects of the facts. Just as there are rational reasons, short of empirical confirmation, for accepting one theory over another—reasons such as simplicity and heuristic power—so also are there rational reasons—such as consistency or equal treatment— for accepting one value over another.[7]

If not all ethical and methodological values are subjective in a reprehensible way, then advocating some values and being a partisan on their side is philosophically defensible on both epistemological and ethical grounds.[8] In other words, objectivity does not equal neutrality, for at least six reasons:

1 Failure to criticize indefensible or questionable values gives implicit assent to them in practising ethics or public policy. Hence, once one admits that methodological and ethical values are unavoidable in all research, including scientific research, then not to assess those values is to become hostage to them or at least implicitly to sanction them. Hence, to avoid uncritical acceptance of status quo values one must criticize values rather than remain ethically neutral in all cases.

2 Not all ethical and methodological positions are equally defensible. If they are not, then real objectivity requires one to represent indefensible positions as indefensible and less defensible positions as less defensible.

3 To represent objectivity as neutrality in the face of a great hazard or threat is simply to serve the interests of those responsible for the threat.

4 To represent objectivity as neutrality is also to encourage persons to mask evaluational and ethical assumptions in their research and policy and hence to avoid public disclosure of, and control over, those assumptions.

5 To represent objectivity as neutrality is also to presuppose that objectivity is somehow delivered from on high rather than negotiated and discovered socially through the give-and-take of alternative points of view, point and counterpoint.

6 Most disturbing of all, to represent objectivity as neutrality is to sanction ethical relativism and therefore injustice. This is exactly what happened during World War II when some anthropologists from Columbia University were asked about their position on the actions of the Nazis. They said that because conflicts between the Nazis and others represented a controversy over value systems, they had "to take a professional stand of cultural relativity"; they said that they had to be "skeptics" with respect to all judgments of value.[9]

At least three groups in contemporary society would agree that the Columbia University anthropologists should have been skeptics with respect to judgments of value. They would support a resounding no to the question of whether philosophers should be advocates: (1) the fashionable "deconstructive" postmodernists who have tried to destroy the foundations of ethical, social, and epistemological criticism; (2) the unfashionable positivists who nevertheless lurk in the closets of most natural scientists; and (3) the relativist social scientists who have confused silence with objectivity and neutrality. Someone else can have the task of telling how and why these three positions go wrong. For now, I'd like to provide several consequentialist arguments, followed by a number of contractarian or deontological arguments, for advocacy and partisanship in selected cases of environmental scholarship.

Consequentialist Arguments for Advocacy

One of the most powerful consequentialist arguments in favor of environmental advocacy is that without it greater harm would occur, more persons would be hurt, and more important values would be sacrificed. Although it would be difficult to prove, for example, it is arguable that the Nazis' experimentation on prisoners and brutality against Jews, gypsies, and leftists could have been stopped or at least hampered had the Columbia University anthropologists and other scholars taken a different ethical stance and condemned the atrocities. Likewise, it is reasonable to believe that environmental abuses such as global warming, destruction of the ozone layer, and pollution of air and water could be stopped or at least hampered if scholars would take a partisan stance against them.

Of course, the obvious objection to taking a partisan stance on environmental or other issues is that such stances are often wrong and that careful, conservative scholars ought never move beyond the facts. If knowing that one were correct were a necessary condition for taking a position of advocacy, however, then many evils would be so advanced that it would be impossible to stop them. Moreover, in a situation of uncertainty, advocacy encourages counterarguments and public discussion and hence is often itself an important way to resolve uncertainties.

In other words, an important consequentialist argument in favor of environmental advocacy on specific issues is that such advocacy would help to educate the public. Even if particular scholars were wrong in advocating certain courses of action, the advocacy itself would draw out public debate, analysis of the issues, and a will to know the truth. Environmental advocacy would also help to reverse a status quo dominated by the vested interests of industry, greed, big government, and the military. Without such advocacy, our silence or neutrality likely would serve the status quo, especially what is ethically and environmentally indefensible in the status quo. As Abraham Lincoln put it: Silence makes men cowards. Silence or neutrality makes us cowards in telling the truth about the evils that surround us, and therefore our silence sanctions those evils. Scholars' failure to adopt positions of environmental advocacy also might encourage the consequence that less educated persons, some serving their own vested interests, would dictate public policy debate. If scholars and those most lacking in self-interest do not become advocates, then the advocacy will become the prerogative of the worst elements of society, just as a volunteer army has often become the prerogative of ne'er-do-wells and politics has often become the prerogative of the corrupt.

Environmental advocacy is also defensible on largely prudential grounds. If environmental hazards are threatening our lives and well-being, then a purely prudential argument in favor of scholars adopting positions of environmental advocacy is that such advocacy would lead to better protection of human and environmental welfare. It is arguable, following this line of reasoning, that environmental advocacy is justifiable on the grounds of self-defense. We have the obligation to do whatever is necessary to defend our lives and welfare. Therefore, as a consequence, we have the obligation as scholars to engage in environmental advocacy. In other words, one consequence of our acting as environmental advocates is that we would be better able to protect human rights to bodily security and equal protection, both of which are threatened by environmental degradation.[10]

Deontological Arguments for Advocacy

There are also good deontological reasons for believing that those who oppose the advocacy of scholars are wrong. For example, by virtue of their position, the anthropologists who failed to oppose Hitler were being neither objective nor neutral. It is not objective to say that committing atrocities is neither right nor wrong. It is not objective to say that one should be neutral regarding experimentation on prisoners without their consent. It is not objective to be neutral in the face of systematic discrimination against persons on the basis of their religion or race. Genuine objectivity requires calling a spade a spade. An important deontological argument for ethical advocacy of scholars is that objectivity does not require treating a questionable ethical position and a more reasonable one the same. Indeed, as Aristotle recognized, equal treatment does not mean the same treatment; equal treatment means treating equals the same. By virtue of trivializing and treating morally different positions equally, proponents of alleged neutrality actually discriminate and practice bias.

Failure to practice advocacy often amounts to bias. "Telling it the way it is" frequently requires us to take a stand precisely because certain governmental, political, and economic interests are taking either a reprehensible stand or no stand at all against great evils. Vested interests often exercise a highly questionable sort of advocacy, and our raising questions about their stances typically amounts to advocacy for the other side. No one can evaluate the social science methodology of risk perception studies done near the proposed Yucca Mountain radioactive waste site, for example, without examining and condemning the massive, one-sided advertising campaign mounted against the citizens of Nevada by every nuclear utility in the country. When the nuclear industry spends $5.5 million per year (in ratepayer funds) in one state in an attempt to control the results of social science surveys, the students of social science methodology cannot ignore that fact.[11] Scholars need to condemn such bias. In doing so they act as advocates for alternative action.

One reason that researchers need to act as advocates for alternative action is that, often, researchers are the only people with the requisite information to make an informed decision about the rights and wrongs of a particular situation. In other words, an important deontological reason for scholars acting as environmental advocates is that they often have the ability to make a difference; they have a "responsibility through ability." Following the reasoning of moral philosophers such as Peter Singer, if we have the ability to make a difference, and if it would cause us no serious hardship to do so, then we have the duty to attempt to make a difference.[12]

We also have a responsibility through complicity. We have a responsibility to act as environmental advocates because often we have benefited from environmental harm. Frequently, for example, we are responsible for correcting environmental harms because we have paid less for goods produced by manufacturers who fail to curb their pollution. Hence, our monetary benefits have been purchased at the price of harms to the environmental commons. Scholars in developed, Western nations bear a special responsibility through complicity because our standard of living and luxuries frequently are made possible only through environmental degradation and through our using a disproportionate share of environmental resources. Hence, we have a responsibility through complicity to help reverse the environmental damage from which we have profited.[13]

Even if scholars had no responsibility through complicity to act as environmental advocates, we would clearly have a responsibility by virtue of third-party professional obligations. Professional ethics dictates that by virtue of the benefits professionals receive from society, we have an obligation to the public to protect its interests and serve its welfare. Indeed, professionals' obligations to third parties often supersede obligations to first and second parties. In the case of employees of state universities, this third-party obligation is particularly strong and is, indeed, even a first-party obligation, because the people—the taxpayers of the state—are literally our employers. Hence, we have an obligation to protect their interests, a main part of which includes environmental well-being.[14] And if we have an obligation to protect the interests of the public in environmental well-being, then we may have an obligation to engage in environmental advocacy.

Restrictions on Advocacy

Admittedly, of course, if one takes a position of advocacy, then one is bound to provide equal consideration of all relevant interests and to answer all relevant objections of "the other side." This is perhaps the greatest failing of applied philosophers and environmental scholars who take positions of advocacy. They sometimes are more interested in preaching to the converted than in examining both sides, in order to show which is ethically or methodologically preferable. A corollary to presenting alternative sides and to answering relevant objections is to put one's own methodological and ethical judgments up front to determine whether they can bear scrutiny. This again seems to me to be a common failing of applied philosophers working in environmental ethics. They sometimes are more interested in speculative, and often undefended, metaphysics and ethics than in the epistemological justifications for their positions.

Another necessary condition for environmental advocacy is that we meet William Frankena's criterion for discrimination: it must lead to greater overall equality and good, over the long term, for everyone. Otherwise, any discriminatory or partisan arguments, even for environmental goods, are not justifiable and may merely use other persons and their positions as means to our own partisan ends.[15] But herein lies the problem. Those who want to build Yucca Mountain radioactive waste repository and jeopardize our descendants in perpetuity, or those who want to continue destroying thousands of species per day, typically *agree* with principles of equal consideration of interests and with achieving greater equality and good, over the long term. Usually, however, they disagree with us over the facts. They disagree over whether Yucca Mountain will leak over tens of thousands of years, whether species extinction is a natural process, or whether humans can accommodate themselves to increasing numbers of carcinogens. Therefore, one of the most important tasks of the environmental advocate is to understand and defend the factual assumptions that he or she makes.[16]

Indeed, Paul Gomberg argues quite persuasively that moralists can be advocates and even partisans whose killing of others can be ethically justified provided that certain factual and ethical considerations are satisfied.[17] The factual conditions for justifiable advocacy (according to Gomberg) have to do with the gravity of the physical threat and the guilt of those responsible for it.[18] The gravity of the physical threat is an especially important condition in justifying advocacy regarding a particular environmental situation because the graver the threat, all things being equal, the more justified is a partisan position against it. This is why, for example, in his *Just and Unjust Wars,* Michael Walzer claims that "the survival and freedom of political communities . . . are the highest values of international society," and therefore we can countenance even the killing of civilians when the existence of a nation is up for grabs.[19]

But what about Earth First!'s actions? Is one justified in being an advocate and a partisan if one's goal is to protect a greater environmental good—survival of the planet and its resources? If civil disobedience is justifiable, and I think that there are occasions when it is, then analogous arguments might reveal when philosophical disobedience to the alleged norms of disinterested scholarship is likewise justifiable. Also, if Walzer is correct, then one could argue analogously that if the survival of the earth and its inhabitants is the highest of all values, then even the most extreme forms of advocacy and partisanship, such as killing civilians, can be countenanced when survival is at stake. Obviously, advocating killing is an extreme position. Equally obviously, it is justified only in the gravest of situations. Hence, much of the key to the justification of scholarly advocacy is the factual context in which it takes place.

Although he did not write about philosophical partisanship, John Locke appears to justify the partisan conception of human relationships when he says: "One may destroy a man who makes war upon him, or has discovered an enmity to his being, for the same reason that he may kill a wolf or a lion, because they are not under the ties of the common law of reason, have no other rule but that of force and violence, and so may be treated as a beast of prey." [20]

Few, if any, of us are likely to find ourselves in situations in which, because others are making war on us, we therefore have the right to destroy them or to advocate their destruction. Nevertheless, those who justify Earth First!'s actions appear to believe that they are in such a situation. Partisan scholarship and advocating particular ethical and policy positions, both amounting to a form of coercion, are obviously more justifiable to the degree that they are necessary to prevent some greater evil. The greater the evil needing to be prevented, the greater the justification for the coercive or partisan scholarship. Although I have doubts about whether he succeeded, that is how Garrett Hardin, for example, attempted to justify the highly coercive measures he defends in "The Tragedy of the Commons" and "Living on a Lifeboat." [21]

One could probably say, however, that the views of persons like Garrett Hardin and Edward Abbey—who said that he would sooner shoot a man than a snake because snakes are important members of ecological communities—and Earth First! members are highly ideological. Because they are highly ideological, one would probably argue that they are incapable of being justified by means of the numerous causal inferences necessary to show that some personal or environmental catastrophe is at stake.

Indeed, epistemological conservatism keeps most of us from assenting to, much less joining in, the actions of Earth First! We also believe that the environmental world is not quite so simple as Earth First! members believe, just as the political world is not so simple as Marxist revolutionaries claim; neither worldview obviously and easily justifies highly partisan actions. It does not seem to be the case, for example, as R. P. Dutt claims,[22] that fascist deeds and acts of war are inevitable under capitalism, because there is never any pure capitalism. Fascism sometimes exists with some degree of democracy because many acts of war are at least partially justifiable. Likewise, I believe that there are few totally unjustifiable acts of environmental degradation. Rather, many environmental actions often involve uncertainty regarding their causal effects, or, if the effects are certain but harmful, their proponents sometimes justify them by appealing to the greater good. In other words, in many cases of environmental controversy there are no "smoking guns."

Although I believe strongly in environmental advocacy, it is not always obvious or provable that environmental catastrophe is inevitable unless we engage in partisan scholarship and activism to promote particular causes, for example, stopping use of all potential carcinogens. We simply do not have that great a fix on the causal chain that results in various environmental damages. Because we don't, our advocacy is never wholly or easily justifiable. For example, recent news reports tell us that there is a cluster of primary brain cancers among residents near the Los Alamos National Laboratory in New Mexico, where nuclear weapons research is conducted. We know radiation causes cancer, and we have a dose-response curve to measure the effects of radiation exposure. We also know that there is a statistically significant increase in the disease rate in the Los Alamos area. The epidemiological studies are inconclusive, however, because we cannot link the effect, cancer, to the alleged cause, radiation exposure, in all cases. For one thing, cancer typically has a latency period and takes several years to show up, because the exposed population often is not studied for a long period of time. Moreover, researchers frequently cannot rule out intervening factors and alternative causes of the cancer, even though increases in the cancer are statistically significant.[23] In other words, many environmental situations are characterized by massive scientific uncertainty. This means that in order to justify environmental advocacy in such a case, one must justify choosing the environmental actions least likely to cause the most serious harm. One must defend a personal rule of scholarship that is based on maximin decisions rather than on utilitarianism or on average expected utility. I shall not take the time to defend such a maximin ethics, both because I have done so elsewhere and because John Rawls has given persuasive arguments that seem to me to be convincing. For both of us, however, perhaps the main key to the acceptability of advocacy directed at maximin choices is the severity of the environmental catastrophe we face. In other words, the key is the factual situation:[24] the greater the catastrophe we face, the greater is the acceptability of advocacy to prevent catastrophe.

If we do engage in partisan scholarship—work that defends and examines only one side of an issue—independent of the correct factual situation, then we should recognize that such coercive tactics may not lead to environmental education. Instead, they may lead to bias, to an inability to engage in rational analysis, and, ultimately, to diminished autonomy and decreased civil liberties for those who seek to be heard on all sides of an issue. Often, the first casualty of those who seek to preserve us from a great social or political evil is civil liberties. Likewise, the first casualty of those who seek to preserve us from a great environmental evil may be loss of autonomy and the ability to rationally analyze a situation.

From a consequentialist point of view, it is possible to defend both partisanship and avoidance of partisanship. Partisan scholarship could lead to the consequences (1) that we as a society lose the ability to engage in rational analysis of a situation, and (2) that because we lose part of our rational abilities, we lose some of our autonomy and some of our capacity for free, informed consent both to environmental hazards and to government actions. Partisan scholarship could also lead to the consequence (3) that from a pragmatic and prudential point of view, experts whose warnings about environmental disaster are proved wrong thereby lose their credibility. Such a loss of credibility would hurt not only society but the profession as a whole.

Avoidance of advocacy and partisan scholarship, on the other hand, could also lead to dangerous consequences. For example, the U.S. Office of Technology Assessment claims that up to 90 percent of all cancers are environmentally induced and theoretically preventable,[25] and we know that one in three persons will die of cancer. Had more people spoken out to advocate reduction of suspected environmental carcinogens, these rates might not be what they are today. Had more moral philosophers argued about the ethical constraints of behavior in a situation of scientific uncertainty, then the carcinogens might not have been so easily accepted. Other consequences of avoiding advocacy might be that those in a position to correct environmentally catastrophic situations would not do so.

For example, when the Chernobyl accident took place, officials in the former USSR said (and continue to say) that only 31 casualties occurred as a result of the accident. They ignored all nonimmediate fatalities, and they forbade medical doctors from inscribing the cause of death on the death certificates of those killed by radiation-related causes. Even the U.S. Department of Energy has admitted that Chernobyl fatalities are likely to go as high as 28,000, and academics at the University of California, Berkeley, have argued that once the statistical casualties are counted, the fatalities could go as high as 475,000.[26] Failure to address the silence of the nuclear industry in such a situation, and failure to be an advocate for the four million persons living near Chernobyl, whose premature deaths could be prevented, were they moved out of contaminated areas, is reprehensible. Environmental advocacy seems required of every scholar who knows the situation.

Sometimes we also might be able to justify our advocacy or our partisanship on the grounds that totally objective dialogue or argument is impossible. The argument here is that those who need to hear nonpartisan analysis would not listen to it, and some of those at fault in situations of environmental degradation have not listened for a long time. This is the same justification suggested by John Locke, who believed that it cannot be taken for granted that two human beings are bound by the same morality or common law of reason. Not all human beings are capable of listening to each other. Rather, a common bond of morality depends on the actual relationships among people, including their intentions toward each other.[27]

In other words, in order to treat "persons on the other side" as being responsible for their actions and able to change, we must believe in their susceptibility to ethical dialogue.[28] If I engage in ethical dialogue with another, I treat the other as ethically responsible. Dialogue both helps to establish and is presupposed by a moral community of agents seeking agreement. Hence, if we understand ascriptions of moral responsibility as entailing the belief that some persons can be affected by dialogue and criticism, then we need to know whether these persons can be so affected. This is a factual question. If they cannot be so affected, and if rational persuasion is impossible, then, presumably, one is not required to present totally neutral, nonpartisan rational arguments in order to persuade them. As Paul Gomberg puts it, if fascist brutality and fascist mindsets are inevitable, then morality is useless.[29]

According to the partisan conception of morality, there may be others with whom one does not share a morality and to whom one's moral duties are limited. This may be why, for example, the quadriplegics and paraplegics who helped to attack Peter Singer in Switzerland did not believe that they shared a common morality with him, whereas they were convinced that he was their enemy, a person whose ideas about euthanasia could result in their destruction. Conversely, persons who were convinced that others did share a common morality with them would not be likely to behave like those who disrupted Singer's talk because they would see no causal connection between a philosopher's beliefs about euthanasia and exterminating the disabled. If one is committed to a universalist morality, one would have trouble believing that another person is "out to get one" or has a design on one's life. In Reuben Ainsztein's words, "Because [Jews] . . . believed in progress and the perfectibility of man, they were the last to realize how bestial the Germans were."[30]

The obvious questions are whether actions are bestial or not and whether people can be written off or not. The obvious problem with environmental advocacy is the epistemological question of whether the factual situation is catastrophic enough to justify advocacy. On the one hand, because most of us do not understand fully the factual conditions around us, we often cannot determine whether or not advocacy is justified. On the other hand, factual uncertainty requires ethically conservative actions, actions not likely to harm either persons or the environment. Hence, factual uncertainty can be grounds for advocating ethically conservative actions.

Because we believe in progress and the perfectibility of humans, we likewise are often too slow to recognize the need for advocacy or the extremity of the environmental catastrophe that we face. This is somewhat like what Kris Kristofferson (the same Kristofferson who wrote "Me and Bobbie McGee" and "Help Me Make It Through the Night") said of his own transformation. He went from being an army brat and volunteering for Vietnam to being a Rhodes scholar, a longtime antiwar activist, a supporter of the United Farm Workers, and an opponent of United States policy in Central America. His own idealism about both humans and the government, however, kept him from recognizing the severity of the military and environmental dangers around him and therefore from taking a position of advocacy. He says: "Growing up, I was never aware of the fact that only white males who owned property were covered in the Constitution and could vote, and the whole country was built on genocide, the murder of natives. I've often thought that the more I read, the more I realized that our Government may never have stood for the things I believe in. But they made a mistake. Somewhere along the line they taught me that's what we stood for, and now I demand it."[31] We must demand it as well.

NOTES

1 Peter Singer, "On Being Silenced in Germany," *New York Review of Books* 38, August 15, 1991, 36–42.

2 Kristin Shrader-Fréchette, "Helping Science Serve Society," in *Hoe Toonaangevend is de Universiteit?* ed. H. de Ward (Groningen, Netherlands: University of Groningen Press, 1989), 75, 78.

3 Shrader-Fréchette, "Helping Science Serve Society," 79.

4 Shrader-Fréchette, "Helping Science Serve Society," 77–78.

5 Shrader-Fréchette, "Helping Science Serve Society," 78.

6 See Helen Longino, *Science as Social Knowledge* (Princeton: Princeton University Press, 1990); also Shrader-Fréchette, *Science Policy, Ethics, and Economic Methodology* (Boston: Reidel, 1984), 73. Finally, see Shrader-Fréchette, *Risk and Rationality* (Berkeley: University of California Press, 1991), 40ff.

7 Shrader-Fréchette, *Science Policy,* 73–74.

8 Shrader-Fréchette, *Science Policy,* 183.

9 Shrader-Fréchette, *Science Policy,* 88.

10 A. Gewirth, *Human Rights: Essays on Justification and Applications* (Chicago: University of Chicago Press, 1982), 181ff.

11 Yucca Mountain PR expenditures were revealed through the investigative reporting of D. Olinger, in "Nuclear Industry Targets Nevada," *St. Petersburg Times,* December 1, 1991, D1, D5.

12 Shrader-Fréchette, *Risk,* 160–62.

13 Shrader-Fréchette, *Risk,* 162–63.

14 See Michael Bayles, *Professional Ethics* (Belmont, Calif.: Wadsworth, 1981), 92–109.

15 William Frankena, "The Concept of Social Justice," in *Social Justice,* ed. R. Brandt (Englewood Cliffs, N.J.: Prentice-Hall, 1962), 15; see also Shrader-Fréchette, *Risk,* chap. 8, for discussion of this argument.

16 Paul Gomberg, "Can a Partisan Be a Moralist?" *American Philosophical Quarterly* 27 (January 1990): 71.

17 Gomberg, "Partisan," 71–79. Following Gomberg, I take *partisan* to mean "a division of human beings into those on my side, whose interests or judgments count positively, and my enemies" (75).

18 Gomberg, "Partisan," 72–73. What principle of proportionality is relevant to justify partisanship and advocacy? Clearly what is not appropriate is partisanship and advocacy that somehow exceed the gravity of the harm arising from the situation one advocates. What is not appropriate is what Hersh Smoliar, a leader of partisans from the Minsk Ghetto, describes: "Each one of them had his own account to square. . . . Two eyes for one, the whole mouth for one tooth" (quoted in Gomberg, "Partisan," 73). This attitude bespeaks revenge rather than impartial justice; presumably such revenge is appropriate only in the most extreme cases in which one's enemy is outside one's moral community and is bent on annihilation.

19 Michael Walzer, *Just and Unjust Wars* (New York: Basic Books, 1977), 254.

20 Quoted in Gomberg, "Partisan," 75.

21 See Garrett Hardin, "The Tragedy of the Commons," *Science* 162 (1968): 1243–48; and Hardin, "Living on a Lifeboat," *BioScience* 24 (1974): 561–68.

22 R. P. Dutt, *Fascism and Social Revolution* (Chicago: Proletarian Publishers, 1978), 16ff., 44ff., 91, 296ff.

23 J. M. Cousteau, "Nuclear Weapons Testing Casts a Deadly Shadow on the Environment," *Calypso Log* 18 (October 1991): 3.

24 See Shrader-Fréchette, *Risk*, chap. 8.

25 See Shrader-Fréchette, *Risk*.

26 Cousteau, "Nuclear Weapons Testing," 5.

27 Cited in Gomberg, "Partisan," 75.

28 See Lawrence Stern, "Freedom, Blame, and Moral Community," *Journal of Philosophy* 71 (1974): 72–84.

29 Gomberg, "Partisan," 75.

30 Quoted in Gomberg, "Partisan," 76.

31 Rosa Jordan, "Kris Kristofferson," *Progressive* 55 (September 1991): 36–38.

ALASTAIR S. GUNN

Can Environmental Ethics Save the World?

This essay is something of a mongrel, or, as politically correct dog lovers might say, a mixed breed. It started as an account of new developments in environmental ethics (with opinionated comments) in the first section of the conference to which I was originally asked to contribute. The program format changed, however, and my essay was moved to next-to-last.

A disadvantage of giving a presentation at the end of a conference is that many of what one had fondly imagined were brilliantly original thoughts turn out to have occurred to other speakers also. Still, this disadvantage is offset by the opportunity to learn from earlier speakers and review their ideas. This is a fortunate position. It allows me to comment extensively on their contributions without them having had the opportunity to do the same to mine. More usefully, perhaps, it enables me to identify some of the themes that emerged in the conference.

The title of the conference, "Theory Meets Practice," sums up for me the justification for pursuing, at the taxpayers' expense, a career in applied ethics. People need to get involved as advocates, in the manner described and exemplified by Kristin Shrader-Fréchette. As I explain in more detail later, however, I have yet to see much evidence that theory *is* achieving much that will save the world. In fact, I am sometimes tempted to say that we philosophers should declare a moratorium on grand theorizing. More realistically, and acknowledging that without theory there could be no application, environmental philosophers should at least contribute in a practical way as well as engaging in theory construction. In order of priority, we should proceed as follows: first, which should not take long, we should agree that the world needs to be saved. Second, we should work out how to save the world, putting our solutions into practice as we go. Third, if we get lucky and do manage to save the world, there will be time to work out why it was a good idea to have done so.

Some of what I heard at the conference, in particular the interdisciplinary nature of the presentations, encouraged me to believe that environmentalist academics are capable of making a substantial contribution. Not one presentation was "pure" philosophy, science, economics, or law; and while all contained challenging ideas, none was too technical or theoretical. Still, I have two worries. The first is the apparent rejection of technology, especially engineering and science. Listening to some environmentalists, one would never guess that they spend their lives personally recycling nutrients and inorganic chemicals, let alone traveling around in cars and airplanes, producing their papers on word processors, and faxing, e-mailing, or, as a last resort, airmailing photocopies to their friends around the world. Yet if eight to ten billion people are to live anything like happy and sustainable lives on this planet, we will need more and better science and technology, not a retreat from science and technology.

A second worry, about which I will have more to say later, is that environmental ethics as practiced in the United States and Britain, and to a lesser extent in continental Europe and Australia, exhibits a rather disturbing monoculturalism. As a cultural pluralist, I consider the search for a universal environmental ethic that will apply at all places and at all times to be not merely a fantasy but a highly dangerous one. While all environmentalists talk of global problems, they are not always so quick to acknowledge or even notice the possibility of different cultural perspectives on environmental issues. Global problems are frequently no more than aggregated local ones, whose solutions are therefore also local. While it is true that climate change, for instance, is an international problem, it does not follow that it is equally important and pressing to everyone. Nor will its solution necessarily be found by setting up international task forces, which to poor countries will be seen as primarily serving the interests of the rich countries that created most of the world's environmental problems and are now demanding that everyone else stop developing. This is the main reason why there has been so much skepticism in poor countries about the United Nations Commission on Environment and Development Earth Summit. International agreements and institutions, for instance, international mail and telephone systems, work only when they are perceived to be in the interests of all countries. As Udo Simonis argues, we can forget the idea of international agreements on emissions unless all parties can agree on what is fair.

Environmental Ethics or Environmental Philosophy?

My initial reaction to the phrase *new environmental ethics* was that it incorporates a redundancy. Environmental ethics itself is so new that there is no "old" environmental ethics with which to compare. And it is indeed very new. In 1975 I began, tentatively, to introduce into my ethics courses questions about the moral status of animals and whether species, mountains, and ecosystems could be said to have rights. Most of the students—who were more than happy to discuss the ethics of nuclear weapons, racism, sexism, drug use, and so on—were incredulous at these bizarre ideas. Yet, four years later, my new environmental ethics course attracted more than eighty students—and now it has more than two hundred.

Unfortunately—perhaps because of this sudden enthusiasm, but also because they had been influenced by the literature—many students came to the course with a simplistic and romantic view of environmental ethics. They had discovered that there was one dominant paradigm of rapacious exploitation—cowboy, or frontier, ethics—attributable to "the West." There were two alternatives: conservation (later renamed "sustainable development"), and a holistic or land ethic, which was attributed to Aldo Leopold and all "non-Western" societies. Environmental ethics consisted of trashing the dominant paradigm, rejecting conservation because of its anthropocentrism, and advocating a (or *the*) land ethic. It was not necessary to explain with any precision what an environmental ethic actually committed one to doing, though riding bicycles, hiking in the wilderness, and just being glad that Antarctica was still there were very desirable.

The term *environmental ethics* is sometimes said to be a misnomer: Eugene Hargrove (1989b) says it should have been called "environmental philosophy." Ethics does not come into existence without a social, intellectual, and general philosophical context. As Corrado Poli emphasizes, epistemological and ethical questions are fundamentally connected. The focus of interest of disciplines other than philosophy has come to include the environment. Biologists' preoccupation with taxonomy and anatomy has given way to an interest in ecology; economists are recognizing the importance of externalities, especially environmental ones. Moreover, there is a public recognition that unlike earlier generations, we have the power to damage severely the life prospects of our descendants. This is the context in which philosophers have become professionally interested in environmental issues.

Environmental ethics, however, developed in a way different from other areas of ethics. For one thing, many of its practitioners seem to have been attracted because of their (initially nonphilosophical) interest in the protection of wildlife and wild places—in my case, endangered species. Environmental philosophers are often highly specialized, too. The ethical theorists of the past—in the European tradition, Plato, Aristotle, Thomas Hobbes, David Hume, Immanuel Kant, and so on—were each innovators in many branches of philosophy. As a result, their ethical writings are in a clear and explicit context. Hobbes, for instance, begins *Leviathan* by, as it were, setting up the world. The first chapters are devoted to epistemology, metaphysics, philosophy of mind, and philosophy of science; then he tells us about human nature, metaethics, and political, social, and legal philosophy. His account of society and of a particular form of state would make little sense without the context. But the context—the assumptions, the worldview—that lies behind environmental ethics is often not made explicit, so that its philosophers appear to be using either the terms of the standard "Western" account of the world, which many believe is inconsistent with an environmental ethic, or else no discernible context at all. In the long run, successful environmental ethics will need to be part of a wider philosophical position.

As my colleague Michael Fleming has pointed out to me, however, none of this implies that environmental ethics needs a new philosophical base, a whole new philosophy. To assume that it does is to beg what is sometimes considered the central question of anthropocentric versus nonanthropocentric environmental ethics. *If* a completely new ethic is needed, maybe a new philosophy on which to build it is needed as well. If we can deal adequately with ethical questions about the environment from a purely human-centered perspective—as we appear to be doing in professional and business ethics—then maybe we can build on what we have.

Meanwhile, environmental ethicists have endeavored both to build on existing philosophical foundations and to develop alternative approaches such as deep ecology, ecofeminism, and postmodernism. An interesting feature of recent environmental ethics is a sort of eclecticism among philosophers who are broadly within the "Western" tradition but wish to make use of the insights of alternative approaches.

Rather than try to survey and evaluate recent developments in environmental ethics, I have chosen to focus on what I consider to be a promising theme: pluralist alternatives to the standard universalistic approach to ethics. I present some doubts about the ability of environmental ethical theories to influence environmental policy and practice. Finally, I suggest some ways in which philosophers can help promote an environmentally sustainable culture.

Questioning Universalism

The standard, oversimplified metaethical position is that all ethical theories fall into one of two groups, generally labeled (1) universalist, objectivist, or cognitivist; and (2) relativist, subjectivist, or noncognitivist. The first group includes all ethical theories whose main principles are supposed to be knowable and timelessly true and to apply to all situations and relationships: for instance, the theories of Plato, Aristotle, Kant, John Stuart Mill, and George Edward Moore; and among modern environmental philosophers Paul W. Taylor, J. Baird Callicott, and perhaps Christopher Stone and Eugene Hargrove. The second position, represented by the theories of Hobbes, Hume, and most existentialist writers, and falsely attributed by Moore to Mill, is that all ethical principles are no more than individual or aggregated preferences, and there is no sense in which one individual's or society's values is better than any other's: there is no moral progress or regress, only change. Universalists tend to lump together all forms of "mere" (or "rank") relativism as reductionist and nonmoral: "An ethical theory is a theory about how we *ought* to behave. But ultimately neither personal nor cultural relativism deals in 'oughts.' Cultural relativism reduces to a study of what most people in a particular culture approve of, and personal relativism reduces to a study of what individuals feel" (Carroll et al. 1985:9).

If values-as-preferences really were the only alternative to universalism, the relativist position would surely be untenable. Such accounts give no basis for rejecting any value, no matter how hostile to human survival, or accepting any other. Fortunately, however, just as there are several variants of universalism, there are also a number of alternative nonuniversalist positions. Perhaps the single most important feature they have in common is the view that there is no such thing as value in isolation from a perspective: there are Christian, Buddhist, Maori, liberal, and feminist values, but none can claim to be "true" in isolation from Christian or other doctrines as a whole. Stuart Hampshire, who rejects relativism, characterizes it as "the thesis that ways of life . . . are not the subject of moral judgment, because there is no independent ground from which they can be evaluated" (1983:151).

Indeed, to ask whether a value is "true" in this sense is to demand that we "transcend our scheme of justification and try to examine it as a whole from outside," which we cannot do because "there is no point we can occupy from which this scrutiny could take place" (McNaughton 1988:156). Elizabeth Dodson Gray points out that this sort of universalism is implicit in the traditional hierarchical pyramid views of the universe.

To reject universalism is not necessarily to require that ideologies claimed by (some of) their adherents to be universal should be abandoned, since the content of an ideology is logically (and should be psychologically) independent of the extent of its application—like a weather forecast whose accuracy is unaffected by the fact that it applies only to a defined area. What is rejected is the claim to be universal. In this view, Jesus should not have said, "I am the Way"; he is *a* way.

Some critical social theorists, especially postmodernists, go beyond this position. In a violent attack on Jacques Derrida, Richard Rorty, and Jim Cheney, J. Baird Callicott (1990) characterizes their branch of postmodernism as "essentially nihilistic" and likely to lead to a "new dark age . . . a *Realpolitik* of difference in a shattered and fragmented world." He also acknowledges, though without apparent enthusiasm, the claims of "constructive" postmodernism to be a kind of transition to whatever is supposed to replace modernism. In fact, postmodernists seem to me to be doing what philosophers have always been expected to do: they question accepted beliefs and authorities, act as intellectual gadflies, prick the pretensions of elaborate and grandiose theorizing, and continue Locke's enterprise of clearing away rubbish. Perhaps this is somewhat obscured by the extravagant, not to say arrogant, tone of much postmodernist literature.

Stripped of its doomsday language, Callicott's criticism has some validity. As Aristotle (and, dare I say it, the Athenians who judicially murdered Socrates) realized, philosophers who do no more than undermine existing beliefs do not perform a useful service unless they or someone else can come up with something better. Canvas cleaning may be good if a better picture is to be painted, or "negotiated," but it is not clear that postmodernism allows for such judgments.

Ecofeminism, in contrast, has a program that is both critical and positive. In emphasizing the importance of intuition, feelings, and commitment, ecofeminism provides both a corrective to the excessive rationalism that has pervaded philosophy and a new direction. In emphasizing the particular and the personal, ecofeminists have drawn our attention away from the meaningless "big picture" environmental crisis view of the world expressed in (often unknowable) billions of this and remaining years of that. Real environmental problems are the problems of real people, in their ecological, cultural, and interpersonal context. To illustrate: "Only" 1 percent of the earth's water is fresh, so we had better not waste or pollute it. But is 1 percent a little or a lot? "Only" 1 percent of the solar radiation reaching earth is utilized by living things, but this does not seem to inhibit life on earth. An adequate environmental ethics would be primarily concerned with, for instance, the relation between water availability and particular places and organisms, such as the effects of a hydroelectric dam on downstream rural women and wildlife.

Recently, a number of writers have defended "moral pluralism," as distinct from "moral monism." The main criticism to date has come from Callicott (1990). Christopher Stone (1987:13) characterizes monism as follows: "The conventional view of ethics is to put forward a single coherent body of principles . . . and to demonstrate how it guides us through all moral dilemmas more satisfactorily than its rivals."

The ambition of monists is to unify all ethics within a single framework that is capable of yielding the One Right Answer. Moral pluralism, in contrast, invites us to conceive of morality as several distinguishable activities, as partitioned into several distinct frameworks, each governed by distinct principles and logical textures. Thus the analysis of good character might be carried out in a framework different from that of good acts; obligations to future generations, family, or other societies will not necessarily be determined by the same rules. A somewhat similar view is presented quite independently by Andrew Brennan (1988, 1991), who believes both that "different considerations apply in different cases" (1991:28) and that "each case can be viewed from more than one perspective" (1991:30). For instance, the question of whether the killing of bowhead whales is justifiable cannot be answered without reference to context. It makes a difference whether the killers are Inuit people, who have been killing and fully utilizing the products of a small number of whales for centuries, or the commercial fishing fleets of a rich country systematically exterminating whole species to make pet food and candles.

Stone's rejection of monism, however, is universalistic rather than relativistic in the sense that he often writes as if the different principles that are to be used in different frameworks could be appropriate at all times and in all cultures. According to Stone, the pluralist "can hold that there are really (and not relatively) universal right answers to moral quandaries, as immutable as the value of pi" (1987:246).

While he does not commit himself to this view (which, if the choice of analogy is taken seriously, implies that ethical principles are a priori true), he does admit to "much sympathy" for the view "that ethics is committed to seek moral truth, much as, in science, there is a commitment to find scientific truths" (1987:249).

Soon I will present some of my reservations about universalism and sympathetically examine as an alternative a form of cultural pluralism.[1] In rejecting universalism I do not, of course, mean to rule out the possibility that there may turn out to be common elements in many or even all cultures. Humans are organisms with biological needs for which all cultures make provision. Needs can be met in a variety of ways, however, and ecological constraints ensure that successful ways of life differ from place to place. Also, culture provides for much more than biological survival.

As I noted in my introduction to this essay, it is my impression that most of the participants in the "Theory Meets Practice" conference are committed to some form of universalism. Only Yu-shi Mao's essay presents the value of cultural diversity unambiguously. Frank Golley's position, a version of bioregionalism that defines regions both biologically and culturally and in which the knowledge of scientific ecology is likened to the traditional knowledge of successful cultures, also respects culture. But I thought he slightly undermined his position by implying that we might somehow take the best elements of many cultures and construct a global ethic. From which perspective are we to select the best elements? Pessimistically, we may end up with Mexico represented by Taco Bell, Australia by Crocodile Dundee, and Britain by Fergie and Di. More seriously, such a globalized ethic is likely to end up as no more useful than Esperanto, a language that is highly logically structured and therefore easy to learn, but which almost nobody speaks because it is nobody's language.

Universalistic elements that are really just unconscious globalizations of the common elements of the Euro-American cultures are sometimes very subtly and quite unintentionally included. For instance, during Holmes Rolston's otherwise very fine presentation, he presented a video tracing changes in the biosphere. In one corner of the screen was a time line to show which historical periods corresponded with the environmental changes. But while the video was stressing the global nature of environmental change, the time line was entirely Eurocentric: the period labeled "Islamic" referred purely to the centuries of major Islamic influence in Europe; later there were references to "the Middle Ages" and even "the New World."

The United States has become the cultural colonizer that several European nations aspired to be, with consequent destructive effects on indigenous cultures. To illustrate: not many years ago, performances of the traditional *wayang kulit* (shadow puppet) in Java attracted packed houses. When I watched several performances in the large city of Yogyakarta, Java, in late 1991, the audience consisted of a few foreigners and one or two locals. Everyone else, I was told, was at home watching "New Attitude," "The Cosby Show," or "MacGyver" (with Indonesian subtitles), or listening to tapes of Madonna, Megadeath, or the Beastie Boys. Perhaps it is because cultural transfer in recent decades has been largely one-way that universalism is more taken for granted in the United States and former colonial nations of Europe than elsewhere.

Richard Sylvan, a leading advocate of cultural pluralism, sees a need for "we in the Antipodes to break loose from the damaging cultural assumptions and practices of the industrialized North and work towards establishment of a different, less environmentally destructive culture, towards a certain regional autonomy" (1986:1). This would be necessary even if the culture if the North were not "damaging," he thinks, because culture is "a comprehensive social paradigm" (103) that provides social cohesiveness and is "the glue of a group" (108).

It is a truism that human evolution has proceeded mainly by cultural rather than physical change; viewed in evolutionary terms, ethics is simply part of the adaptive behavior that constitutes culture. The fact that a culture exists at all means that it works to some extent. As the anthropologist Colin Turnbull notes: "Culture, as anthropologists define it, is learned behavior and traditions that by and large are adaptive and work towards survival" (1985:176). In this sense all cultures are at least partially successful, just as a short-lived species is partially successful in evolutionary terms. But some cultures are more successful than others—they are sustainable for a longer period just as some species live longer than others. Some cultures are also more resilient than others. Syncretism occurs when cultures are resilient enough to absorb would-be ecumenical movements and make them their own. Thus the forms of Buddhism, for instance, practiced in Japan and Sri Lanka have very little in common. New Zealand Catholic women take the birth control pill at about the same rate as their non-Catholic sisters. The Muslim sultan of Yogyakarta in Java is married symbolically to the sea goddess, and every year on their wedding anniversary, animistic and Hindu-Buddhist offerings are made and ceremonies performed. The Balinese may even be strong enough to cope with that most colonizing of all phenomena, tourism.

Many societies, by contrast, have had cultures that were very successful but not very resilient, frequently because of historical isolation. There seems to be a disturbing parallel between the fates of colonized island fauna and isolated peoples. Notoriously, the transfer of European environmental attitudes and practices to the rest of the world has often destabilized ecologies (Crosby 1986) as much as the imposition of Christianity has disrupted culture in general.

Clashes between cultures might seem to be the inevitable result of the expansion of societies from their original resource base. And so they are, if one of the cultures subscribes to a universal ethic. On a jaundiced view of ethical universalism, it is liable to form the theoretical basis of the activities of cultural imperialists such as missionaries who set out to convert the heathen to the only true faith—the Catholic or British or Maoist or Muslim way of life. E. H. Carr quotes a fine example from Cecil Rhodes: "I contend that we are the first race in the world, and that the more of the world we inhabit, the better it is for the human race" (Carr 1939:76). Mill himself makes it quite clear that the European nations have a mission to bring civilization to the ignorant and unenlightened: "Despotism is a legitimate mode of government in dealing with barbarians, provided the end be their improvement" (Mill 1859 and 1972:73).

Arun Balasubramaniam (1990) argues that such an "ecumenical" approach to one's culture may end up as the theoretical foundations of an ethical imperialism that destroys thriving cultures. Often, all that is left is an inappropriate ersatz version of the now dominant culture that retains only those elements of the original culture that are compatible with the newly globalized paradigm. Brennan similarly (though perhaps inconsistently with the passage quoted earlier) rejects "ethical colonialism, whereby those situated in certain kinds of society, surrounded by certain kinds of goods and activities, declare that they have discovered certain universal truths which do no more than reflect, in a suitably generalized way, their own local aspirations and ideals" (1988:176).

Mill's position, clearly, is that liberal values ought to apply at all times and in all places. In making this universalistic claim, however, Mill may undermine the much more defensible claim that certain rights are historically and (I argue in Gunn 1983) logically tied to a particular view of human nature and society that is central to the broadly liberal democratic tradition and should be defended even at considerable cost and sacrifice. Supposedly universal values avowedly lack any historical, ecological, or cultural context; this is supposed to be their strength, that they do not stand "merely" in relation to a particular context. Yet being rootless, they cannot be defended except by appeal to intuition. In contrast, it may be argued that the anchoring of value to a culture provides the best support for rights.

Within a culture, the natural resource base—individual animals and plants, species, rivers, natural features—is valued. Thus each tribe in New Zealand has its sacred places; for instance, the sacred mountain of a tribe is typically the one that was first seen by the tribe's ancestors on their arrival from the mythical homeland, Hawaiiki. In the case of one tribe, the Ngati-Porou, Mount Hikurangi is doubly valuable since by tradition the ancestral canoe is buried in the crater lake. It is impossible to understand the value of this mountain for the Ngati-Porou without understanding the relevant aspects of their culture, and to ask whether Hikurangi is "really" valuable is as silly as asking whether it is "really" sacred. A mining company that recently proposed to prospect for gold on the mountain saw Hikurangi only as a valuable source of minerals. Although the company proposed to put right any damage by restoration, this was unacceptable to the Ngati-Porou because mining would destroy the mountain's *mana*   its spiritual authority—while the company could do no more than merely restore the physical appearance. Since the Crown, not the landowner, owns mineral rights under New Zealand law, the tribe had to make a case against the granting of prospecting rights. Their main argument in successfully blocking the application was certainly not that mountains (or this one) are objectively and intrinsically valuable, but that Hikurangi is central to their culture and should not be sacrificed to provide short-term gain for outsiders.

It is important to note that adherence to the values of one's culture is not merely a matter of having preferences. As Mark Sagoff (1986) argues, our attachment to equality and opposition to slavery are not merely personal preferences for having the one and not the other: they are commitments to a certain sort of society. They are values of the community into which the individual has been socialized. Bernard Williams (1985) argues that there is a plurality of social worlds, perhaps something like Wittgensteinian forms of life, to each of which different moral principles (or "moral reality") are appropriate. For instance, a samurai warrior's socialization has equipped him to cope in his world but not in ours, and our socialization would not be appropriate to his world. This does not commit us to say that no judgments about the merits of samurai society (or our society) can be made. It does require us to acknowledge that the values of samurai (or our) society should be considered in context.

Some Doubts about Environmental Ethics

If we accept Aristotle's dictum that the end of ethics is not *knowing* but *doing*, it follows that the purpose of environmental ethics is to tell us how to act in respect of the environment.

According to Hargrove, however, "Environmental ethics has as yet had little practical influence on environmental affairs and is unlikely to have much in the immediate future" (1989a:4). In Stone's view, "Part of the problem is that we have yet to establish a clearly defined sense of mission" (1988:139).

When I presented some of the ideas in this essay at a 1991 conference in Sydney, two philosophers in the audience made very perceptive remarks. David Bennett said: "What you're objecting to is that environmental philosophy is *philosophy*." John Passmore commented that what I was objecting to was the scholasticism that, in his view, is the bane of the mainstream Western academic tradition and is now taking over environmental philosophy. Hardly any of the great philosophers of the past were professionals, and their writings are not generally festooned with scholarly references and bibliographies. A work in the style of Ludwig Wittgenstein's *Tractatus* would probably not get published today.

If Passmore is right, the exciting new theories of today will be the bureaucratized dogmas of the next century, complete with vast bodies of literature consisting of replies, rejoinders, commentaries, and, when all else fails, review articles. Though Antonio Gramsci and, in due course, Jacques Derrida may spin in their graves, their self-proclaimed intellectual heirs will exhibit precisely the "colonizing" and "totalizing" that the movement was supposed to prevent. In case this pessimistic prospect proves to be correct, environmental philosophers who want to make a difference to the world had better go to it now, while the field is still young and vigorous.

Unfortunately, too much recent environmental philosophy has been marred by obscurantism, debates about the merits of high-level theories, and romantic and simplistic stereotypes of diverse cultures. A major short-coming of some environmental ethics is that it is written abstractly, some-times in language largely unintelligible to anyone but a handful of scholars. The opening sentence of a recent article in *Environmental Ethics,* a journal intended to be widely accessible, reads, in part: "in the light of postmod-ernist deconstruction of modern totalizing and foundationalist discussion, can we any longer make sense of the idea of privileged discourse?" (Cheney 1989:117). Probably not. In fact, the views presented in the article are timely and interesting, but many readers of *Environmental Ethics,* however well educated and intelligent, are unlikely to get beyond the first sentence.

Much academic environmental debate is unlikely to be very productive for a second reason: the participants often already agree about *what* ought to be done, but they endlessly debate *why* it ought to be done. I am guilty of this myself: I have published articles on rare species protection that largely assume that we ought to preserve species, the "interesting" question being why we should do so (Gunn 1980, 1984).

The academic environmental philosophy movement has been accused of overemphasizing the importance of theory. One critic writes, "There seems to be an important assumption of philosophers that the major problems in environmental ethics are metaethical and normative, and that questions of empirical data are less important" (Lemons 1985:187).

It may be said that the movement has a near obsession with theoretical distinctions, especially oversimplistic distinctions. This is odd, given that environmental philosophers are (rightly) prone to reject rigid, dualistic, either/or approaches to philosophy such as the simplistic distinctions be-tween subjective/objective, meaningful/meaningless, and mind/body. Yet, despite criticisms of such approaches (e.g., Rolston 1982; Callicott 1985; Norton 1986; and Frank Golley, this volume), numerous articles continue to be published defending or assuming sharp distinctions between anthro-pocentric and nonanthropocentric attitudes to nature, between views of nature as intrinsically and instrumentally valuable, between ethical sub-jectivity and ethical objectivity. Arguments rage as to whether the domi-nant paradigm is centrally flawed by anthropocentrism or androcentrism, whether or not we must adopt a Marxist economic analysis before trying to understand environmental problems, and about the respective merits of different cultures (usually arranged by the writers into two classes to suit their own agenda). Thus, for instance, *one* Western, northern, materialistic, developed, colonialist, modernist culture is contrasted with *one* Eastern,

Third World, traditional, tribal, indigenous, aboriginal, spiritual culture. This is not to say that such contrasts cannot be drawn, nor that it is not worthwhile to draw them. What I do want to insist is that, as Descartes should have learned, we cannot build a whole philosophy on a bumper sticker.

At its worst, this approach to ideological mapping is reminiscent of the good guys–bad guys categorization in movies such as *The Green Berets* and *Dances with Wolves*—the virtual identification of such diverse approaches as ecofeminism, postmodernism, deep ecology, and (all?) Native American cultures (see, for instance, Cheney 1989; Booth and Jacobs 1990). The tendency to divide cultures into Western and Eastern is especially unfortunate, for a number of reasons. I shall mention three here.[2]

First, as a recent critic notes, in the writings of many deep ecologists, "complex and internally differentiated religious traditions—Hinduism, Buddhism, and Taoism—are lumped together as holding a view of nature as believed to be quintessential biocentric" (Guha 1989:76). This view of Eastern philosophies (and day-to-day cultural practices) is, he notes, romantic, monistic, and simplistic.

To talk of a monolithic Western culture is equally crass. David Harmon (1987:156) argues that "cultural diversity among modern social groups should be afforded as much recognition as that which is given to the juxtaposition of traditional with modern societies." Moreover, as others such as Mark Sagoff, Eugene Hargrove, Roderick Nash, and Bryan Norton have persuasively argued, the Anglo-American tradition is a rich cultural resource for environmentalism.

A second reason for rejecting the simplistic distinction is that it does not fit the facts. As Harmon notes, "When people involved in the management of protected areas use these terms [traditional, native, and indigenous], the distinction they seem to want to make is between those who live harmoniously (in a strictly ecological sense) with their immediate environment and those who don't. In the current management literature it is too often presumed that traditional societies, native peoples, and indigenous peoples do; modern societies, colonists, and other non-indigenous peoples don't" (1987:156).

Third, the alternative models presented for our emulation are often unrealistic. Granted, people in industrialized countries live a wasteful, unsustainable life-style, which they need to change, but most do not want to become subsistence hunter-gatherers, nor are they equipped to do so. Admiration of a greatly simplified low-entropy life-style has been characterized as typically a "postaffluent" phenomenon. "Only those who have been reared in affluent suburbs can rebel against over-consumption and the banality of materialism" (Faramelli 1973:191). In contrast, a welfare rights organizer, speaking to a group of young ecology radicals, notes: "We will have some difficulty understanding one another, for our welfare mothers want what you are rejecting" (quoted in Faramelli 1973:191).

People in poor countries often see environmentalists from rich countries as deluded romantics, sometimes with good reason. For instance, most Southeast Asians are more at home in villages, towns, and cities than in a rain forest; 300–400 of the 9,000 Penan of Sarawak are probably the only hunter-gatherers remaining in Asia. Human beings around the world generally seek a reasonably secure and comfortable life, increasingly a "Westernized" life-style. Whether this is good for them in the opinion of philosophers is irrelevant. If it is what people actually want, it is what they will pursue. The challenge is not to preach the virtues of the simple life but to discover and support ways of living that enable both human flourishing and ecological stability.

Making Ourselves Useful

I argued earlier that we philosophers should be shifting our emphasis away from highly theoretical and abstract analysis and theory construction and toward problem solving. There are two reasons why this is not only desirable but a positive duty. The first is the urgency of environmental problems. Solving many of the issues with which academics deal—the four-color problem, the origins of the Japanese people, the function of the megaliths on Easter Island—is not very pressing. But even though the "last decade" rhetoric of 1970 has worn thin, it is clear that we do not have long to save the world.

The second reason is that, at least at the popular level, it is often very easy to reach agreement on very abstract and impersonal questions, but it becomes progressively more difficult to get people to agree on specific policies to implement the theories. An interesting example was presented at a conference on waste management:

Do we [Australians] all agree that wastes should be minimized?
Do we all agree that not all wastes can be effectively recycled?
Do we all agree that we need to treat intractable wastes?
Do we all agree that there is a need for a high-temperature incinerator?

Do we all agree that the incinerator should be located in New South
    Wales?
Do we all agree that the incinerator should be located in or near
    Sydney?
Do we all agree that the incinerator should be located at suburb X?

It is easy enough to construct other environmental examples, such as
going from "Do we all agree that environmental collapse should be prevented?" to "Do we all agree that we should stop using private cars?" or
"Do we all agree that this pulp mill should close down?"

Whether we think that (for instance) the ozone layer or an endangered
species is intrinsically or only instrumentally valuable will not matter when
it comes to the formation and implementation of policy. What matters
is that we *do* accept that they are valuable and that we do something to
protect them. It does not matter whether we do so because we think that
species are valuable as the children of the god Tane, as the Maori believe,
or as natural kinds (Rescher 1980) or because they are a useful source of
materials and energy (Myers 1983) or as aesthetic and scientific resources
(Ehrlich and Ehrlich 1981) or as environmental indicators (Russow 1981).
And the reason why it does not matter is that the need for environmentally sustainable policies is overdetermined: there are many reasons, each
of which on its own is sufficient.

I suggest that we act as if the following points had been settled:

Ecological processes and their maintenance are very valuable, if any-
    thing is, and their protection is the highest priority. Whether this is
    because humans need them to survive or for their own sake does not
    matter.
Humans and nature are interrelated: we have a right to be here as well
    as an obligation not to destroy ecological processes.
There is no one environmentally correct way of doing things; different
    ways of life are appropriate for different environments. Even if there
    were one correct way there would be no time to convince everyone
    to adopt it. Therefore we must mobilize *existing* local and regional
    cultural resources in support of ecologically sound policies.

I believe that, as philosophers, we have an obligation to make ourselves
useful in our professional practices. Perhaps philosophers studying environmental problems cannot help philosophizing about them, nor should
we try to do so. As I noted earlier, ecofeminists and others such as War-

wick Fox have drawn our attention to the excessive rationalism of much Western philosophy. Still, reasoning is central to philosophy, just as observation is central to science; and philosophers have an obligation to subject opinions to rational examination. This is a *professional* obligation, incidentally, both because we are experts at this and because it is in the public interest that we do so.

We do need an environmental ethic, in the sense that we need to incorporate environmental sustainability into our culture. The purpose of a culture is the flourishing of its members and of whatever they think is significant. What counts as flourishing and significant will depend on the culture's beliefs and values; there have been many successful cultures. The success of a culture depends in the long term on its staying within the resources available to it. Thus on one level it is absurd to compare the very different cultures of the people of the Nullabor, Kiribati, the Aleutians, or Sarawak, or to expect that people in Wellington, New Zealand, will find anything there to emulate. On a different level, though, and perhaps this is part of what Frank Golley meant, all successful cultures do have a great deal in common. They do not do the same things, nor do they hold the same or even similar beliefs. They do share a match, a fit between their culture—their beliefs, attitudes, technology—and where they live. This does not mean that Wellingtonians, for instance, should all go back to living as the pre-European Maori did. It does mean that they should ensure that their way of life is as compatible with long-term flourishing as was that of the traditional Maori. Their life may include computer terminals and compact disc players powered by hydroelectricity; it will not include dumping milliscreened sewage, as at present, into the harbor, or driving one ton of car to the corner store to buy one liter of milk—a process that is less than 0.1 percent efficient.

Philosophers can contribute to the development of an environmentally sustainable culture. While much of what follows may seem obvious to ethicists, it is certainly not obvious to everyone, as a glance at the letters page of any local newspaper will show. Philosophers can challenge the assumptions of those who profess to think that there is no environmental problem. Often, it is enough to make those assumptions explicit and analyze them. For instance, in New Zealand as in the United States, mining companies, foresters, and people who want to drain wetlands still maintain that "a balance must be struck between environmental protection and development." Of course. But a balance is achieved when the scales end up equal. What we have is a gross *imbalance* because most of the forest has already been logged, and the wetlands drained. If we want to achieve a balance, we should immediately stop logging and draining and start restoring—that is all that "achieving a balance" could possibly mean in this context. Pointing this out does not make miners, loggers, and drainers go away, of course, but at least it should remove some of the garments of righteousness they have assumed. Also, as Aristotle noted, some things cannot be balanced. There is no compromise between exterminating and saving a species, mining and not mining a sacred mountain, constructing a hydroelectric dam and maintaining a wild river.

Bad arguments against environmentally sound action abound, especially where proposed changes require that people give up something they are used to. For instance, a crude short-term consequentialism often forms the basis of claims that there is no point in changing our environmentally destructive behavior because it will not make any difference. Suppose I gain considerable pleasure from driving long distances at high speeds on deserted roads in a classic Mustang and taking a nightly soak in winter in an outdoor Jacuzzi—which I admit I would, were the opportunity available. Or, more prosaically, suppose that I enjoy reading many newspapers and magazines that I discard with the trash because there is no convenient way to recycle them in my community. Clearly my life-style is environmentally damaging, yet there seems to be no point in denying myself these pleasures, because that would have next to no effect on the environment. Similar arguments are sometimes presented against ethical vegetarianism, to the effect that small changes in demand do not affect the supply of mass-produced products such as chickens, so by giving up eating chicken I do not prevent any animal suffering at all.

Arguments, or unstated assumptions, of this kind are extremely common. Philosophers should undertake to undermine them, both among their circle of acquaintances and publicly. My favorite counterexample is that if making a difference is all that matters I might as well make good money selling crack outside my local high school, since if I do not, someone else will and the supply will be the same. Environmentally damaging activities, like drug peddling, can also be questioned on the basis of virtue ethics: what sort of person does not care whether he or she wastes natural resources or destroys the lives of adolescents? Is that the kind of person you want to be?

It can also be pointed out that acting ethically is not just a matter of private behavior change. As Peter Singer (1975) points out, the ethical vegetarian does not merely stop eating animal products; he or she should be endeavoring to create a movement, urging supermarkets and restaurants to cater to vegetarians, lobbying government, and so on. Also, as Kristin Shrader-Fréchette notes, behavior can have a symbolic or demonstration effect that stirs the complacent to thought. Here again, a crude analysis of the direct costs and benefits will not suffice to evaluate the desirability of a change. The costs to New Zealand of its policies of banning all nuclear weapons and nuclear-powered vessels from its land and territorial waters and vigorously opposing French nuclear testing in the South Pacific include an act of state terrorism by France in blowing up the Greenpeace flagship *Rainbow Warrior* in Auckland, in which a crew member was killed, and years of cool relations with the United States government, estimated to have cost hundreds of millions of dollars in lost trade. Still, without wishing to appear self-righteous, the vast majority of New Zealanders believe that these policies are examples of responsible policy. Individuals can do the same, often at much higher cost, like the Buddhist monks who immolated themselves during the Vietnam War. Of course, the one carrying out the demonstration action can never know what, if anything, it will achieve.

We can also contribute to clarifying and arguing for concepts and values that are central to an environmentally sustainable culture. For instance, in New Zealand law, *intrinsic value* is not defined, even though it is a key term in statutes such as the Resource Management Act (1991). Curiously, that act defines terms such as *aircraft* and *working day* even though everyone knows what they mean. In law, an undefined term is to be understood in its ordinary sense. There is no ordinary sense of *intrinsic value,* which is a term of art, yet its interpretation will be crucial in making policy and eventually before the courts when planning decisions are challenged. The view of the powerful New Zealand Treasury Department, as I understand it, is that all values are preferences, like tastes in flavors of ice cream, and that all preferences count equally. If this is accepted, the right policy is the one that is supported by the most preferences, whether measured by numbers, loudness, or willingness to pay. But if there is such a thing as intrinsic value, it will not be reducible to preferences. Philosophers can help here. As I noted earlier, Mark Sagoff (1986) has argued clearly and persuasively for a distinction between values and preferences, not just theoretically but in the context of policymaking. Warwick Fox, who has contributed enormously to our understanding of value positions in the context of which intrinsic value might be understood, has conducted influential workshops for the New Zealand Ministry for the Environment. I myself have endeavored to characterize intrinsic value in a New Zealand context in a report commissioned by the New Zealand Department of Conservation and at planning hearings as an expert witness.

Most important, as Ignazio Musu stresses, is education. In particular, we philosophers can expand our work with environmental professionals and laypeople. We should be able to emulate medical ethics, whose success in New Zealand and elsewhere is attributable partly to the willingness of applied ethicists to get involved, to work with (not preach at) health care professionals and the community. The result is a strong ethics input to professional education and practice via ethics courses in medical and nursing degrees, hospital ethics committees, and so on. As well as working on projects with environmental groups and professionals, philosophers should be pushing for ethics courses to be part of the education of environmental professionals such as engineers, planners, and architects.

Finally: an environmental ethic will work if it is both widely accepted and integrated into everyday life. Several Maori people whom I have consulted tell me that (insofar as one can generalize about Maori culture) they never had an environmental ethic, in the sense of a special set of environmental values, additional to their other values. Sustainability was just integral to their way of life. Environmental awareness and responsibility should equally not be restricted to a small group of Greenies, nor should it be something that we all do, but only on Sundays.

NOTES

Most of this essay was written during short periods of sabbatical leave spent at the National University of Singapore and the University of Georgia. Grateful thanks are due to Peter Hartel and Jean Billingsly of the Department of Agronomy and Frederick Ferré of the Department of Philosophy, all at Georgia, and to Goh Swee Teh, Arun Balasubramaniam, and Padmasiri de Silva of the Department of Philosophy, Singapore, for their hospitality and helpful comments.

1 Since the conference I have had the opportunity to read Bryan Norton's (1991) *Toward Unity among Environmentalists,* in which he makes, more elegantly, some of the points I raise about cultural pluralism.

2 The next four paragraphs are a much abbreviated version of a section in my paper "Environmental Ethics and Tropical Rainforests: Should Greens Have Standing?" *Environmental Ethics* 16 (1994).

REFERENCES

Balasubramaniam, Arun. 1990. "Traditional and Modern Cultures: A Marriage of Cultures or Holy Matrimony?" Paper presented at International Philosophy Congress on Traditional Cultures, Philosophy and the Future, Jakarta, January.

Booth, Annie L., and Harvey L. Jacobs. 1990. "Ties That Bind: Native American Beliefs as a Foundation for Environmental Consciousness." *Environmental Ethics* 12:27–43.

Brennan, Andrew. 1988. *Thinking about Nature.* Athens: University of Georgia Press.

———. 1991. "Moral Pluralism and the Environment." *Environmental Values* 1:15–33.

Callicott, J. Baird. 1985. "Intrinsic Value, Quantum Theory, and Environmental Ethics." *Environmental Ethics* 7:257–77.

———. 1990. "The Case Against Moral Pluralism." *Environmental Ethics* 12:99–124.

Carr, E. H. 1939. *The Twenty Years Crisis.* 2d ed. London: Macmillan, 1962.

Carroll, Mary Ann, et al. 1985. *Ethics in the Practice of Psychology.* Englewood Cliffs, N.J.: Prentice-Hall.

Cheney, Jim. 1989. "Postmodern Environmental Ethics: Ethics as Bioregional Narrative." *Environmental Ethics* 11:117–34.

Crosby, Alfred W. 1986. *Ecological Imperialism: The Biological Expansion of Europe, 900–1900.* New York: Cambridge University Press.

Ehrlich, Paul, and Anne Ehrlich. 1981. *Extinction.* New York: Random House.

Faramelli, Norman J. 1973. "Ecological Responsibility and Economic Justice." In *Western Man and Environmental Ethics,* ed. Ian G. Barbour, 188–203. Reading, Mass.: Addison Wesley.

Fox, Warwick. 1991. *Towards a Transpersonal Ecology.* Boston: Shambala.

Gary, Romain. 1974. Introduction to his *Vanishing Species.* New York: Time-Life.

Guha, Ramachandra. 1989. "Radical American Environmentalism and Wilderness Preservation: A Third World Critique." *Environmental Ethics* 11:71–83.

Gunn, Alastair S. 1980. "Why Should We Care about Rare Species?" *Environmental Ethics* 2:17–37.

———. 1983. "Traditional Ethics and the Moral Status of Animals." *Environmental Ethics* 5:133–53.

———. 1984. "Preserving Rare Species." In *Earthbound,* ed. Tom Regan. New York: Random House.

———. 1994. "Environmental Ethics and Tropical Rainforests: Should Greens Have Standing?" *Environmental Ethics* 16:21–40.

Hampshire, Stuart. 1983. *Morality and Conflict.* Cambridge: Harvard University Press.

Hargrove, Eugene. 1989a. *Foundations of Environmental Ethics.* Englewood Cliffs, N.J.: Prentice-Hall.

Harmon, David. 1987. "Cultural Diversity, Human Subsistence, and the National Park Ideal." *Environmental Ethics* 9:156–57.

———. 1989b. "The Future Is Now." *Environmental Ethics* 11:291–92.

Lemons, John. 1985. A Reply to "On Reading Environmental Ethics." *Environmental Ethics* 7:185–88.

McNaughton, David. 1988. *Moral Vision.* Oxford: Basil Blackwell.

Meine, Curt. 1988. *Aldo Leopold.* Madison: University of Wisconsin Press.

Mill, John Stuart. [1859] 1972. *On Liberty.* London: J. M. Dent.

Myers, Norman. 1983. *The Primal Source.* Boulder: Westview Press.

Nash, Roderick. 1989. *The Rights of Nature: A History of Environmental Ethics.* Madison: University of Wisconsin Press.

Norton, Bryan. 1986. "Conservation and Preservation: A Conceptual Rehabilitation." *Environmental Ethics* 8:195–220.

Rescher, Nicholas. 1980. "Why Save Endangered Species?" In *Unpopular Essays on Technological Progress.* Pittsburgh: University of Pittsburgh Press.

Rolston, Holmes, III. 1982. "Are Values in Nature Subjective or Objective?" *Environmental Ethics* 4:125–51.

Russow, Lily-Marlene. 1981. "Why Do Species Matter?" *Environmental Ethics* 3:101–12.

Sagoff, Mark. 1974. "On Preserving the Natural Environment." *Yale Law Journal* 81:205–67.

———. 1986. "Values and Preferences." *Ethics* 96:301–16.

Singer, Peter. 1975. *Animal Liberation.* New York: Avon Books.

Stone, Christopher D. 1987. *Earth and Other Ethics: The Case for Moral Pluralism.* New York: Harper and Row.

———. 1988. "Moral Pluralism and the Course of Environmental Ethics." *Environmental Ethics* 10:139–54.

Sylvan, Richard. 1986. "Culture and the Roots of Political Divergence." Research School of Social Sciences, Australian National University.

Turnbull, Colin. 1985. "Cultural Loss Can Foreshadow Extinction." In *Animal Extinctions,* ed. R. J. Hoage, 175–92. Washington, D.C.: Smithsonian Institute Press.

Williams, Bernard. 1985. *Ethics and the Limits of Philosophy.* Cambridge: Harvard University Press.

HOLMES ROLSTON III

Winning and Losing in Environmental Ethics

No evil can come to a good man.—Socrates, *Apology*

Can and should humans win or lose when they do the right thing caring for nature—for animals, wildflowers, endangered species, old-growth forests? That simple question has a multidimensional answer. Reaching back into the philosophical past, remember that Socrates said that no evil can come to a good man. But Socrates evidently was wrong, since good persons suffer nearly all the misfortunes of ordinary people, and sometimes they even suffer as a result of their goodness. Was not Socrates, himself a good man, condemned to death? Still, aphorisms can be true in ways not at first evident. Socrates claimed to know with certainty that good people do not lose.[1]

Winning Wrong and Losing Right?

In environmental ethics, many of us hold two beliefs, typically present in some cognitive dissonance. First, we think that values are in conflict. What some gain, others lose; decisions are a win-lose game. Economists routinely calculate costs versus benefits. They ask about opportunity costs. If one uses a consumable resource one way, one cannot use it another way. One cannot eat a piece of pie twice. Either a tract is timbered or made wilderness for recreation, not both. Either a wetland is drained and plowed as farmland or is left as wetland for waterfowl hunting, not both. Life is always an economics of value gain and value loss. There must be winners and losers among the humans who are helped or hurt by the condition of their environment.

Also, humans can gain or lose vis-à-vis nature. When we cut down a forest to gain timber and make a plowed field, the fauna and flora lose; humans gain. How much of the time should humans win—all of the time or only part of the time? We cannot lose all of the time, but, at the other extreme, we may also hold that humans ought not always and invariably be the winners. There must be a net gain for humans if we are to flourish, but that tenet still allows that humans can and ought sometimes to constrain their behavior for the good of plants and animals.

Second, in tension with this value conflict, we also believe that it is really in our human self-interest to conserve a decent environment. If we really get it right there need be no win-lose solutions. Norwegian prime minister Gro Harlem Brundtland, speaking for the United Nations Commission on Environment and Development, called for "a new holistic ethic in which economic growth and environmental protection go hand-in-hand around the world." [2] Caring properly for the natural world can combine with a strategy for sustainability, a win-win solution. A bumper sticker reads: Re-cycling: Everyone wins. That is almost an aphoristic model for the whole human-nature relationship. If we are in harmony with nature, everyone wins.

The Science Advisory Board of the Environmental Protection Agency concludes in a report that "although natural ecosystems—and the linkages among them—are not completely understood, there is no doubt that over time the quality of human life declines as the quality of natural ecosystems declines." [3] This is the entwined destinies view.

If we consult Socrates with these puzzles in mind, it might seem that he does not offer much help. For he is not talking about winning or losing environmental goods. He is about to die; his attention is on his own character. He is focusing too inwardly. Whoever wrongs another person always damages his own well-being more than his victim's. Socrates claims that the only true harm befalls one's character—he calls this "the soul"—and, at that focus, doing the wrong thing ruins the soul, the worst result imaginable. Doing the right thing ennobles the soul, beyond which there is nothing higher to be won. We should attach the highest value not to living but to living well, which is to live honorably and justly. [4]

Socrates seems to be claiming that doing the right thing brings such a great benefit that even if considerable other harms come as a result, the just

person never loses. No accumulation of resulting harms can weigh nega-
tively more than doing the right thing weighs positively. Doing the right
thing gains an *arete,* an excellence, a virtue, and gaining that more than
compensates for other losses, such as one might suffer in business, political,
or social affairs. But has this much promise for environmental ethics?

No net loss comes to those who do right if they place a high enough
value on doing right. If so, it is impossible to lose by doing right. This is the
high-character-gain–no-net-loss view. But it is not just the doing right that
is valued; the act itself is valued because it brings good to the character.
Justice pays off with excellence. So this is a noble-soul view. The result is
a virtue ethics. Virtue is its own reward. That might work in environmental ethics; people who do the right thing by environmental conservation
are better people. On top of the benefits of a wise use of resources there
comes a still higher excellence: personal satisfaction in having done the
right thing. That is so true that even in some cases in which humans lose
by a reckoning that counts only their consumption of goods, the character
benefit means that the "losers" have gained something far better than they
lost.[5] Environmental ethics pays off.

But now we begin to wonder about motivations. We are uncomfortable
with saying "good ethics is good business" and stopping at that. We may
think that good ethics and good business are compatible enough; but still,
if I have good ethics only because it is good for business, because it pays off,
then am I not being more prudent than moral? Extrapolating, we can now
say: Doing the right thing environmentally, you may not gain in business
at all. But you will gain elsewhere more than you lose in business. There is
still a payoff. Winning soul has become the determinative thing, although
gains to nature are closely coupled with gains to the high soul. Gains to
nature are always gains to the lofty character—win-win. Why be moral?
Because it offers the best chance for happiness.

Perhaps what we need is a paradoxical view. We must lose to gain, gain
to lose. The high-character-gain–no-net-loss view is too shallow; there is a
paradox at the heart of morality. We really ought to sacrifice self for others,
and when we do this without expectation of further reward, a surprising thing happens. We are, in fact, blessed in return. Those who care for
others find that these caring relationships bring meaning to life. One cannot care for others in order to gain reward, looking for stars in one's crown,
but neither can one care for others selflessly without being rewarded. So
we would have to crack a paradox to lose and win at the same time in
environmental ethics.

Let us try another account—the winning right account. In the course of learning morality, we come to be corrected from a misperception. One wins because one gets his or her values right. The issue is not trade-off, nor is it paradox; it is error correction. The loser will be worse off by his lights, but his lights are wrong; and if he or she gets things in the right light, there is no loss, only gain. We can couple this with another of Socrates' startling beliefs: that those who do wrong do so involuntarily because they act in ignorance.[6] It doesn't do any good to win if one is wrong, and the win isn't a win. One can't win wrong. Really, one can only win right.

Let us take an example from southern history. Suppose the South had won the Civil War: slavery would have continued, the United States would have been weakened and fragmented, and industrial development would have lagged. And the South would not be anywhere close to the prosperous society that exists today, where whites and blacks have more genuine and more productive relationships, trade flourishes, people are autonomous, human rights are defended, and so on. The South may have lost the war, but it did not really lose, because the war was wrong. When the right thing was done, things turned out win-win in the long term.

Similarly with the liberation of women. Some men lost job opportunities; others have to do housework they did not have to do before. Males lost their dominance, they lost power. But relationships are now more just and humane; male-female interpersonal relationships are more genuine. The talents and skills of women, formerly often wasted, now are more fully utilized in the work force; family incomes are higher, marriages are richer, and so on. Males have much to gain if women are liberated—far more than they have to lose—and what they have to lose ought to be lost because it is chauvinistic.

There is a parallel in environmental ethics. The person reforms, re-forms his or her values. In reformation of soul, focus shifts from its own excellence and is refocused on environmental values. Such a soul is ennobled, but it is not ennobled alone and isolated; it is ennobled just as it is reconnected into a larger value web. The soul knows its ecology.

Redefining Winning

Some will protest that we insist that humans can win but then we redefine winning, change the rules of the game while the game is in progress. We win by moving the goalposts. That is cheating, like showing a net positive balance in your checkbook by revising the multiplication tables. You will win by losing at the old game and then playing a new game. Some persons did lose, in the sense that losing had when this argument started. They lost timber or opportunities for development or jobs. But when *winning* is redefined, they do not lose. Reevaluating, they gain character excellence. That does not establish anything true about the world; it is just a redecision about how to use words.

Yes, you do have to move the goalposts to win. That might be cheating if the game is football, and the two teams have agreed on where the goals are. The goals are arbitrary. But in environmental ethics, there is a disanalogy. You move the goalposts because you discover that they are in the wrong place. And that is really to win, because getting to the wrong goal is not winning but losing. You have more ability to value. You find more values in the natural world than you did before. You stop exploiting nature and become a member of a human and a biotic community residing on a richer, more meaningful earth.

The person who is doing the wrong thing will, quite likely, not think that it is the wrong thing. Socrates was sure that the person doing the wrong thing thinks that decision and action are the right things. Whoever acts in a way that jeopardizes species must think that the action does not really jeopardize species, or, if jeopardy is known, that there are overriding considerations. The members of the Denver Water Board must have thought something like this when they spent large amounts of money, energy, and time trying to build the Two Forks Dam, even though it might have jeopardized the whooping cranes and the sandhill cranes as well as the Pawnee montane skipper. Loggers who press to cut more old-growth forest in the Pacific Northwest must think something like this. The action must seem good to the person who does it. One way or another, the person has calculated what seems right and expects to win.

If such a person is wrong, the goalposts, since they are misperceived, will have to be moved. But that is not cheating to win, that is facing up to the truth: what was before thought to be winning is losing. Consider the Pacific Northwest. There will be some losers, in the sense that some people will have to change jobs. They will, meanwhile, come to reside in a community that is stable in its relationship with the forests in which it is embedded, and that makes them winners. They once lived in a community with a worldview that saw the great forests of the Northwest as a resource to be taken possession of, exploited. But that is not an appropriate worldview; it sees nature as a commodity for human gratification and nothing else. The idea of winning is to consume, the more the better. When the goalposts are moved, these "losers" at the exploitation game will come to live in a community with a new worldview, that of a sustainable relationship with the forested landscape, and that is a new idea of winning. What they really lose is what it is a good thing to lose: an exploitative attitude toward forests. What they gain is a good thing to gain: a land ethic.

Or take the Denver Water Board. They believed that their dam project would not jeopardize the whooping crane, but it would have. They believed that their dam, with its life of fifty years, was more important than the whooping crane, which has lived here five million years and might continue another million, if unperturbed or restored by humans. But they were wrong. They lost the Two Forks decision; the dam they proposed as a good thing, to supply more water to Denver and its suburbs, will not be built. They lost their case; they lost the water.

So what do they now have? They have the opportunity to introduce conservation measures—recycling water, reducing water on lawns, switching from bluegrass to native grasses, curbing water-intensive industries. They have to turn to agricultural water saved from improved agricultural techniques. And, of course, they—those on the board and Denverites and Coloradans—have the Two Forks Canyon in all its splendor, available for recreation. Now, did those who fought *for* the dam really lose? They lost the dam, but the dam was a loser anyway. And when one loses a loser, one really wins.

A dynamic rather than a static view of interests is necessary to decide whether we win or lose. Our desires change over time, are shaped and reshaped by the affiliations of our careers. The goalposts are constantly moving. Values won are as prospective as retrospective. It may take a decade or two to know whether one won or lost, because interests and values shift over time. In a society that is already perhaps the wealthiest in the world, environmental integrity is likely to become ever more valuable. Chances are, those who lost an opportunity for development really won natural values they, their children, and their grandchildren will cherish.

Self-interest, Self-transformation, and Altruism

A win-win ethics is not much ethics at all, because to be self-interested in a trade-off is not to be particularly ethical; it is simply to be prudent. No doubt there are win-win situations, and these are to be delighted in, but they are not ethical situations. If I purchase a new car, I get what I want (the car), the automobile salesman gets what he wants (my $12,000), and we are both happy. The deal is a good thing, but it is not an action in which either of us is to be praised for our charity, or even our morality, though the trade does require a minimal honest dealing.

Philosophers' protest that ethics is not really ethics until one is prepared to lose in the cause of justice is likely to be met by a counterprotest from biologists that a loser ethics is biologically impossible. We are often told by biologists that humans are full of selfish genes; they are constituted by human nature to act in terms of self-interest. It is easily shown that such self-interest can lead to several kinds of cooperation. Such reciprocal altruism is really disguised self-interest, enlightened by the facts of mutual support in culture. And when we learn our ecology, we will act further to save our environment and thereby to save ourselves. But humans cannot act as real losers—unless by mistake.

After the biologists, economists are ready enough to add their weight to the gathering insistence, against ethicists, that humans cannot really be expected to behave as losers in the economies in which they operate. Indeed, the very definition of a *rational* person, as an economist uses this term, is one who acts to maximize self-interest. For example, we expect that persons will earn the most money they can and get the most possible for what they spend. It is irrational to do otherwise. The economy is fueled by persons acting in intelligent self-interest. No economy can work if people are intent on being losers. No ethics can expect people to be steady losers; that flies in the face of what people have to do to eat, clothe themselves, put shelter over their heads, and look after their offspring.

Nor ought an ethics expect them to lose. If one wants to get people to do the right thing, one must give them incentives. If one wants them to do the right thing by way of saving endangered species or recycling their wastes or controlling their pollutants, one must make it to their advantage to do these right behaviors, otherwise failure is certain. Probably one can persuade a few people to do these things out of charity some of the time, but if one wishes to elicit these behaviors from most of the people most of the time, people must be allowed to do right by themselves at the same time that they do right by the environment. It will have to be a win-win situation.

In reply to this portrait of humans as constitutionally self-interested winners, environmental ethicists take three somewhat divergent routes; they move the goalposts to somewhat different locations. The first position transforms winning by satisfying self-interest to winning by self-transformation. The once-isolated self, defending itself against the community it inhabits, is reenvisioned, extended, so that the self is smeared out in the community. By the account of deep ecology and Arne Naess, when the self realizes its wide "identification" with others, "we must see the vital needs of ecosystems and other species as our own needs; there is thus no conflict of interests. It is a tool for furthering one's own realisation and fullness of life. . . . So, if we progress far enough, the very notion of 'environment' becomes unnecessary." "Self-realization" is indistinguishable from "self-realization for all beings!"[7]

That is an interesting win-win situation. The self wins by enlarging itself to include all other selves, or, put another way, the self becomes indistinguishable from other selves. This is said to follow a principle of ecology that everything is what it is not in isolation, but where it is, integrated into its community. Interdependence is more true than independence. Although it appeals to a holistic ecology, this position is also a metaphysical monism or holism, and it often has a decidedly religious flavor, perhaps that of a pantheistic naturalism or an Eastern nondualism. Whether or not one adopts this position all the way, enlarging the self does seem to be moving in the right direction. If we add ecology to genetics, biology is just as insistent that selves are what they are in the web of their communities as they are full of selfish genes.

Now it is becoming hard to say, however, exactly where the goalposts are. We discover that the self is so enlarged that there is no longer any environment. Environmental ethics has made the environment unnecessary! Perhaps we should say that the environment has won, since the self is enlarged into it and all selves are realized. Perhaps we should wonder whether the environment wins if it becomes unnecessary. Winning and losing are not terms that have much meaning if we cannot distinguish self from other.

The second kind of win-win self-transformation is the self-ennobled view, an environmental virtue ethics. The world remains a plural contest of values. Though humans must win often enough to have their vital needs met, they can and ought to behave with caring concern for fauna and flora because the result is that they become quite excellent humans. With an elevated idea(l) of human excellence, we win. We reply to the selfish-gene biologist and to the rational self-interested economist that there is yet a further, philosophical concept of self, the Socratic self, that wishes character above all else. Excellence can best be gained by doing the right thing in environmental ethics. So environmental ethics is really self-actualizing; it is the pursuit of human excellence, if we get our goalposts right. There will be only winners, excellent winners.

On a no-lose–high-soul account, the environmentally virtuous person seems to be valuing natural things for what they are in themselves, but in the end the primary value sought turns out to be human excellence. But if all value of and in nature is derived from the virtuous actions of human agents, then nature is, after all, a kind of moral resource. This does not sound any more like such a high-souled account. It seems unexcellent—cheap and philistine, in fact—to say that excellence of human character is what we are after when we preserve endangered species. We want virtue in the beholder. Is value in the species a just tributary to that? Excellence of human character does indeed result from a concern for these species, but if this excellence of character really comes from appreciating otherness, then why not value that otherness in wild nature first? Let the human virtue be tributary to that.

There are various intrinsic goods that the self desires and pursues in relation to others that are not self-states of the person who is desiring and pursuing. These are satisfactions of which I will speak in a moment. The preservation of the bald eagle is not covertly a cultivation of human excellences; the life of the eagles is the overt value defended. An enriched humanity results, with values in the eagles and values in persons compounded—but only if the loci of value are not confounded.

Both of the responses discussed above—concerning the totally enlarged self and the greatly ennobled self—are troublesome even in principle. They could be even more troublesome in practice, since there would have to be widespread self-reformation for the environmental crisis to be solved. Either movement would have to become popular enough to make a difference, and that seems unlikely. One must not say, of course, that an ethics has to be popular to be right; to the contrary, ethics has often set ideals that are only partially attainable. It may be that there are such win-win ideals and that a few high-souled persons attain such character, but now the win problem shifts. Winning requires success that is attainable by only a very few persons. Most of the members of the Denver Water Board, most timber operators in the Pacific Northwest, and most ordinary citizens will remain ordinary selves interested both in taking care of themselves and in doing right by the environment. What can we say about them?

We cannot expect people to be steady losers, but neither must we expect them to be aggrandizing maximizers. Self-interest is not the only rule in the game, though it is one of the indispensable rules. It may be, for instance, that self-interest is satisfied with "enough" (the root, etymologically, of *satis-faction*), and that thereafter, with enough for self, self becomes more interested in its relations with others, in the community the self inhabits and from which it increasingly draws meanings and further satisfactions. In this community, "right" relations are what is most satisfying, though they need no longer add to personal property accumulations.

That brings us to a third response to the question of whether the self wins or loses, to another way of combining self-interest, self-transformation, and altruism. This is the satisfied-self view. The world remains plural; the self does not dissolve in it. The self is interested in excellence, but that is not the only determinant of behavior. The self finds its satisfactions, first, in capturing enough values from the natural world to have vital needs met, to be prosperous; that is a consumer self. Second, the self finds satisfaction in meaningful relations with the cultural world that the self inhabits as citizen, and also with the natural world in which the self resides. This is the communitarian self. Winning involves more than one set of goalposts. People do continue to shift goalposts. Human development reaches levels where we say "Enough!" and shift our value focus, because to win more of what we already have enough of is not to win any more. To the contrary, it is to begin to lose.

This view of human nature does not require that persons lose self-identity in the monistic whole, or even that they be particularly excellent, high-souled individuals. Nor does it see them as full of selfish genes and nothing more. Human nature has multiple satisfactions, multiple values that the person can take an interest in defending, multiple goalposts on the field of play. There are multiple natural values in which humans can and ought to take an interest. The possibilities in human nature and the possibilities in nature are such that in the present culture, no one needs to lose when doing the right thing in environmental ethics, though many will have to learn different satisfactions. Winning is here redefined from the "scoring the most points" of the aggrandizing self to the "satisfied life" of the person enjoying an optimal value richness in his or her community.

It is not that what we choose is satisfying, and that brings our good. Rather, what is satisfying is our good, and the environmental component is that we find the ecology we inhabit satisfying. This ecology can be satisfying if and only if it is both resource and residence, only if we use it while living in a meaningful community. We are not choosing it for our happiness, but our happiness is bound up with it.

Would we choose these things if they did not involve our happiness? That is a difficult question, and not because we think we ought to answer yes or are reluctant to say no. Rather, we do not know how to answer either yes or no. We are constituted in these relationships, and we find such a constitution to be satisfying; and we also find these things satisfactory fits in their places, whether or not we are there to be satisfied with our experiences of these relationships. We do want to say: "Yes, we want those things to flourish whether or not we are around to be happy; we want them there without our happiness."

If we answer: "No, we would not choose these things without our happiness," then simply not choosing them makes us unhappy, unsatisfied. Having moved the goalposts to where they now are, constituted by our ecology,[8] there is no other happiness to be chosen elsewhere. There are other ingredients to happiness, but they now are conjoined with this ecological one. Repudiating the natural world in which we reside, repudiating our ecology, is itself unsatisfying. Not choosing these ecological goods in order to gain happiness, therefore, is a logical and empirical impossibility. All the other, nonnatural goods, whatever they are, are undermined by the loss of these natural values.

Two kinds of satisfactoriness constitute the relationship established by doing right: (1) the satisfactoriness of the natural world, a complex web of adapted fits in a prolific ecosystem, is continued; and (2) human-taking satisfaction in this natural world is continued likewise. These things have a good of their own; they are located in a good place, they are desired for their own sake, and desiring them is my satisfaction. That is a win-win situation. Oppositely, losing them is losing the satisfaction that comes based on them; that is a lose-lose situation.

Being ethical sometimes means having to place the interests of others above our own, and that means that certain of our interests will not be satisfied, at least not in the degree that they might have been had we no ethical concern. If my interest is in making a profit, that interest will not be satisfied in the degree before. If my interest is in building a cabin on a parcel of bayshore land that the state wishes to include in a nature conserve for eagles, I lose that opportunity. Do I lose? Yes, if there is no other way to make a profit; yes, if I have no shelter over my head. But no, if there are other sectors of the economy in which these desires can be satisfied; no, if my enlarged value set means that I subsequently find higher satisfactions than I did before residing on a landscape replete with the native fauna and flora.

In addition to promoting personal self-interests, we want to have integrity, to be responsible members of a community. That sense of belonging to a healthy society—and, in environmental ethics, of belonging to a healthy ecosystem—is also part of self-interest, but now the self is entwined with the community destinies. One cannot be healthy if the ship on which one is sailing is sinking. We win when we assume responsibility for heritages that are greater than we are.

We make a mistake if we have too private a view of interests, too dualistic a view of winning. Certain things have to be won together. Our sense of our common interest merges with the welfare of the community we inhabit. At this point we may need even to redefine what Socrates thought winning meant. He thought winning was gaining a noble soul. His noble soul was concerned about a community, the political community of Athens. But Socrates did not have much concern about the biotic community. "You see, I am fond of learning. Now the country places and trees won't teach me anything, and the people in the city do."[9]

Environmental ethics is not inclined to focus just on the human community or, if that fails, to retreat into the isolated self with its excellence and justice. Valuing others, valuing nonhuman others, is itself a satisfactory act. That is what is wrong with the human excellence view; it has fallen into a concern with what is a satisfactory, satisfying view of self. But what we are really satisfied by is not just the excellence of an own self, but a display of excellences in the surrounding world. We are so satisfied by the flourishing of these others that there is no sense of loss at all. Your gain is my gain; not my gain in any selfish sense, but my gain in living in a richer, more value laden, meaningful world.

Nature Harmed for Culture?

Is there some peculiar human excellence that requires that nature be harmed? When culture wins, must nature lose? That question has a timebound answer; and I fear that the first answer to this question has to be yes. Culture is the peculiar human excellence, and advanced agricultural and technological culture is not possible except as it is superimposed on nature in such a way that it captures natural values and redirects them to cultural use. Take forestry. Civilization on the earth over the last twenty centuries is almost unthinkable without the use of wood for structure and fuel. The scale of timber and fuel needed to support a developing civilization will invariably modify forest ecosystems adversely. It is to be hoped that such an extractive resource use can be put on a sustainable basis; trees can be well tended, fertilized, and sprayed. But even so, when a forest is made a resource for culture, the natural forest as a wild ecosystem will be harmed. The integrity of the primeval forest ecosystem is sacrificed, more or less, when it is harnessed to culture.

Or, consider agriculture. Plowing the soil disturbs the native forest or grassland that preceded it. In this sense, all agricultures harm the ecosystems on which agriculture is superimposed. Perhaps the ecosystem can retain its health; an agriculture can be fitted intelligently into the ecological process of a landscape. Nevertheless, agriculture proportionate to its extent disturbs and harms the pristine integrity of the landscape. It rebuilds the landscape to meet the needs of the farmers. The farmers win; the pristine grasslands and forest are sacrificed to their benefit, and the city folk have bread in their supermarkets.

Or, consider animals raised both for food and for other products, such as their skins. When animals are domesticated—as with cows, sheep, and goats—they must be tended. The welfare of the cows is entwined with the welfare of the cowboy; that of the sheep is entwined with that of the shepherd. But the animals become artifacts of culture. They are bred for the qualities humans desire: tender meat or soft wool. Their reproduction is manipulated by breeders, they are traded in markets, and so on. They are not necessarily unhappy; the chickens I remember on my grandfather's farm in Alabama seemed to like it where they were. Nevertheless, all domestic animals are captured for human uses. On the farm we butchered in the fall, sheared sheep in the spring, and ate chicken every Sunday.

Consider beasts of burden. It is difficult to think that civilization could have developed to its advanced state without beasts of burden. If no human had ever ridden a beast nor laid a load on its back, humans would not have figured out how to build motorcars and trucks. It is true that a horseman attends to the welfare of his horse, and that most of these animals would never have existed without their breeders; nevertheless, they became artifacts of culture.

The point is that culture does require the capture and sacrifice of specific kinds of natural values. The cultural phase of human history not only must be superposed on natural history, it must also adapt and rebuild that natural history to its own benefit. And, from here onward, any society that we can envision must be scientifically sophisticated, technologically advanced, globally oriented, as well as (I hope) just and charitable, caring for universal human rights and for biospheric values. This society will try to fit itself in intelligently with the ecosystemic processes on which it is superposed. But it will also have to redirect those processes to its benefit. In that sense nature must be harmed if culture is to continue. Culture is a postevolutionary phase of our planetary history; it must be superposed on the nature it presupposes. At the same time, humans should build sustainable cultures that fit in with the continuing ecological processes. So, the first principle of culture is that it rebuilds wild nature; the second principle of culture is that culture ought to be sustainable on the ecological processes that support it.

"Sustainable development," J. Ronald Engel tells us, "may be defined as *the kind of human activity that nourishes and perpetuates the historical fulfilment of the whole community of life on Earth*."[10] That statement sounds vaguely reasonable so long as it is kept reasonably vague, but closer analysis shows that historically, the fulfillment of the human community does not result in simultaneous fulfillment of the whole biotic community. When Iowa is plowed up to plant corn, it can hardly be said that the grasslands of Iowa reach their historical fulfillment. The bison must scatter, and there will be fewer bobolinks—all sacrificed so that Europeans may build their culture on the North American continent. The most we can say is that Iowans can and ought to sustain their agriculture within the hydrology, soil chemistries, nutrient-recycling processes, and so on, that operate on the Iowa landscape. But there is no sustainable development of Iowa agriculture that leaves the natural history of Iowa unblemished. Legitimate human demands for culture cannot be satisfied without the sacrifice of nature. That is a sad truth.

Culture Harmed for Nature?

That is looking past. What is ahead? Must we further harm nature to develop culture? The answer to that question, again, is timebound; and, at least in the developed countries, is no, a satisfactory culture is quite possible without further degrading nature. Indeed, further degrading nature is likely to make culture less satisfactory. This is an empirical claim. About 2 percent of the contiguous United States is wilderness (1.2 percent designated; 1 percent under study); 98 percent is developed, farmed, grazed, timbered, or designated for multiple use. Another 2 percent might be suitable for wilderness or semiwild status—cutover forests that have reverted to the wild, or areas as yet little developed. On the 96 percent that is domesticated, vast natural processes—rainfall, streamflow, soil fertility, photosynthesis, nutrient recycling, native fauna and flora—often remain, though these processes have typically been much degraded: pollutants in the streams and soils, soils lost, native fauna and flora decimated, species endangered, exotics introduced.

Remembering the root of *satisfactory,* we are far past the point where enough is enough, and the mix of cultural values and natural values ought not be further skewed in the direction of the cultural. It is already so disproportionate that in many areas of the United States it is the natural values that are in short supply, not the cultural ones. These natural values ought to be preserved for their own ends, but when they are preserved, they simultaneously enrich the culture that is otherwise impoverished of natural values. When Columbus arrived in the Americas in 1492, there was a vast amount of wilderness. In the five hundred years since, there has been an explosion of European culture rebuilding the landscape, and that rebuilding has now reached a point where further expansion of culture at the price of nature will be counterproductive, even for culture. The next five hundred years simply cannot be like the last five hundred years without a tragic loss of natural values that will harm humans as well as harm what nature today remains on the landscape.

That is the way to interpret what happened with the Two Forks Dam. The good dam sites in the nation have long since been occupied; the water available in the American West has been appropriated, often without regard for the so-called in-stream benefits of riparian flows that maintain the native fauna and flora. Further damming of the rivers and further dewatering the streams will not be good for nature or culture either, since it will deprive culture of the benefits carried by nature. That is the way to interpret what is happening in the Pacific Northwest. The old-growth forest has been massively cut, and further cutting of the old growth is not going to be good for the fauna and flora, not good for the spotted owl. It is not going to be good for the culture in the Pacific Northwest either, because it will throw the natural values there into increasingly short supply, and it will only further prolong an already unsustainable culture, increasing the disaster when the crash comes.

The end of ethics is more life, increased quality of life, more experience of neighborhood. It is a sad truth that life preys on life, that culture does have to eat nature, but that is not the only truth; there is a glad truth that culture can be satisfied, can only be satisfactory, if its destiny is entwined with nature. I do not say that there is no further cultural development needed, only that we do not need further cultural development that sacrifices nature for culture, that enlarges the sphere of culture at the price of diminishing the sphere of nature. Nor will culture be harmed if we do not get it.

We can put this claim into empirical form by examining a human population growth curve over the last century (Figure 1). The realm of culture has exploded relative to the realm of nature, and this is true in both the

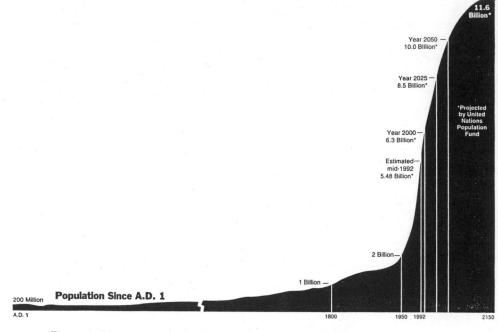

Figure 1. Human Population Growth Curve, A.D. 1–2150.
Copyright 1992 by the New York Times Company. Reprinted by permission.

developing and the developed countries. Not only have people grown in numbers, their expectations have grown as well, so that we have one exploding curve on top of another one. A superficial reading of such a graph is that humans really start winning big in the second half of the twentieth century. But when we come to our senses, we realize that this kind of winning, if it keeps on escalating, is really losing. When we get the goalposts in the right place, we see that we are headed in the wrong direction. Humans will lose, and nature will be destroyed as well. Cultures have become consumptive, with an ever-escalating growth of insatiable desires. Culture does not know how to say "Enough!" Starkly put, the growth of culture has become cancerous. That is hardly a metaphor, for a cancer is essentially an explosion of unregulated growth.

Individual persons caught up in this cancerous growth can and will be—even ought to be—harmed in terms of their immediate perceived personal goals, perhaps even deprived of their bodily needs. This could be prevented by a just distribution of the goods of culture, now often so inequitably distributed. Few persons would need to go without "enough" if we could use, justly and charitably, the produce of the already domesticated landscape. If such redistribution does not take place, people will be hurt. But it is better to try to fix this problem where it arises, within society, than to try to enlarge the sphere of society by the sacrifice of remnant natural values.

Growth is not what we want, even though it seems a short-range solution meeting what seem like legitimate personal needs. The species curve indicates that *Homo sapiens* will not be harmed if the cancerous growth is stopped. We win when there is no more development. And our win is simultaneously nature's win. However painful the surgery, no one is harmed when a cancer is stopped.

Inheriting the Earth

Can and should humans lose? The world is a complicated place. There is no simple answer: the answer is first yes and later no; sometimes yes, sometimes no; in some ways and places yes, in others no; superficially yes and at depth no; yes for self-aggrandizing humans, no for communitarian humans; yes for humans caught up in the inequities of culture, no for humans doing the right thing by nature. Perhaps the proper response is not to be dismayed that the question is so elusive, but to be glad instead that the answers are so open-ended. We have a great deal to gain by doing the right thing, and even when it seems that we lose by doing it, we typically do not; not if we get our goalposts in the right place, not if we can refocus our goals off the narrow self and enlarge them into the community we inhabit. There is always a deeper, philosophical sense in which it seems impossible to lose; that is all the more incentive to do the right thing.

Socrates did not think he could be a loser in Athens, and we have discovered a bigger truth. Humans ought not be losers on the earth; they belong on their home planet. Earth is a planet with promise, a planet of great value. Our human experience has characteristically been devoted to the promise of the culture in which we live and move and have our being. But our human experience must also devote itself to the promise of nature, in which we also live and move and have our being. For not only are humans the only species capable of enjoying the promise of culture, we are also the only species capable of enjoying the splendid panorama of life that vitalizes this planet.

NOTES

1 *Apology,* 41d. Note the certainty, despite Socrates' insistence earlier that he has only ignorance (*Apology,* 21–23). The epigraph is from *Plato,* vol. 1, trans. H. N. Fowler, Loeb Classical Library, vol. 36 (Cambridge: Harvard University Press, 1977), 145.

2 Quoted in *Ethics of Environment and Development,* ed. J. Ronald Engel and Joan Gibb Engel (London: Belhaven Press, 1990), 1.

3 Science Advisory Board of the United States Environmental Protection Agency (EPA), quoted in Brad Knickerbocker article, *Christian Science Monitor,* 23 December 1991, 8.

4 *Crito,* Loeb Classical Library, vol. 1 (Cambridge: Harvard University Press, 1917), 48.

5 Thomas E. Hill, Jr., "Ideals of Human Excellence and Preserving Natural Environments," *Environmental Ethics* 5 (1983): 211–24.

6 Socrates holds that anyone who knows the good is going to value the good so much that he or she will do it. So only those who are ignorant do the wrong thing. We may not agree with Socrates that this is always true, but it is often true; see *Protagoras* 352b–c, in *The Dialogues of Plato,* trans. B. Jowett (New York: Random House, 1937), 1:352–53.

7 David Rothenberg, introducing the position of Arne Naess, in *Ecology, Community and Lifestyle* (Cambridge: Cambridge University Press, 1989), 10–11.

8 We are also constituted by our culture, and we trade off these double constitutions, as I discuss later.

9 *Phaedrus,* 230d, Loeb Classical Library, vol. 1 (Cambridge: Harvard University Press, 1917), 423–24.

10 J. Ronald Engel, "Introduction: The Ethics of Sustainable Development," in *Technics of Environment and Development,* 1–23; citation on 10–11, emphasis in original.

BRYAN NORTON AND

EUGENE HARGROVE

Where Do We
Go from Here?

Norton: Urging Philosophy to
Become Practical

Which comes first, theory or practice? I offer a brief
plea for the priority of practice and for the remarkable ability of real-world
problems to focus the philosophical mind.

Let me begin to explain the importance of practice by introducing a
distinction between two kinds of nontheoretical philosophy; I call them
applied philosophy and practical philosophy. Although these terms are
sometimes used interchangeably, I use them here to correspond to two
somewhat different roles for philosophers in the process of public policy
formation. *Applied philosophy* refers to the application of general philosophical principles in adjudications among policy goals and options. Applied philosophy's method is usually to develop general, abstract, and universal principles and then to apply these principles to specific cases; or,
sometimes, to discuss only hypothetical, carefully circumscribed cases. In
the latter event, applied philosophers apparently expect that policymakers
will be the ones to actually apply the philosophical principle in particular situations. Since these universal principles are expected to function as
essential premises in an argument that one or another policy is justified,

agreement on a policy option will emerge only if the general principle is accepted by all parties to the dispute. If agreement does not occur, then the applied philosopher must retreat to theoretical arguments and attempt to establish more definitively the key principle or premise before returning to applications.

Practical philosophy is more problem oriented. Its chief characteristic is its emphasis on theories as tools of understanding, tools that are developed to resolve specific policy controversies. It shares with applied philosophy the goal of contributing to problem solution, but practical philosophy does not assume that useful theoretical principles will be developed and established independent of the policy process. It works toward principles by struggling with real cases rather than by establishing theory and then "applying" it to real cases.

Practical philosophers introduce theories only insofar as they help in understanding specific management problems. It is often possible to generalize from problems toward general theories of management and even toward general moral principles, but practical philosophers avoid adopting theoretical principles on purely a priori grounds. According to practical philosophers, principles are ultimately generated from practice, not vice versa. It is in this sense that I believe practice is prior to theory. There are, of course, echoes of pragmatism, especially of John Dewey's passionate commitment to philosophical engagement in practical affairs, in this line of reasoning. My version of pragmatism seeks to avoid dogma, arguing only for the practical urgency of addressing real-world management problems. I do not argue that theory is worthless; on the contrary, theory building that addresses real-world problems, in the spirit of Dewey and Aldo Leopold, is absolutely essential if the environmental movement is to develop a vision for the future. In the meantime, however, theoretical differences need not impede progress in developing current policy; if all disputants agree on central management principles, even without agreement on ultimate values, management can proceed on these principles.

As an advocate of practical philosophy, my approach is similar to the circular reasoning outlined by John Rawls in his search for a theory of justice that constitutes a "reflective equilibrium": We struggle toward better theory by alternating attempts to formulate theory and application of theory to cases (Rawls 1971). In this way we constantly check our principles against our intuitions about what should be done in particular situations. I differ, perhaps, from Rawls in arguing specifically for the importance of starting from real-world problems as cases, and putting less importance on imagined cases of philosophers (Norton 1991). Imagined test cases are chosen to test theory at the very limits of its application, where theory is predictably more controversial. Real-world cases often do not require the resolution of problems of philosophical principle; in many areas, for example, several worldviews and philosophies converge on the importance of an all-out effort to protect biological diversity. In other cases, mid-level management principles accepted by all disputants in the case can be used as the basis of policy resolution, even when exact formulations of the abstract general principles underlying the mid-level consensus remain under dispute. In environmental policy, most important issues can be resolved, I would argue, by applying mid-level criteria of good management that are common to a sustainability ethic in the anthropocentric stewardship tradition and to an ecocentric perspective (Norton 1991). It is therefore more important, practically, to determine what each of the competing philosophies would agree on as mid-level management principles than to determine which is "correct" in a general philosophical sense.

Philosophers who focus on specific management problems are likely to recognize solutions that satisfy, or nearly satisfy, several widely held values, whereas applied philosophers are likely to opt for one or the other of the incompatible policies implied by their own philosophical principles. I believe the former approach is more helpful in environmental policy formation, because abstract philosophical theories often introduce value categories that are useless for the problem at hand. Abstract and universal principles are often too general to illuminate the fine-grained differences facing managers in real situations. Consider the fairly common management dilemma of what to do when herbivore populations grow so large that they threaten the integrity of ecological systems. Knowing that our ancestors were wrong to remove predators and Native American hunters from a region decades ago does not tell us what to do now—an overpopulation of grazers on a predator-free range forces a management decision. Even doing nothing is a form of management, a form that can often be predicted correctly to have disastrous consequences for the ecological integrity of the region. Suppose that all parties to a real-life herbivore versus ecosystem debate were to accept the general principle of biocentrism, which insists on the moral equality of all species, a theory developed by philosophers to counteract the view that only humans have intrinsic value. Biocentrism, so much discussed by applied environmental ethicists, is impotent to decide such cases because the real conflict is between competing species, individuals, and ecosystems; and biocentrists are nowhere near achieving consensus, even among themselves, regarding the correct moral weighting among these competing categories.

The goal of theory is to unify, to achieve rules based on a few ultimate values. The limiting, and ideal, outcome of philosophical discourse, from the viewpoint of theory, is moral monism, defined as a philosophy that seeks "to produce and to defend against all rivals, a single coherent and complete set of principles capable of governing all moral quandaries," and which assumes that this is a determinate goal in the sense that this set of principles will "yield for each quandary one right answer" (Stone 1988). Moral monisms share a reductionistic tendency; biocentrists who reduce all moral values to intrinsic values of all living things are no less reductionistic than are economic utilitarians.[1] Moral pluralists, on the other hand, exhibit a willingness "to develop a conception of the moral realm as consisting in several different schemata, side by side" (Stone 1988). Pluralism has the advantage in practice of allowing agreement on specific cases without requiring agreement on the general formulation of moral principles. If advocates of several moral principles agree on a specific moral directive, this can be seen as corroboration of that directive, and continued discussion of abstract principles can continue at leisure. As management goes forward, consensus embodied in common goals and objectives of major worldviews and ideologies can be used to explain and support environmental actions.

The impact of the differences between applied and practical philosophers is well illustrated by the great Olympic goat controversy. Well-meaning park managers introduced mountain goats into Washington State's Olympic National Park during the 1920s. Their population grew at a rate of about 9 percent per year and reached a total 1,200 in 1983, when the National Park Service began removing the goats by live-capture because they were destroying lichen populations, threatening nine species of unique endemic plants, and causing erosion in drier regions of the park. The population has been reduced to less than 400, and the Park Service proposes to continue removing the goats, shooting those they cannot capture and relocate, and eventually eliminating the goats from the core of the park. The Fund for Animals opposes the policy (Scheffer 1993).

An applied philosopher would look at this case as turning on questions of moral theory such as whether or not goats, plants, or ecosystems have moral standing. From that point forward the applied philosopher has two options: (1) opt for a particular monistic principle—anthropocentric utilitarianism, biocentric egalitarianism, or ecocentric holism—and then lecture environmental managers about what they should do, based on the preferred moral principle; or (2) less certain of his or her own principles or hoping for the broader support of consensus, return to the philosophy journals. In the latter case, the applied philosopher must eschew recommendations until rational discussion and debate determine a moral theory capable of resolving all environmental policy disputes. In the philosophy journals, goats and lichens will be cited, at best, as case studies illustrating the limits of principles.

But a practical philosopher will not use specific controversies as case studies for examining moral principles; a practical philosopher will consider it a challenge to reduce the distance between the two sides in the controversy by finding a general policy direction that can achieve consensus and define a range of actions that are morally acceptable to a wide range of worldviews. In searching for solutions to the problem, the practical philosopher will see that a second issue, much less general than ultimate moral principles, is perhaps more important in resolving this dispute. The Park Service's position is based on a management principle; the service seeks to maintain natural systems, especially their self-organizing structures and processes, and to protect the systems from rapid change caused by the introduction of new species. Agreed-upon scientific principles suggest that introduction of a large herbivore into a system into which it has not been integrated by natural, multigenerational competition and adaptation will likely result in destruction of vegetation and extirpation of species and will threaten the ecosystem's integrity.

A closer look at the Olympic goat controversy reveals that philosophers who treat this problem as a conflict in basic moral principles miss a more important, and less general, disagreement: in fact, the Park Service and the Fund for Animals disagree about the zoological history of the Olympic peninsula. The Park Service decided to remove the animals because they accepted the evidence that the goats are exotics; the Fund for Animals entered the debate, opposing the removals and citing evidence that mountain goats existed on the Olympic peninsula before 1900. In this specific policy disagreement, the Fund for Animals, by recognizing the importance of whether or not the goats are exotics (Fund for Animals 1992), retreated from an absolute principle that animals (mammals)—because of their greater mental awareness as individuals—should always be given priority over plants and healthy ecological systems. If that had been the principle of their argument, they would never have entered the scientific controversy by offering evidence of earlier sitings; that evidence would be irrelevant if goats have, in all situations, moral priority over plants and ecosystems. The goat controversy, therefore, in practice turns essentially on an ecological fact—the historical existence of mountain goats on the Olympic peninsula.[2]

Although the evidence against this historical existence seems stronger than the evidence for it (Scheffer 1993), my point is not to resolve that issue but rather to use the case to illustrate the difference between practical philosophy and applied philosophy. The applied philosopher will see this case as governed by an abstract moral principle such as utilitarianism (in which case the issue will be the comparative levels of sentience of goats, on the one hand, and threatened plants and ecosystems, on the other) or as a question of which living things have rights or some other form of moral standing. The issue for applied philosophers, then, is whether the goats have moral standing and whether this moral standing is sufficient to override other moral considerations, including the rights and interests of future generations to experience intact ecosystems and any morally considerable interests of plants and other animals affected.

The practical philosopher, who sees the problem as one of resolving a public policy dispute rather than as a test case for abstract principles, will not emphasize these difficult general issues because both parties to the policy dispute have accepted the principle that the Park Service can and should manage areas based on historical ecological information. Since the Fund for Animals has argued that the mountain goat is an indigenous species and that the 1920s translocation of goats was a restoration rather than an introduction, practical philosophers can join the search for an acceptable compromise, such as binding adjudication by a panel of scientific experts assembled to provide the best scientific opinion on the historical issue. If the historical ecological information definitively shows the goats are exotics, the goats may be or should be removed. If scientists cannot agree, perhaps further study will be required. But even this situation implies progress. While the scientific determination of the historical range of mountain goats remains a difficult controversy with some evidence available to support both conclusions, it is an empirical controversy for which scientific evidence can be sought and cited. Here, the role of applied philosophers will be to assist in weighing the evidence by clarifying the standards of evidence appropriate to the debate, rather than in asserting and defending a general and controversial moral principle such as ecocentrism, mammalcentrism, biocentrism, or anthropocentrism.

The prevailing tendency of environmental ethicists to see problems in environmental policy as interesting cases with which to test philosophical principles rather than as real problems requiring rational resolution has isolated environmental ethics from policy discourse and debate. Given the urgency of environmental problems and the serious controversies about what should be done in difficult cases, the goal of environmental ethics and environmental philosophy should be to contribute to resolving real debates. A greater emphasis on the facts of disputed cases and an eagerness to find common moral and philosophical ground among disputants—a move away from applied philosophy and toward practical philosophy—would redirect environmental ethics away from abstract debates and toward resolution of urgent and important public controversies. I believe it would also contribute to clarity in discussions of philosophical principles, but that discussion must remain to be joined at another time.

Another practical consequence of the broadly pragmatic approach I advocate here may be the abandonment of philosophy departments by environmental philosophers, who may instead take up residence in schools of natural resources, schools of planning, and schools of public policy. They might even find employment with environmental advocacy groups or in management agencies of government. Moving across campus or out of academia will not, of course, resolve the abstract problems of environmental ethics; but it would change the focus of questions that would be addressed by practicing environmental philosophers. If so, these moves would enhance the contribution of philosophers to public policy dilemmas.

Hargrove: Urging Environmentalists to Become Philosophical

In the early 1970s, the time of the first Earth Day, there was a widespread consensus among environmentalists that the foundations of the environmental crisis on our planet were philosophical. Although the origin of this belief is not completely clear, most environmentalists probably came to it by reading Aldo Leopold's famous essay "The Land Ethic," in *A Sand County Almanac*.[3] Armed with this belief, they began trying to persuade philosophers involved in environmental groups to undertake work on environmental ethics, a field that did not exist at that time. Most environmentalists expected that the development of an environmental ethics would be a relatively simple matter. Some philosopher would simply write a short book on applied ethics as it relates to the environment, which environmentalists could then consult when necessary. The actual scenario was quite different.

It took most of the 1970s for those philosophers willing to answer the environmentalists' calls just to determine what a field called environmental ethics might be like. In the 1980s those philosophers wrestled with the relation of the new field of environmental ethics to animal liberation. Deciding that there was no relation, they examined the environmental claim that "nature ought to have rights." Finding that such a claim could not be justified, they then undertook a historical examination of the history of philosophy and concluded that environmental ethics was incompatible with philosophy in all three periods of Western civilization. Finally, they turned to an examination of intrinsic value as it might or might not relate to nature, anthropocentrically or nonanthropocentrically, but reached no definite conclusion.

While all this activity was going on, environmentalists grew first impatient, then frustrated, and then bored. Concluding that environmental ethics was too theoretical, they decided to take matters into their own hands once again and began arguing for nature in terms of positions that they previously had considered the causes of the environmental crisis. To counter the argument that only humans matter, they argued that nature should be protected to protect humans because only humans matter. Concluding that only economic arguments seemed to work, they then tried to subvert economic cost-benefit and risk-benefit analyses to their own purposes. Uncomfortable with intrinsic value arguments, they returned to instrumental arguments, or possible instrumental arguments: Nature should be protected because something in it that we have not yet discovered might be a cure for cancer (or, most recently, a cure for AIDS). These changes in approach were considered by environmentalists to be a step back to a factual, objective strategy: they were now arguing facts, not values; science, not ethics. It was, essentially, a rejection of environmental ethics theory in toto. Environmentalists decided to forget about environmental ethics and play their opponents' games. Having concluded that environmental ethics was too theoretical and historical, and too complicated and imprecise, they determined not to pay any further attention to environmental ethics until philosophers made it simple and practical enough for environmentalists to use without much effort on their part—what they had wanted from the beginning. This move was from the theoretical to the practical, but in such a way that the theoretical was rejected in favor of a nontheoretical, or at least noncritical, practice.

This rejection of philosophy appears to be a reasonable move because it can be defended as a return to factual, value-free argumentation in environmental policy and decision making. It is appearance only, however, because environmentalists are returning to an approach that is itself based on philosophical positions from the nineteenth and early twentieth centuries: specifically, utilitarianism, pragmatism, and logical positivism. Utilitarianism equates pleasure with good, and bad or evil with pain. This redefinition of values (good, bad, evil) as facts (mental or physical manifestations called feelings) permitted the development of a calculus that could be used to determine the greatest good for the greatest number (that is, the greatest amount of pleasure with the least pain). Pragmatism, which focuses on instrumental value (means rather than ends), attacks the idea of intrinsic value as unnecessary on the grounds that all values can be described in instrumental terms. Logical positivism, which claims that statements not scientifically verifiable are meaningless, presents values as the radically subjective, irrational expression of emotion.

These three positions are joined together in "modern" economic thought as the foundation of all public policy and decision making. Economics, which deals with the selfish satisfaction of cravings and desires in a market system, owes its instrumental focus to utilitarianism and pragmatism and its focus on feelings to utilitarianism and the emotivism of logical positivism. Essentially, economics, despite its claim to be a science, is little more than utilitarianism mixed with scientific jargon deriving from logical positivism. Unlike other sciences, economics is predictive in only a limited way: in terms of extrapolations from a market involving moderate scarcity; that is, a market with enough consumer items to permit choice, but not so many that choice between items becomes unnecessary. Of the three positions, pragmatism is probably the least influential. Nevertheless, it is responsible for the widespread inability of most people, including environmentalists, to think in terms of noninstrumental or intrinsic values. Like utilitarianism and logical positivism, it has trickled down from philosophy to ordinary people. The trickle-down effect of utilitarianism, pragmatism, and logical positivism is perhaps the most impressive—though at the same time the least known—influence of Western philosophy in the twentieth century. It is impressive because it has produced a mode of thought that is considered so entirely value free and factual that it needs no defense (certainly not a philosophical one); it is so pervasive that little children pick it up without formal training of any kind. It is little known because its origins in recent philosophy have already been forgotten.

The victory of utilitarianism, pragmatism, and logical positivism over the minds and hearts of both ordinary people and policymakers came almost invisibly and without protest. It is a change, as Mark Sagoff points out very effectively, in which the "citizen" is being replaced by the "consumer."[4] This change in ordinary and educated thinking should be recognized as a paradigm shift. It is not so regarded, however, because most people find it hard to imagine that anyone could have ever thought in another way. It is the inability of twentieth-century people to see this utilitarian, instrumentalist, radically subjective economic thinking as one way of looking at the world among many (as a philosophical position) that gives it its factual flavor and makes it appear invulnerable to attack.

Despite its veneer of invulnerability, utilitarianism cannot be easily defended. First, although the idea of simply defining good as pleasure has been around since at least the ancient Greeks, and probably goes back long before them, it was repeatedly rejected throughout the history of Western civilization because it was a factually false position. As Aristotle points out, humans frequently take pleasure in things and activities that are bad. This "fact" remains a good and obvious reason for rejecting contemporary utilitarianism today. Second, the pragmatic rejection of intrinsic value was not based on an argument that only instrumental values exist, but rather on the argument that it is possible to treat all values as if they are instrumental. The obvious problem with this argument is that it fails to establish that it is desirable to collapse value entirely into instrumental terms. The "fact" that it is not desirable to do so, at least in environmental policymaking, is demonstrated in part by environmentalists' endless, but confused, calls for rights for nature, which, if they could be bestowed, would provide nature with a sake (that is, with intrinsic value). Clearly, if a move toward efficiency produces a widespread feeling that something important is missing, it is not a successful simplification. Third, the logical positivists' claim in the early twentieth century that values are nothing but irrational and radically subjective expressions of emotion is tautological. If one accepts that only facts matter, then ethics and values do not matter. The 2,500 years' worth of theory available before the positivists made their antivalue proclamations was not refuted; it was simply dismissed. The "fact" that most people continue to lead their lives in terms of values, moreover, suggests that the positivist critique of values and ethics may not be true. In particular, the existence of a wide variety of socially accepted values about which there is nearly universal agreement undercuts any claim that values are irrational, radically subjective expressions of emotions. Objectivity can be based on agreement. Such objectivity is impossible only if the alleged radical subjectivity of the individual is taken to preclude all agreement, a claim whose falsity can easily be demonstrated by pointing to examples of agreement (for example, concerning truth telling, promise keeping, and the appreciation of natural beauty).

Accepting the economic paradigm in environmental policy and decision making, even when trying to twist it in favor of environmental goals and purposes, does not necessarily solve the policymaker's problems. It is very hard to make a value-free decision, even when one actually wants to. In practice, a policymaker usually makes a decision based largely on particular values. However, believing that these values are radically subjective expressions of emotion that are therefore indefensible, the policymaker undertakes a search for facts that will support the decision. There are two problems with this approach. First, the policymaker may feel guilty because he or she has seemingly employed an inappropriate decision procedure—one that is not value free. Second, and more important, it is no longer possible to have an objective policy debate. Because the facts brought in at the end are supposed to justify the decision, the debate has to deal with them rather than with the factors that actually determined the decision. The result is a policy approach determined by factors the policymaker finds embarrassing to talk about and defended by "facts" presented in the context of a general philosophical position (utilitarianism, pragmatism, positivistic emotivism) that the policymaker usually does not accept intuitively or morally. Obviously, there ought to be a better way.

I do not deny that it may be possible to subvert the economic approach while accepting all the presuppositions on which that position is based. Nevertheless, given that "modern" economic thought has so far proven to be a very powerful antienvironment weapon in environmental policy, the prospects do not seem to be too good unless environmentalists also try to promote a counterposition that undermines the antienvironmental elements in the economic approach. Such a counterposition, it would seem, would involve some criticism of the utilitarian, pragmatic, and positivistic underpinnings of economics. If so, then environmentalists will probably have to make a new attempt to get philosophers to develop a philosophical counterposition, an environmental ethic, unless they want to remain forever at the cracker-barrel level—doomed to lament over and over again that "nature ought to have rights" or that "there is a mystical bond between humans and nature."

If the move from theory to practice is to be successful this time, environmentalists will have to play a more active role. Simply waiting for environmental ethicists to make the transition for them is unrealistic. First, philosophy professors have very little, if any, practical experience in the vast number of fields, both academic and professional, that make up environmental affairs. It is unlikely that these philosophers, who must meet their academic commitments to provide undergraduate and graduate programs in general philosophy and service courses for various other departments at their institutions, will ever be able to master enough of these environmental fields or their practical applications to develop a practical philosophy. The prospects for success would be increased significantly if environmentalists learned enough philosophy to make some tentative efforts to apply an environmental ethics theory themselves. Such efforts could have a snowball effect, for substantial efforts at application by environmental professionals, however inadequate, could highlight problems of application, providing environmental ethicists with useful insight into matters that they might not understand on their own.

Second, environmental ethicists, if they are to remain professional philosophers, cannot stray too far from theory without endangering their careers. A complete move from theory to practice is more likely to be viewed at tenure and promotion time as good citizenship rather than meritorious professional activity. This problem is obvious in virtually all professional writing in environmental ethics, including the articles in my own journal, *Environmental Ethics*. As a result of the professional need to be both theoretical and practical, most articles are written at a level that permits seemingly contradictory criticism: environmentalists claim that the material is too theoretical, and peer evaluators in professional philosophy claim that the material is too practical to have any professional value.

The requirement that philosophers in the field of environmental ethics provide an application for their theories is a unique demand. If all philosophers in the history of Western civilization had been required to fill in all the blanks themselves, it is unlikely that philosophy would ever have had any influence in human affairs. Existentialism is a good example of a movement in philosophy that has had significant influence over a period of time. Philosophers working in this area did not have to figure out in detail how the general public would or should deal with their writings. Indeed, they frequently produced conflicting views that reached the general public unreconciled. This material (for example, the writings of Jean-Paul Sartre, Albert Camus, Martin Heidegger, and Søren Kierkegaard) was read by interested members of the general public who then created their own individual existential philosophies from bits and pieces of the various positions. There were no calls for existential philosophers to tell their readers how to practice their theories. Similarly, there were no calls for professional philosophers to spell out every detail of the practical applications of utilitarianism, pragmatism, and logical positivism during their critical trickle-down phases in the early twentieth century. Both professional and ordinary people were willing to read the material provided by these philosophers and use it in their work without lamenting that it was not practical enough.

There is actually only one area within applied philosophy in which the move from theory to practice has been a success: medical ethics. Unfortunately, medical ethics cannot provide environmental ethicists and environmentalists with a model. First, medical ethics is a simpler field than environmental ethics. Medical ethics has developed strictly within a traditional framework that aims at the protection and preservation of human life, health, and welfare. As a result, medical ethicists have available to them a huge body of traditional theory from which they can draw at will. In contrast, environmental ethics is viewed as a challenge to the traditional framework insofar as it tries to include concerns about nonhuman living and nonliving entities, including things that do not fit the model of entity very well (e.g., natural processes, species, and ecosystems). Because environmental ethics is a criticism of traditional positions—not only in ethics but in social and political philosophy, philosophy of science, aesthetics, metaphysics, epistemology, and the history of philosophy generally—it has to be more theoretical and less practical than medical ethics. Rather than simply picking and choosing which traditional theory to apply, the environmental ethicist must frequently describe and attack traditional positions that prevent the move from theory to practice (as noted already), such as the roles of utilitarianism, pragmatism, and logical positivism in public policy and decision making.

Second, medical ethics focuses more narrowly on decision making than environmental ethics does. Because most of the general features of medical ethics already have a long history that remains unchallenged, the major concern is the resolution of tough cases involving the application of new medical technologies that were inconceivable until fairly recently (e.g., the transplantation of organs from one human body to another). The use of transplant technology required a decision that doctors themselves were unwilling to make: In order for the transplanted organ to be useful to its human recipient, it must still be alive; in order for it to be removed, however, the human donor must in some appropriate sense be "dead." Philosophers settled this issue, which was considered to be a philosophical rather than a factual matter, by deciding for doctors that brain death was enough. Generally, environmental professionals are not seeking assistance in deciding what to do in tough cases. Rather, they are looking for ways to justify matters that are already intuitively clear to them, even though they cannot explain why even to their own satisfaction. Environmental ethics proceeds in accordance with the medical ethics model only when there are conflicts between environmental intuitions and other ethical intuitions. For instance, species survival breeding programs sometimes produce conflicts between environmental and animal welfare perspectives that in turn require decisions about tough cases similar to those in contemporary medicine.

Third, doctors and other medical professionals are more willing to work with medical ethicists than environmentalists are willing to work with environmental ethicists. Medical professionals are (apparently) more willing because the focus on decision rather than theory, and on traditional theory over new theory development, reduces the need for them to acquire more than a superficial knowledge of philosophy. In addition, the anticipated benefits of interaction with medical ethicists—the creation of a body of prelegal principles that may provide them with protection should court cases arise at a later date—help keep motivation and interest in interaction high. In contrast, environmentalists rarely have a clear idea of what they are trying to achieve when they approach environmental ethicists and, given their frequently abysmal knowledge of philosophy, probably would not be able to recognize that anything had been settled should a conceptual breakthrough occur. Neither environmentalists nor environmental ethicists are sure about what might be a suitable improvement on the vague idea that "nature ought to have rights." The problem is not that philosophers cannot come up with a theoretical improvement over the largely rhetorical call for rights for nature, but rather that they must come up with an improvement that environmentalists will accept at an intuitive level without a need for any significant amount of critical thought or explanation. Environmental professionals who wish to move from mere rhetoric to theory to practice in this matter need to know enough about rights theory and value theory to be able to interact with professionals who deal with such issues. Such basic knowledge is routinely expected when practitioners attempt to work with specialists in other fields. Among most environmental professionals, however, the need for such knowledge of philosophy, even the equivalent of a freshman introductory course, is considered a failure of the field rather than a failure of those who refuse to learn anything about it.

If environmental ethicists are required to shoulder all the responsibility for the development of an environmental ethic, it is unlikely that an environmental ethic will ever be developed. To my knowledge no ethic of any kind has been developed entirely by any one philosopher or group of philosophers. At most, particular philosophers or groups of philosophers have merely conceived, explained, and expressed ethical intuitions that had been developing for a long time. Without some sort of protomoral change at the intuitive level throughout human society, it would be impossible for an ethicist to articulate an acceptable view of any kind. In other words, a position advanced "before its time" would simply be misunderstood or ignored until human society was ready for it. Viewed in this way, the problem is not simply how to go from theory to practice, but also how to go from practice to theory—what Anthony Weston calls "enabling practice"—in such a way that theory and practice develop together.[5]

If environmental ethics remains the primary responsibility of philosophers, then the prospects for further development are grim. At best, philosophers will continue to offer courses at universities and write books that other philosophers will read and use in their classes. Gradually, as interest in the subject grows, more students will take these courses. Eventually, when there is enough interest and enough philosophy teachers have the necessary expertise, every student preparing for work in environmental affairs may be required to take one course on the subject. When multiple courses become available, some students may go beyond the token requirement. Ten to twenty years later, these students will begin to be promoted into positions of authority where, if they still remember anything about their coursework, they may try to put theory into practice. These efforts will then provide practical information about the application of an environmental ethics theory that finally will allow philosophers to improve the theory. Finally, in thirty to forty years, as senior members of their respective environmental fields, some of them might be in a position, and have the desire, to require training in environmental ethics as part of the basic qualifications for employment in environmental affairs. Interaction between philosophers and environmental professionals in this final phase, in the late twenty-first and early twenty-second centuries, will then produce the environmental ethic that we want and need today.

This prospect is a grim one because an environmental ethic that is fully in place only in the late twenty-first century might be too late to do humans or the planet much good. Yet, the commitment needed to speed up the process may be beyond that which environmentalists, government, industry, and ordinary citizens (as consumers) are willing to make. At a minimum, we face a forty- to sixty-year delay as environmental professionals without any training in environmental ethics are slowly replaced by newcomers armed with a single course in the subject.

To develop environmental ethics on a timetable that will allow it to make a difference, the hundreds of thousands of environmental professionals who are working and studying now will have to be trained in environmental ethics as quickly as possible. They will require more than a single course; they will need to spend a significant amount of time (preferably in one-year leaves of absence) becoming familiar with the values and facts. They will need to become comfortable with the idea of dealing with values as part of environmental policy and decision making and to start defending those values as part of objective (or, for sticklers, quasi-objective or intersubjective) policy debate.

Without such a commitment we might as well continue lamenting the "facts" that weathermen cannot predict the weather better, physicists cannot provide us with fusion reactors on a more timely basis, politicians cannot provide us with the ideal democratic society, economists cannot predict and control economic cycles, and philosophers cannot create an environmental ethic all by themselves. Without such a commitment, the problem of theory and practice will remain an "academic" issue in a derogatory sense only.

The situation is made more difficult because we are at a turning point in the history of Western civilization. The modern period is in the process of being replaced by a yet unnamed "postmodern" period. This period of transition is hardly a good time to try to develop a new environmental philosophy, given that the basic presuppositions of the last three centuries have been discarded and the new presuppositions are not yet in place. It is not unimaginable that the philosophical foundations of the next period could develop in such a way that environmental concerns become increasingly difficult to express. The stakes are very high. The development of environmental ethics could either profoundly shape the direction of the next period or become irrelevant.[6] With so much at stake, it is not good sense to wait for philosophers to provide what is needed. If we are ever to move from theory to practice, we must all do our part.

NOTES

1 I have detailed my broader objections to theories of intrinsic and inherent value in Norton (1992).
2 I do not deny that some members of the Fund for Animals might oppose the implication that their efforts to demonstrate that goats are indigenous to the peninsula commits them to an admission that individual exotics can in all cases be removed from an overgrazed range. If they do deny this connection, another philosophical issue remains: Under what conditions does the goal of protecting the integrity of ecosystems outweigh the "interests" of exotic animals? Note that this issue also turns on the conflict between individuals and ecosystems; and this conflict is not resolved by the acceptance of the general principle of species equality. Again, environmental philosophers will contribute to policy resolutions only if they have something to say about which species must be protected in a specific situation, with all the nuances of interspecific competitions, ecological risks, and human intrusions.
3 Aldo Leopold, *A Sand County Almanac* (New York: Ballantine Books, 1970).
4 Mark Sagoff, *The Economy of the Earth* (New York: Cambridge University Press, 1988).
5 Anthony Weston, "Before Environmental Ethics," *Environmental Ethics* 14 (1992): 321–38.
6 See Jim Cheney, "Postmodern Environmental Ethics: Ethics as Bioregional Narrative," *Environmental Ethics* 11 (1989): 293–325.

REFERENCES

Fund for Animals. 1992. "Historic and Scientific Evidence That Mountain Goats Are Native to the Olympic Peninsula." Future Farmers of America, Northwest Region, press release, Salem, Oreg.
Norton, Bryan G. 1991. *Toward Unity among Environmentalists*. New York: Oxford University Press.
———. 1992. "Epistemology and Environmental Values." *Monist* 75:209–26.

Rawls, John. 1971. *A Theory of Justice*. Cambridge: Harvard University Press.
Scheffer, Victor B. 1993. "The Olympic Goat Controversy: A Perspective." *Conservation Biology* 7:916–19.
Stone, Christopher. 1988. *Earth and Other Ethics*. New York: Harper and Row.

FREDERICK FERRÉ

Epilogue

Reflecting on the Reflections

Our book ends with an appeal for everyone to take part in both theory and practice. In the Introduction, Victoria Davion opposes the dichotomy itself and argues that it is not finally sustainable, but she does recognize that the poles of ethics and policy tend to pull us in opposite directions. Her effort is to keep these poles in contact for the sake of the light they can provide when linked. Bryan Norton, though he urges philosophers to get involved in helping to solve penultimate, local, concrete questions, acknowledges that getting theory right is important and worthwhile. This is true, he argues, even if (especially if!) such theory is at a level of abstraction far short of ultimate comprehensiveness. Finally, Eugene Hargrove appeals for volunteers from the trenches to spend time in what may seem like the ivory towers of philosophy—but any time spent cultivating theory, he insists, is not important just for rest and recreation. It may, from the other side, help practice and theory meet in fruitful ways.

This book contains essays by those who emphasize theory and those who emphasize policy. If these essays contribute to a better appreciation of the pains and potentials of philosophy to people who normally work close to practice, and if they contribute to a more concrete sense of the real world where environmental problems demand solution by thoughtful policy, then the book will have fulfilled its purpose.

253

Works Cited

Aitken, R. 1980. "Gandhi, Dogen and Deep Ecology." *Zero* 4:52–57.

Allen, T. F. H., and T. B. Starr. 1982. *Hierarchy: Perspectives for Ecological Complexity.* Chicago: University of Chicago Press.

Anselm. 1903. *Proslogium.* Trans. S. N. Dean. La Salle, Ill.: Open Court.

Aquinas, T. 1955. *Summa Contra Gentiles.* Book I. Trans. A. C. Pegis. Garden City, N.Y.: Doubleday.

Aristotle. 1941. *The Basic Works of Aristotle.* Ed. R. McKeon. New York: Random House.

Arrhenius, E. A., and T. W. Waltz. 1990. "The Greenhouse Effect: Implications for Economic Development." World Bank Discussion Paper 78, Washington, D.C.

Austin, R. C. 1988. *Beauty of the Lord: Awakening the Senses.* Atlanta: John Knox Press.

Ayres, R. U. 1989. *Energy Efficiency in the U.S. Economy: A New Case for Conservation.* Laxenburg: IIASA Publications.

Bach, W., and A. K. Jain. 1991. *Von der Klimakrise zum Klimaschutz.* Münster: Institut für Geographie. (extension of a 1988 manuscript).

Bacon, F. 1960. *The New Organon.* New York: Library of Liberal Arts Press.

Barbier, E., D. Pearce, and A. Markandya. 1989. *Blueprint for a Green Economy.* London: Earthscan.

Barbour, I. 1982. *Energy and the American Values.* New York: Praeger.

Barrett, H. M. 1940. *Boethius: Some Aspects of His Times and Work.* Cambridge: Cambridge University Press.

Barrett, S. 1989. "Global Warming: Economic of a Carbon Tax." In *Blueprint for a Green Economy,* ed. D. Pearce et al. London: Earthscan.

———.1990. "The Problem of Global Environmental Protection." *Oxford Review of Economic Policy,* pp. 68–79.

Bateson, G. [1972] 1987. *Steps to an Ecology of Mind.* Northvale, N.J.: Jason A. Ponson.

Bayles, M. 1981. *Professional Ethics.* Belmont, Calif.: Wadsworth.

Benedick, R. E. 1991. *Ozone Diplomacy: New Directions in Safeguarding the Planet.* Cambridge: Harvard University Press.

Bergen. 1990. *Action for a Common Future.* Bergen: Ministry for the Environment.

Berle, A. A. 1965. "Property, Production and Revolution." *Columbia Law Review* 65:1–20.

Berman, M. 1981. *The Reenchantment of the World.* Ithaca: Cornell University Press.

Bernstein, R. 1985. *Habermas and Modernity.* Cambridge: MIT Press.

Berry, W. 1977. *The Unsettling of America: Culture and Agriculture.* San Francisco: Sierra Club Books.

Bertalanffy, L. von. 1967. *Robots, Men, and Minds.* New York: Braziller.

Bett, H. 1925. *Johannes Scotus Eriugena: A Study in Medieval Philosophy.* Cambridge: Cambridge University Press.

Bohm, D. 1980. *Wholeness and the Implicate Order.* London: Routledge and Kegan Paul.

Bolin, J., et al., eds. 1986. *The Greenhouse Effect, Climate Change, and Ecosystems.* New York: Scope 29.

Bonus, H. 1991. "Umweltpolitik in der Sozialen Marktwirtschaft." *Aus Politik und Zeitgeschichte,* (March 1): 37–46.

Booth, A. L., and H. L. Jacobs. 1990. "Ties That Bind: Native American Beliefs as a Foundation for Environmental Consciousness." *Environmental Ethics* 12:27–43.

Bormann, F. H., and G. E. Likens. 1979. *Pattern and Process in a Forested Ecosystem.* New York: Springer Verlag.

Botkin, D. 1990. *Discordant Harmonies: A New Ecology for the Twenty-first Century.* New York: Oxford University Press.

Brandt Report. *See* Independent Commission on International Development Issues.

Brennan, A. 1988. *Thinking about Nature.* Athens: University of Georgia Press.

———. 1992. "Moral Pluralism and the Environment." *Environmental Values* 1:15–33.

Brisbin, I. L., and C. E. Dallas. 1984. "Estimation of the Uptake and Distribution of Radiocesium by Migrating Water Fowl Following the Chernobyl Incident." *Proceedings of the Society Environmental Toxicology and Chemistry* (SETAC): 41.

Bronowski, J. 1973. *The Ascent of Man.* Boston: Little, Brown.

Brown, L. F. 1976. "Reclamation at Climax, Urad and Henderson Mines." *Mining Congress Journal* (April).

Brown, L. R., et al. 1984–92. *State of the World*. New York: W. W. Norton/World Watch Institute.

Brown-Weiss, E. 1989. *In Fairness to Future Generations: International Law, Common Patrimony, and Intergenerational Equity*. Tokyo: Transnational Publishers.

Brubaker, L. B. 1988. "Vegetation History and Anticipating Future Vegetative Change." In *Ecosystem Management for Parks and Wilderness*. Seattle: University of Washington Press.

Brundtland, G. 1987. *Our Common Future*. Oxford: Oxford University Press. *See* World Commission on Environment and Development.

Burgess, J. C. 1990. "The Contribution of Efficient Energy Pricing to Reducing Carbon Dioxide Emissions." *Energy Policy* (June): 449–55.

Cahen, H. 1988. "Against the Moral Considerability of Ecosystems." *Environmental Ethics* 10:195–216.

Callicott, J. B. 1985. "Intrinsic Value, Quantum Theory, and Environmental Ethics." *Environmental Ethics* 7:257–77.

———. 1986. "The Metaphysical Implications of Ecology." *Environmental Ethics* 8:301–16.

———. 1990a. "The Case Against Moral Pluralism." *Environmental Ethics* 12:99–124.

———. 1990b. "The Metaphysical Transition in Farming: From the Newtonian-Mechanical to the Eltonian-Ecological." *Journal of Agriculture Ethics* 3:36–49.

———. 1991a. "That Good Old-Time Wilderness Religion." *Environmental Professional* 13:378–79.

———. 1991b. "The Wilderness Idea Revisited: The Sustainable Development Alternative." *Environmental Professional* 13:235–47.

Capra, F. 1975. *The Tao of Physics: An Exploration of the Parallels Between Modern Physics and Eastern Mysticism*. Boulder: Shambala.

Carr, E. H. 1962. *The Twenty Years Crisis*. 2d ed. London: Macmillan.

Carraro, C., and D. Siniscalco. 1991. "The International Protection of the Environment." Fondazione ENI Enrico Mattei, Milan. Mimeo.

Carrol, J., ed. 1988. *International Environmental Diplomacy*. Cambridge: Cambridge University Press.

Carroll, M. A., et al. 1985. *Ethics in the Practice of Psychology*. Englewood Cliffs, N.J.: Prentice-Hall.

Carson, R. [1962] 1987. *Silent Spring*. Boston: Houghton Mifflin.

Chandler, W. U., ed. 1990. *Carbon Emission Control Strategies: Case Studies in International Cooperation*. Baltimore: World Wildlife Fund and the Conservation Foundation.

Chaplin, C. 1935. *Modern Times*. Hollywood, Calif.: United Artists.

Cheney, J. 1989. "Postmodern Environmental Ethics: Ethics as Bioregional Narrative." *Environmental Ethics* 11:117–34.

Cherrett, J. M. 1980. "Key Concepts: The Results of a Survey of Our Members' Opinions." In *Ecological Concepts: The Contribution of Ecology to an Under-*

standing of the Natural World, ed. J. M. Cherrett. Oxford: Blackwell Scientific Publications.

Chichilnisky, G. 1991. "Global Environment and North-South Trade." Columbia University, New York. Mimeo.

Ci Hai [Encyclopedia of Words; in Chinese]. 1985. Ed. Shu-Xin-chen, Chen Wang-dao, et al. Shanghai: Shanghai Encyclopedia Publisher.

Clagett, M. 1963. *Greek Science in Antiquity.* New York: Collier Books.

Clements, F. E. 1916. "Plant Succession: An Analysis of the Development of Vegetation." Carnegie Institution, Washington, D.C.

Commission on Research and Resource Management Policy. 1989. *National Parks: From Vignettes to a Global View.* Washington, D.C.: National Parks and Conservation Association.

Committee on Science, Engineering, and Public Policy. 1991. "Policy Implications of Greenhouse Warming." National Academy of Sciences, Washington, D.C.

Committee on the Role of Alternative Methods in Modern Production Agriculture. 1989. *Alternative Agriculture.* Washington, D.C.: National Academy Press.

Commoner, B. 1971. *The Closing Circle: Nature, Man, and Technology.* New York: Knopf.

Condorcet. 1989. *Esquisse d'un tableau historique des progrès de l'esprit humain.* Boston: Beacon Press.

Cornes, R., and T. Sandler. 1987. *The Theory of Externalities, Public Goods and Club Goods.* Cambridge: Cambridge University Press.

Costanza, R., B. G. Norton, and B. Haskell, eds. 1992. *Ecosystem Health: New Goals for Environmental Management.* Washington, D.C.: Island Press.

Cousteau, J. M. 1991. "Nuclear Weapons Testing Casts a Deadly Shadow on the Environment." *Calypso Log* 18 (October): 3.

Crosby, A. W. 1986. *Ecological Imperialism: The Biological Expansion of Europe, 900–1900.* New York: Cambridge University Press.

Daly, G., P. R. Ehrlich, H. A. Mooney, and A. H. Ehrlich. 1991. "Greenhouse Economics: Learn Before You Leap." *Ecological Economics* 4:1–10.

Daly, H., and J. Cobb. 1989. *For the Common Good.* Boston: Beacon Press.

Darwin, C. 1874. *The Descent of Man and Selection in Relation to Sex.* 2d ed. London: John Murray.

Day, G. M. 1953. "The Indian as an Ecological Factor in the Northeastern Forest." *Ecology* 34:329–46.

Descartes, R. 1911a. "Discourse on the Method of Rightly Conducting the Reason and Seeking for Truth in the Sciences." In *The Philosophical Works of Descartes.* Trans. E. S. Haldane and G. R. T. Ross. Cambridge: Cambridge University Press.

———. 1911b. "Meditations on First Philosophy in Which the Existence of God and the Distinction Between Mind and Body Are Demonstrated." In *The Philosophical Works of Descartes.*

———. 1911c. "The Principles of Philosophy." In *The Philosophical Works of Descartes.*

Dr. Seuss. 1954. *Horton Hears a Who!* New York: Random House.

Ducasse, P. 1958. *Histoire du techniques.* Paris: Presses Universitaires de France.

Dutt, R. P. 1978. *Fascism and Social Revolution.* Chicago: Proletarian Publishers.

Ehrlich, P., and A. Ehrlich. 1981. *Extinction.* New York: Random House.

Elliott, C. 1990. Foreword to *Natural History of China.* London: William Collins.

Engel, J. R. 1990. "Introduction: The Ethics of Sustainable Development." In *Ethics of Environment and Development,* ed. J. Ronald Engel and Joan Gibb Engel. London: Belhaven Press.

Enquête-Kommission. 1990a. *Schutz der Tropenwälder: Eine internationale Schwerpunktaufgabe.* [Also in English.]

———. 1990b. "Vorsorge zum Schutz der Erdatmosphäre des Deutschen Bundestages." In *Schutz der Erdatmosphäre: Eine internationale Herausforderung.* 3d ed. Bonn: Deutscher Bundestag, Referat für Oeffentlichkietsarbeit. [Also in English.]

———. 1991. *Schutz der Erde: Eine Bestandaufnahme mit Vorschlägen zu einer neuen Energiepolitik.* Vols. 1 and 2. [Also in English.]

Epstein, R. 1985. *Takings: Private Property and the Power of Eminent Domain.* Cambridge: Harvard University Press.

Evans, F. C. 1956. "Ecosystem as the Basic Unit in Ecology." *Science* 123:1127–28.

Evernden, N. 1985. *The Natural Alien.* Toronto: University of Toronto Press.

Executive Office of the President of the United States. 1992. *Budget of the United States Government, Fiscal Year 1992.* Washington, D.C.: U.S. Government Printing Office.

Fang-zhong, L. 1989. *Historical Statistics of Chinese Households. Cultivated Land and Tax* [in Chinese]. Shanghai: Shanghai People's Publishing House.

Faramelli, N. J. 1973. "Ecological Responsibility and Economic Justice." In *Western Man and Environmental Ethics,* ed. I. G. Barbour. Reading, Mass.: Addison Wesley.

Feldman, A. 1980. *Welfare Economics and Social Choice Theory.* Boston: Martinus Nijhoff.

Finamore, B. A. 1985. "Regulating Hazardous and Mixed Waste at Department of Energy Nuclear Weapons Facilities: Reversing Decades of Environmental Neglect." *Harvard Environmental Law Review* 9:83–141.

Flavin, C. 1988. "Slowing Global Warming: A Worldwide Strategy." Worldwatch Paper 91, Washington, D.C.

Foster, H., ed. 1983. *The Anti-aesthetic: Essays on Postmodern Culture.* Port Townsend, Wash.: Bay Press.

Fowler, H. N., trans. 1917. *Apology* and *Crito.* Loeb Classical Library, vol. 1. Cambridge: Harvard University Press.

Fox, S. 1981. *John Muir and His Legacy: The American Conservation Movement.* Boston: Little, Brown.

Fox, W. 1991. *Towards a Transpersonal Ecology.* Boston: Shambala.

Frankena, W. 1962. "The Concept of Social Justice." In *Social Justice*, ed. R. Brandt. Englewood Cliffs, N.J.: Prentice-Hall.

Fromhold, A. T. 1981. *Quantum Mechanics for Applied Physics and Engineering*. New York: Academic Press.

Fudenberg, D., and J. Tirole. 1991. *Game Theory*. Cambridge: MIT Press.

Galilei, G. 1957. "The Assayer." In *Discoveries and Opinions of Galileo*. Trans. S. Drake. Garden City, N.Y.: Doubleday.

Gary, R. 1974. Introduction to *Vanishing Species*. New York: Time-Life.

Gehring, T. 1990. "Das internationale Regime zum Schutz der Ozonschicht." *Europa Archiv* 23:703–12.

Gewirth, A. 1982. *Human Rights: Essays on Justification and Applications*. Chicago: University of Chicago Press.

Giddens, A. 1990. *The Consequences of Modernity*. Stanford: Stanford University Press.

Glantz, M., ed. 1988. *Forecasting by Analogy: Societal Responses to Regional Climate Change*. Boulder: National Center for Atmospheric Research.

Goldemberg, J., et al. 1987. "Energy for a Sustainable World." World Resources Institute, Washington, D.C.

Golley, F. B. 1987. "Deep Ecology from the Perspective of Ecological Science." *Environmental Ethics* 9:45–55.

Gomberg, P. 1990. "Can a Partisan Be a Moralist?" *American Philosophical Quarterly* 27 (January): 71.

Gomez-Pompa, A., and A. Kaus. 1988. "Conservation by Traditional Cultures in the Tropics." In *For the Conservation of the Earth*, ed. V. Martin. Golden, Colo.: Fulcrum.

Gray, E. D. 1978. *The Energy Oratorio*. New York: Energy Study Project of the National Council of Churches of Christ.

———. 1982. *Patriarchy as a Conceptual Trap*. Wellesley, Mass.: Roundtable Press.

Gribben, J. 1984. *In Search of Schrödinger's Cat: Quantum Physics and Reality*. New York: Bantam Books.

Grubb, M. 1989. *The Greenhouse Effect: Negotiating Targets*. New Haven: Yale University Press.

Guha, R. 1989. "Radical American Environmentalism and Wilderness Preservation: A Third World Critique." *Environmental Ethics* 11:71–83.

Gunn, A. S. 1980. "Why Should We Care about Rare Species?" *Environmental Ethics* 2:17–37.

———. 1983. "Traditional Ethics and the Moral Status of Animals." *Environmental Ethics* 5:133–53.

———. 1984. "Preserving Rare Species." In *Earthbound*, ed. Tom Regan. New York: Random House.

———. 1994. "Environmental Ethics and Tropical Rainforests: Should Greens Have Standing?" *Environmental Ethics* 16:21–40.

Guthrie, W. K. C. 1962–78. *A History of Greek Philosophy.* 5 vols. Cambridge: Cambridge University Press.

Haas, P. M. 1990. "Obtaining International Environmental Protection Through Epistemic Consensus." *Millennium Journal of International Studies* 19:347–63.

Habermas, J. 1983. "Modernity: An Incomplete Project." In *The Anti-aesthetic: Essays on Postmodern Culture,* ed. H. Foster. Port Townsend, Wash.: Bay Press.

Haeckel, E. 1866. "Generelle Morphologie der Organismen." In *Allgemeine Grundzuge der organischen Formen-Wissenschaft, mechaisch begrundet durch die von Charles Darwin reformirte Descendenz-Theorie.* 2 vols. Berlin: Reimer.

Hahn, R. W., and G. L. Hester. 1989. "Marketable Permits: Lessons for Theory and Practice." *Ecology Law Quarterly* 16:301–406.

Hall, J. D. 1986. *Imaging God: Dominion as Stewardship.* Grand Rapids, Mich.: W. B. Eerdmans; New York: Friendship Press, for the Commission on Stewardship, National Council of Churches of Christ.

Hampshire, S. 1983. *Morality and Conflict.* Cambridge: Harvard University Press.

Hardin, G. 1968. "The Tragedy of the Commons." *Science* 162:1243–48.

———. 1974. "Living on a Lifeboat." *BioScience* 24 (October): 561–68.

Harmon, D. 1987. "Cultural Diversity, Human Subsistence, and the National Park Ideal." *Environmental Ethics* 9:156–57.

Harrison, R. 1964. *Animal Machines: The New Factory Farming Industry.* London: Stuart.

Harsany, J., and R. Selten. 1988. *A General Theory of Equilibrium Selection in Games.* Cambridge: MIT Press.

Hartje, V. J. 1989. Studienbericht E9a. "Verteilung der Reduktionspflichten: Problematik der Dritte-Welt-Staaten." Enquête Kommission, Vorsorge zum Schutz der Erdatmosphäre. Berlin. MS.

Harvey, D. 1989. *The Condition of Postmodernity.* Oxford: Basil Blackwell.

Havelock, E. A. 1963. *Preface to Plato.* Cambridge: Harvard University Press.

Heal, G. 1991. "International Negotiations on Emission Control." Columbia University, New York. Mimeo.

Hecht, S., and A. Cockburn. 1989. *The Fate of the Forest: Developers, Destroyers, and Defenders of the Amazon.* London: Verso.

Heisenberg, W. 1962. *Physics and Philosophy: The Revolution in Modern Science.* New York: Harper and Row.

Heizer, R. F. 1955. "Primitve Man as an Ecologic Factor." Kroeber Anthropological Society Papers, no. 13, Berkeley, Calif.

Hekstra, G. P. 1989. "Global Warming and Rising Sea Levels: The Policy Implications." *Ecologist* 19:4–15.

Hill, T. E., Jr. 1983. "Ideals of Human Excellence and Preserving Natural Environments." *Environmental Ethics* 5:211–24.

Hoel, M. 1991. "How Should International Greenhouse Gas Agreements Be Designed?" Oslo University. Mimeo.

Hoeller, P., A. Dean, and J. Nicolaisen. 1990. "A Survey of Studies of the Costs of

Reducing Greenhouse Gas Emissions." OECD, Department of Economics and Statistics, Working Paper no. 89, Paris (December).

Hughes, J. D. 1983. *American Indian Ecology.* El Paso: Texas Western Press.

Hume, D. 1960. *A Treatise of Human Nature.* Oxford: Clarendon Press.

Independent Commission on International Development Issues. 1980. *North-South: A Programme for Survival.* Cambridge: MIT Press. [Brandt Report.]

Jackson, W. 1989. *New Roots for Agriculture.* Lincoln: University of Nebraska Press.

Jeffers, R. 1963. *Selected Poems.* New York: Vantage Books, Random House.

Jochem, E. 1991. "Reducing CO_2 Emissions: The West German Plan." *Energy Policy* (March): 119–26.

Jonas, H. 1984. *The Imperative of Responsibility.* Chicago: University of Chicago Press.

Jones, E. L. 1981. *The European Miracle.* Cambridge: Cambridge University Press.

Jordan, R. 1991. "Kris Kristofferson." *Progressive 55* (September): 36–38.

Jowett, B., trans. 1937. *The Dialogues of Plato.* Vol. 1. New York: Random House.

Juda, L. 1979. "International Environmental Concern: Perspectives and Implications for the Developing States." In *The Global Predicament: Ecological Perspectives on World Order,* ed. D. W. Orr and M. S. Soroos. Chapel Hill: University of North Carolina Press.

Kats, G. H. 1990. "Slowing Global Warming and Sustaining Development." *Energy Policy* 18:25–33.

Keepin, W., and G. H. Kats. 1988. "Greenhouse Warming: Comparative Assessment of Nuclear and Efficiency Abatement." *Energy Policy* 16:538–61.

Kellner, D. 1990. *Television and the Crisis of Democracy.* Boulder: Westview Press.

Kelly, M., et al. 1990. *Cities at Risk.* Norwich: School of Environmental Sciences, University of East Anglia.

Kemp, D. 1990. *Global Environmental Issues.* New York: Routledge.

Kennedy, P. 1987. *The Rise and Fall of the Great Powers.* New York: Random House.

Kirk, R. H., and C. Hayshark. 1972. *Personal Health in Ecologic Perspective.* St. Louis: Mosby.

Koestler, A. 1978. *Janus: A Summing Up.* New York: Random House.

Kohák, E. 1987. *The Embers and the Stars.* 2d ed. Chicago: University of Chicago Press.

Kox, H. 1991. "Integration of Environmental Externalities in International Commodity Agreements." *World Development.*

Koyré, A. 1965. *Newtonian Studies.* Chicago: University of Chicago Press.

Kuhn, T. S. 1957. *The Copernican Revolution: Planetary Astronomy in the Development of Western Thought.* Cambridge: Harvard University Press.

Lake, S. 1981. *Television's Impact on Children and Adolescents: A Special Interest Resource Guide in Education.* Phoenix: Oryx Press.

Lashof, D. A., and D. Tirpak, eds. 1990. *Policy Options for Stabilizing Global Climate*. Washington, D.C.: U.S. Environmental Protection Agency.

Lemons, J. 1985. "Reply to 'On Reading Environmental Ethics.'" *Environmental Ethics* 7:185–88.

Leopold, A. 1949. *A Sand County Almanac and Sketches Here and There*. London: Oxford University Press.

———. 1987. Foreword [to the 1947 MS of "Great Possessions," later titled *A Sand County Almanac*]. In *Companion to a Sand County Almamac*, ed. J. B. Callicott. Madison: University of Wisconsin Press.

Leopold, A., S. A. Cain, C. M. Cottam, I. N. Gabrielson, and T. L. Kimball. 1963. *Wildlife Management in the National Parks*. Washington, D.C.: U.S. Department of the Interior.

Lewis, H. T. 1973. *Patterns of Indian Burning in California: Ecology and Ethnohistory*. Ballena Anthropological Papers, no. 1, Berkeley, Calif.

Lippmann, W. 1922. *Public Opinion*. New York: Macmillan.

Locke, J. 1961. *An Essay Concerning Human Understanding*. Vol. 1. London: J. M. Dent.

Longino, H. 1990. *Science as Social Knowledge*. Princeton: Princeton University Press.

McKibben, B. 1989. *The End of Nature*. New York: Random House.

McLuhan, M. 1965. *Understanding Media: The Extensions of Man*. New York: McGraw-Hill.

McNaughton, D. 1988. *Moral Vision*. Oxford: Basil Blackwell.

Maler, K. G. 1990. "International Environmental Problems." *Oxford Review of Economic Policy*, pp. 80–108.

Manne, A. S., and R. G. Richels. 1990. "CO_2 Emission Reductions: An Economic Cost Analysis for the USA." *Energy Journal* 11:51–74.

Mark, F. 1973. *The Pattern of the Chinese Past*. Stanford: Stanford University Press.

———. 1991. "International Trade in Carbon Emission Rights: A Decomposition Procedure." *American Economic Review* 81:146–50.

Markandya, A. 1989a. "Economics and the Ozone Layer." In *Blueprint for a Green Economy*, ed. D. Pearce et al. London: Earthscan.

———. 1989b. "Global Warming: The Economics of Tradeable Permits." In *Blueprint for a Green Economy*.

Marks, Elaine, and Isabelle de Courtivron, eds. 1980. *New French Feminisms: An Anthology*. Amherst: University of Massachusetts Press.

Martin, C. 1973. "Fire and Forest Structure in the Aboriginal Eastern Forest." *Indian Historian* 6:38–42, 54.

Martin, P. S. 1973. "The Discovery of America." *Science* 179:969–74.

Mathews, J. T., ed. 1991. *Greenhouse Warming: Negotiating a Global Regime*. Baltimore: WRI Publications.

Mead, M. [1949] 1975. *Male and Female: A Study of the Sexes in a Changing World.* New York: Morrow Paperback, William Morrow.

Meeks, L. B. 1991. *Health: A Wellness Approach.* Columbus: Merrill.

Meine, C. 1988. *Aldo Leopold.* Madison: University of Wisconsin Press.

Merryman, J. H. 1985. *The Civil Law Tradition.* 2d ed. Stanford: Stanford University Press.

Mill, J. S. 1969. "Nature." In *Three Essays on Natural Religion.* New York: Greenwood Press.

―――. [1859] 1972. *On Liberty.* London: J. M. Dent.

Mintzer, I. M. 1987. *A Matter of Degrees: The Potential for Controlling the Greenhouse Effect.* Washington, D.C.: World Resources Institute.

Mooney, H. A., and J. Drake, eds. 1986. *Ecology of Biological Invasions of North America and Hawaii.* New York: Springer Verlag.

Morgenstern, R. D. 1991. "Towards a Comprehensive Approach to Global Climate Change Mitigation." *American Economic Review* 81:140–45.

Morrisette, P. 1989. "The Evolution of Policy Responses to Stratospheric Ozone Depletion." *Natural Resources Journal* 29:793–820.

Moulin, H. 1988. *Axioms of Cooperative Decision Making.* Cambridge: Cambridge University Press.

Muir, J. 1901. *Our National Parks.* Boston: Houghton Mifflin.

Mumford, L. 1934. *Technics and Civilization.* New York: Harcourt, Brace.

Myers, N. 1983. *The Primal Source.* Boulder: Westview Press.

Myerson, R. 1991. *Game Theory.* Cambridge: Harvard University Press.

Naess, A. 1973. "The Shallow and the Deep, Long-Range Ecology Movement: A Summary." *Inquiry* 16:95–100.

―――. 1990. "Sustainable Development and Deep Ecology." In *Ethics of Environment and Development,* ed. J. R. Engel and J. G. Engel. London: Bellhaven.

Naess, A., and D. Rothenberg. 1989. *Ecology, Community and Life Style: Outline of an Ecosophy.* New York: Cambridge University Press.

Nash, R. 1982. *Wilderness and the American Mind.* 3d ed. New Haven: Yale University Press.

―――. 1989. *The Rights of Nature: A History of Environmental Ethics.* Madison: University of Wisconsin Press.

Newton, I. 1962. *Mathematical Principles of Natural Philosophy.* Trans. A. Motte, ed. F. Cajori. Berkeley: University of California Press.

Nietzsche, F. 1974. *The Gay Science: With a Prelude of Rhymes and an Appendix of Songs.* Trans. Walter Kaufman. New York: Random House.

Nitze, W. A. 1990. *The Greenhouse Effect: Formulating a Convention.* London: Royal Institute of International Affairs.

Nordhaus, W. D. 1990. "Greenhouse Economics: Count Before You Leap." *Economist* 7 July, 19–22.

Norton, B. 1986. "Conservation and Preservation: A Conceptual Rehabilitation." *Environmental Ethics* 8:195–220.

————. 1991. *Toward Unity among Environmentalists*. New York: Oxford University Press.

————. 1992. "Epistemology and Environmental Values." *Monist* 75:209–26.

Nyerere Report. 1990. *The Challenge to the South: The Report of the South Commission*. Oxford: Oxford University Press.

Oates, W. J. 1948. *The Basic Writings of Saint Augustine*. 2 vols. New York: Random House.

Ockham, W. 1957. *Philosophical Writings: A Selection*. Ed. P. Boehner. Edinburgh: Thomas Nelson, 1957.

Odum, E. P. [1953] 1971. *Fundamentals of Ecology*. Philadelphia: W. B. Saunders.

Ogawa, Y. 1991. "Economic Activity and the Greenhouse Effect." *Energy Journal* 12:23–36.

Okken, P. A., R. J. Sorart, and S. Zwerver. 1989. *Climate and Energy: The Feasibility of Controlling CO_2 Emissions*. Dordrecht: Kluwer Academic Publishers.

Olinger, D. 1991. "Nuclear Industry Targets Nevada." *St. Petersburg Times*, 1 December, D1, D5.

Ominde, S. H., and C. Juma, eds. 1991. *A Change in the Weather: African Perspectives on Climatic Chance*. Nairobi: African Centre for Technology Studies.

O'Neill, R. V., D. L. DeAngelis, J. B. Waide, and T. F. H. Allen. 1986. *A Hierarchical Concept of Ecosystems*. Princeton: Princeton University Press.

Ong, W. 1982. *Orality and Literacy: The Technologizing of the Word*. New York: Methuen.

Opschoor, J. B., et al., 1989. *Economic Instruments for Environmental Protection*. OECD Publications 19 and 92. London: Royal Institute of International Affairs.

Ordeshook, P. 1986. *Game Theory and Political Theory*. Cambridge: Cambridge University Press.

Passell, P. 1990. "Rebel Economists Add Ecological Cost to Price of Progress." *New York Times*, 27 November, B5–B6.

Passmore, J. 1968. *A Hundred Years of Philosophy*. Harmondsworth: Penguin Books.

Pearce, D. 1991. "The Global Commons." In *Greening the World Economy*, ed. D. Pearce et al. London: Earthscan.

Phillips, K. 1990. *The Politics of the Rich and Poor: Wealth and the American Electorate in the Reagan Aftermath*. New York: Random House.

Pinchot, G. 1947. *Breaking New Ground*. New York: Harcourt, Brace.

Poli, C., and P. Timmerman, eds. 1991. *L'etica nelle politiche ambientali*. Padua: Gregoriana Editrice.

Pollan, M. 1992. *Second Nature*. New York: Dell Laurel.

Pyne, S. J. 1982. *Fire in America: A Cultural History of Wildland and Rural Fire*. Princeton: Princeton University Press.

Qing-lian, H. 1988. *Population, a Suspended Sword Toward China* [in Chinese]. Chongqing, Sichuan: Sichuan People's Publishing House.

Rachels, J. 1990. *Created from Animals: The Moral Implications of Darwinism.* New York: Oxford University Press.

Rádl, E. 1946. *U'ticha z filosofie.* Prague: Leichter.

Rawls, J. 1971. *A Theory of Justice.* Cambridge: Harvard University Press.

Reid, W. V. C., and M. C. Trexler. 1991. *Drowning the National Heritage: Climate Change and Coastal Biodiversity in the United States.* Baltimore: WRI Publications.

Rescher, N. 1980. "Why Save Endangered Species?" In *Unpopular Essays on Technological Progress,* ed. N. Rescher. Pittsburgh: University of Pittsburgh Press.

Robertson, D. 1990. "The Global Environment: Are International Treaties a Distraction?" *World Economy* 13:111–27.

Rolston, H., III. 1982. "Are Values in Nature Subjective or Objective?" *Environmental Ethics* 4:125–51.

———. 1988. *Environmental Ethics: Duties to and Values in the Natural World.* Philadelphia: Temple University Press.

Rosenberg, N. J., et al. 1989. *Greenhouse Warming: Abatement and Adaptation.* Washington, D.C.: RFD Proceedings.

Rothenberg, D. 1989. *Ecology, Community and Lifestyle.* New York: Cambridge University Press.

Ruse, M. 1979. *The Darwinian Revolution: Science Red in Fang and Claw.* Chicago: University of Chicago Press.

———. 1986. *Taking Darwin Seriously: A Naturalistic Approach to Philosophy.* New York: Basil Blackwell.

Russow, L.-M. 1981. "Why Do Species Matter?" *Environmental Ethics* 3:101–12.

Ru-zhen, L. 1955. *Jing Hua Yuan* [in Chinese]. Beijing: People's Literature Publishing House.

Sagoff, M. 1974. "On Preserving the Natural Environment." *Yale Law Journal* 81:205–67.

———. 1986. "Values and Preferences." *Ethics* 96:301–16.

Samuelson, P. 1954. "The Pure Theory of Public Expenditure." *Review of Economics and Statistics,* pp. 387–89.

Sand, P. H. 1990. *Lessons Learned in Global Environmental Governance.* Baltimore: World Resources Institute.

Sax, J. 1971. "Takings, Private Property and Public Rights." *Yale Law Journal* 81:149–86.

Scheffer, V. B. 1993. "The Olympic Goat Controversy: A Perspective." *Conservation Biology* 7:916–19.

Schipper, L. 1991. "Improved Energy Efficiency in the Industrialized Countries: Past Achievements, CO_2 Emission Prospects." *Energy Policy* (March): 127–37.

Schneider, S. H. 1989. "The Greenhouse Effect: Science and Policy." *Science* 243:771–81.

Schumacher, E. F. 1973. *Small Is Beautiful: Economics As If People Mattered.* New York: Harper and Row.

Sedjo, R. A. 1990. "Forests to Offset the Greenhouse Effect." *Journal of Forestry* (July): 12–15.

Seed, J., et al. 1988. *Thinking Like a Mountain*. Philadelphia: New Society Publishers.

Shrader-Fréchette, K. 1984. *Science Policy, Ethics, and Economic Methodology*. Boston: Reidel.

———. 1989. "Helping Science Serve Society." In *Hoe Toonaangevend is de Universiteit?* ed. H. de Ward. Groningen, Netherlands: University of Groningen Press.

———. 1991. *Risk and Rationality*. Berkeley: University of California Press.

Simonis, U. E. 1990. *Beyond Growth: Elements of Sustainable Development*. Berlin: WZB.

Simons, M. 1992. "Europeans Worry about Ozone-eating Chemicals." *New York Times,* 3 March.

Singer, P. 1975. *Animal Liberation*. New York: Avon.

———. 1991. "On Being Silenced in Germany." *New York Review of Books* 38, 15 August, 36–42.

Skolnikoff, E. B. 1990. "The Policy Gridlock on Global Warming." *Foreign Policy* 79:88ff.

Smith, D. A., and K. Vodden. 1989. "Global Environmental Policy: The Case of Ozone Depletion." *Canadian Public Policy* 15:413–23.

Smith, J., and D. Tirpak, eds. 1988. *Potential Effects of Global Climate Change on the United States*. Washington, D.C.: U.S. Environmental Protection Agency.

Smuts, J. C. 1926. *Holism and Evolution*. New York: Macmillan.

Snyder, G. 1990. *The Practice of the Wild*. San Francisco: North Point Press.

Solomon, B. D., and D. R. Ahuja. 1991. "International Reductions of Greenhouse-Gas Emissions." *Global Environmental Change* (December): 343–50.

Soulé, M. E., and K. A. Kohm. 1989. *Research Priorities for Conservation Biology*. Washington, D.C.: Island Press.

Speth, J. G. 1989. "Coming to Terms: Towards a North-South Bargain for the Environment." World Resources Institute, Washington, D.C.

Spulber, D. 1987. *Regulation and Markets*. Cambridge: MIT Press.

Stern, L. 1974. "Freedom, Blame, and Moral Community." *Journal of Philosophy* 71:72–84.

Stewart, R. B. 1985. "Economics, Environment, and the Limits of Legal Control." *Harvard Environmental Law Review* 9:1–22.

Stone, C. 1974. *Should Trees Have Standing?: Toward Legal Rights for Natural Objects*. Los Altos, Calif.: William Kaufmann.

———. 1987. *Earth and Other Ethics: The Case for Moral Pluralism*. New York: Harper and Row.

———. 1988. "Moral Pluralism and the Course of Environmental Ethics." *Environmental Ethics* 10:139–54.

Streeten, P. 1989a. "Global Institutions for an Interdependent World." *World Development* 17 (1989):1349–59.

———. 1989b. "International Cooperation." In *Handbook of Development Economics,* ed. H. Chenery and T. Srinivasan. Amsterdam: Elsevier.

Struther, J. 1940. *Mrs. Miniver.* New York: Grosset and Dunlap.

Sugden, R. 1986. *The Economics of Rights, Cooperation and Welfare.* Oxford: Basil Blackwell.

Swanson, T. 1991. "Conserving Biological Diversity." In *Greening the World Economy,* ed. D. Pearce et al. London: Earthscan.

Tansley, A. G. 1985. "The Use and Abuse of Vegetational Concepts and Terms." *Ecology* 16:284–307.

Taylor, M. 1987. *The Possibility of Cooperation.* Cambridge: Cambridge University Press.

Thoreau, H. D. 1962. "Walking." In *Excursions.* New York: Corinth Books.

Tietenberg, T. H. 1985. *Emissions Trading: An Exercise in Reforming Pollution Policy.* Baltimore: Resources for the Future.

Tolba, M. K. 1990. "A Step-by-Step Approach to Protection of the Atmosphere." *International Environmental Affairs* 1:304–9.

Topping, J. 1991. "Global Warming: Impact on Developing Countries." Overseas Development Council, Washington, D.C.

Trexler, M. C. 1991. *Minding the Carbon Store: Weighing U.S. Forestry Strategies to Slow Global Warming.* Baltimore: WRI Publications.

Turnbull, C. 1985. "Cultural Loss Can Foreshadow Extinction." In *Animal Extinctions,* ed. R. J. Hoage. Washington, D.C.: Smithsonian Institute Press.

Tyson, J. L. 1989. "Why China Says Ozone Must Take Back Seat in Drive to Prosperity." *Christian Science Monitor* 23 March.

U.S. Central Intelligence Agency. 1990. Map of Antarctic Research Stations. Central Intelligence Agency, Washington, D.C.

Usher, M. B. 1988. "Biological Invasions of Nature Reserves: A Search for Generalizations." *Biological Conservation* 74:119–35.

Usher, P. n.d. "Climate Change and the Developing World." *Southern Illinois University Law Journal* 14:257–64.

Walzer, M. 1977. *Just and Unjust Wars.* New York: Basic Books.

Warren, Karen J. 1990. "The Power and the Promise of Ecological Feminism." *Environmental Ethics* 12:125–46.

———. 1991. "Feminism and the Environment: An Overview of the Issues." APA Newsletter, *Feminism and Philosophy.*

Webb, T. 1986. "Is Vegetation in Equilibrium with Climate?: How to Interpret Late-Quaternary Pollen Data." *Vegetatio* 67:75–91.

———. 1987. "The Appearance and Disappearance of Major Vegetational Assemblages in Eastern North America." *Vegetatio* 69:177–87.

Wen-lan, F. 1965. *The General History of China* [in Chinese]. Vol. 1. Beijing: People's Publishing House.

Wilkinson, C. F. 1981. "The Public Trust Doctrine in Public Land Law." In *The Public Trust Doctrine in Natural Resources Law and Management: Conference Proceedings,* ed. H. C. Dunning. Davis: Regents of the University of California.

Williams, Bernard. 1985. *Ethics and the Limits of Philosophy.* Cambridge: Harvard University Press.

Williams, R. H. 1990. "Low-Cost Strategies for Coping with CO_2 Emission Limits." *Energy Journal* 11:35–59.

World Commission on Environment and Development. 1987. *Our Common Future.* Oxford: Oxford University Press. [Brundtland Report.]

Worster, D. 1977. *Nature's Economy: The Roots of Ecology.* San Francisco: Sierra Club Books.

Wright, H. E., and D. G. Frey, eds. 1965. *The Quaternary of the United States.* Princeton: Princeton University Press.

Yang, L. 1990. "Zhou Yi and Ecology." In *Zhou Yi and Chinese Medicine* [in Chinese]. Beijing: Beijing Science and Technology Publisher.

Zhi-cheng, M. 1992. "To Learn a Little Bit of 'Anti-Culture.' " *China Environmental News* 14 January [in Chinese].

Contributors

J. BAIRD CALLICOTT is Professor of Philosophy and Natural Resources at the University of Wisconsin at Stevens Point, where he designed and taught the world's first course in environmental ethics in 1971. Since then he has been one of the scholars at the forefront of the development of environmental ethics and has written more than fifty journal articles and book chapters. He is the author of *In Defense of the Ethic: Essays in Environmental Philosophy* and the editor of *Companion to a Sand County Almanac: Interpretive and Critical Essays;* he coedited *The River of the Mother of God and Other Essays*, by Aldo Leopold, and *Nature in Asian Traditions of Thought.*

VICTORIA DAVION (moderator) is Assistant Professor of Philosophy at the University of Georgia. She has published articles in the areas of environmental ethics, ethics, and feminist philosophy. Examples of her work include "Passivism and Care," published in *Hypatia: Journal of Feminist Philosophy,* and "How Feminist Is Ecofeminism?" in a forthcoming book, *Ecological Feminism,* edited by Karen J. Warren.

FREDERICK FERRÉ (moderator and conference co-coordinator) is Research Professor of Philosophy at the University of Georgia. His main interests are the philosophy of technology, religion, and enviromental ethics. He is the author of many articles and books and a speaker in great demand. His first book was *Language,*

Logic, and God (1961), and the most recent is *Hellfire and Lightning Rods: Liberating Science, Technology, and Religion* (1993). He also serves as the general editor of *Research in Philosophy and Technology.*

FRANK B. GOLLEY is Research Professor of Ecology at the University of Georgia and also a professor in the Departments of Zoology and Environmental Design. His main interests are in environmental ethics, environmental history, and human ecology. He is the author of numerous technical monographs and articles in biogeochemistry and in mammalian, tropical, and ecosystem ecology. He is the editor in chief of *Landscape Ecology* and an editor of the Springer Verlag Ecological Studies Series. He has served as the president of the International Association for Ecology (INTECOL) and currently coordinates an advanced course on rural planning at the Instituto Agronómico Mediterraneo de Zaragoza, Spain.

ELIZABETH DODSON GRAY is Codirector of the Bolton Institute for a Sustainable Future and Coordinator for the Theological Opportunities Program at the Harvard Divinity School. She is a feminist theologian and the author or coauthor of five books, including *Growth and Its Implication for the Future* (1975), *Green Paradise Lost* (1979), and *Patriarchy as a Conceptual Trap* (1982).

ALASTAIR S. GUNN is Senior Lecturer of Philosophy at the University of Waikato in Hamilton, New Zealand. He has published numerous articles on environmental and engineering ethics and is a coauthor of *Environmental Ethics for Engineers.* He chairs the Waikato Area Health Board Committee on Ethics and is a member of the New Zealand National Committee for Man and the Biosphere.

EUGENE HARGROVE (moderator) is the Chair of the Department of Philosophy and Religion Studies at the University of North Texas. He is the editor of the journal *Environmental Ethics* and author of *Foundations of Environmental Ethics* (1989). He has edited several books as well, including *Religion and Environmental Crisis* (1986), *Beyond Spaceship Earth: Environmental Ethics and the Solar System* (1986), and *The Animal Rights/Environmental Ethics Debate: The Environmental Perspective* (1992).

PETER HARTEL (conference co-coordinator), a soil microbiologist by training, is a member of the Department of Crop and Soil Sciences at the University of Georgia. He is the program coordinator for the Environmental Ethics Certificate Program and teaches agricultural ethics with Frederick Ferré.

ERAZIM KOHÁK is Professor of Philosophy at Charles University in Prague. Previously a professor of philosophy at Boston University, he returned to his native Czechoslovakia after forty-two years of exile in the United States. In 1991 he represented Czechoslovakia at the Conference of Environmental Ministers at Dobříš. Though his publications include numerous books and articles in both Czech and English, he is best known in environmental circles for his philosophical inquiry into the moral sense of nature, *The Embers and the Stars*.

YU-SHI MAO is Senior Research Fellow at the Institute of American Studies at the Chinese Academy of Social Sciences and Professor of Economics at the China Institute of Mining and Technology in Beijing. He is the author of *The Optimal Allocation Principle: The Mathematical Foundation of Economics* (1985) and *Morality and Benefit* (1989). In addition to serving as the chief editor or consulting editor on four journals relating to economics, science, and technology, he has published more than a hundred articles on economics, ethics, energy policy, environmental policy, and institutional reform in China.

IGNAZIO MUSU is Professor of Economics at the University of Venice and Professor of International Environmental Economics at the Bologna Center of Johns Hopkins University. The author of numerous articles on economics and environmental policy, he serves as chairman of the Scientific Council of the Fondazione Einaudi (Rome) and as a member of the Executive Committee of the European Association of Environmental and Resource Economists. He also serves as a member of the advisory board of several scientific journals.

BRYAN NORTON (moderator) is Professor in the School of Public Policy at the Georgia Institute of Technology. In addition to numerous articles about attitudes toward other species and the value of the natural world, he is the author of two books on biological diversity: *The Preservation of Species: The Value of Biological Diversity* (1986) and *Why Preserve Natural Variety?* (1987). More recently, he has written *Toward Unity among Environmentalists* (1991) and is a coeditor of the forthcoming book *Ecosystem Health: New Goals for Environmental Management*.

CORRADO POLI is Scientific Director and Director of Ethics and Environmental Policies at the Fondazione Lanza in Padua, Italy, where he coordinates the Ethics and Environmental Policies Program. Formerly a senior international fellow at Johns Hopkins University Center for Metropolitan Planning and Research and a visiting professor in the Department of Geography and Environmental Engineering at Johns Hopkins, he is the author of several essays on urban policy and planning.

HOLMES ROLSTON III is Professor of Philosophy at Colorado State University. He is the author of five critically acclaimed books, including *Environmental Ethics* and *Philosophy Gone Wild*. These books have been used as textbooks in more than eighty colleges and universities. In addition, he has written chapters for a dozen books and some seventy articles. His work has been reprinted in numerous other countries. He is a founder and associate editor of *Environmental Ethics* and is currently the president of the International Society for Environmental Ethics.

KRISTIN SHRADER-FRÉCHETTE is Distinguished Research Professor at the University of South Florida. She is the author of more than 120 articles and ten books and monographs, including *Nuclear Energy and Ethics* (1991), *Risk and Rationality* (1991), *Policy for Land: Legal and Ethical Relationships* (1992), *Research Ethics* (1993), and *Method in Community Ecology* (1993). Her theoretical work focuses on methods in hydrogeology and community ecology, and her applied work focuses on probabilistic risk assessment, science technology policy, and environmental ethics. She is the editor in chief of the Oxford University Press monograph series Environmental Ethics and Science Policy and now serves on the editorial boards of twelve professional journals.

UDO E. SIMONIS is Professor of Environmental Policy at the Wissenschaftszentrum (Science Center) in Berlin. He is chairman of the board of the Deutsche Umweltstiftung (German Environmental Foundation) and editor of the *Jahrbuch ökologie* (Ecology Yearbook). He has published on a wide range of developmental and environmental issues, including *Beyond Growth: Elements of Sustainable Development* (1990).

GARY E. VARNER is Assistant Professor of Philosophy in the Center for Biotechnology Policy and Ethics at Texas A & M University. His published papers center on environmental ethics, animal rights, the philosophy of environmental law, and agricultural research policy. Currently he is writing a book on environmental ethics and animal rights tentatively titled "In Nature's Interests? Interests, Animal Rights, and Environmental Ethics."

Index